Collins Primary Maths
Pupil Book 2

5

Series Editor: Peter Clarke

Authors: Andrew Edmondson, Elizabeth Jurgensen,
Jeanette Mumford, Sandra Roberts

Contents

	To use a protractor to measure and draw acute and obtuse angles to the nearest 5° To make patterns from rotating shapes	
Measure: (area and perimeter)	To understand area measured in square centimetres (cm^2)	56–57, 58–59
Measures: (mass)	To use, read and write standard metric units of mass (kg, g), including their abbreviations, and relationships between them To suggest suitable units and measuring equipment to estimate or measure mass	60–61, 62–63, 64–65
Problems involving measures (mass)	To use all four operations to solve simple word problems involving numbers and quantities based on measures (mass), using one or more steps	66–67, 68–69
Organising and interpreting	To solve a problem by representing and data interpreting data in tables, charts, graphs and diagrams, including those generated by a computer, for example: bar line charts, where intermediate points may have meaning (e.g. room temperature over time)	70–71, 72–73, 74–75
Mental calculation strategies (+ and -)/Checking results of calculations	To use known number facts and place value for mental addition and subtraction: add/subtract any pair of two-digit numbers, including crossing 100	76–77
	To add or subtract the nearest multiple of 10 or 100, then adjust	78–79
	To identify near doubles, such as $1·5 + 1·6$	84–85
Rapid recall of addition	To recall addition and subtraction facts for and subtraction facts all numbers to 20	80–81,
	To derive quickly or continue to derive quickly decimals that total 1 or 10	82–83,
Pencil and paper procedures (+)/Rapid recall of addition facts	To extend written methods to addition of more than two integers less than 10 000	86–87, 88–89
	To derive quickly or continue to derive quickly all pairs of multiples of 50 with a of 1000	
Pencil and paper procedures (−)	To extend written methods to subtraction of a pair of decimal fractions, both with one or both with two decimal places	90–91
Properties of numbers and number sequences	To recognise and extend number sequences formed by counting from any number in steps of constant size, extending beyond zero when counting back To recognise multiples of 6, 7, 8, 9, up to the 10th multiple To know and apply tests of divisibility by 2, 4, 5, 10 or 100	96–97, 98–99, 100–101, 102–103

● Read and write whole numbers in figures and words, and know what each digit represents
● Use symbols such as <, >, ≤, ≥, =
● Order a set of integers less than 1 million

Numbers in the hundred thousands

Practice

1 Put each set of numbers in ascending order.

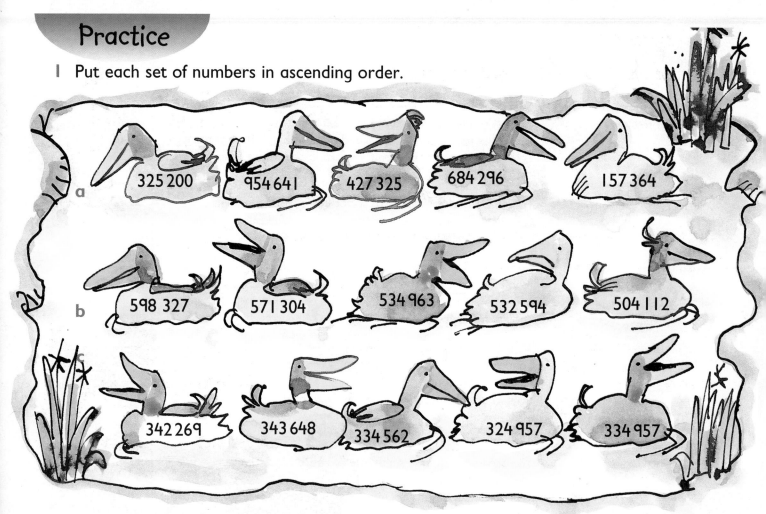

a 325 200   954 641   427 325   684 296   157 364

b 598 327   571 304   534 963   532 594   504 112

c 342 269   343 648   334 562   324 957   334 957

d Choose one number from each set and write it out in words.

2 Copy and complete the statements.

a 542 698 >   b 364 287 >   c 210 954 <

d 308 559 >   e 746 921 <   f 436 952 ≤

g 749 300 ≥   h 869 230 ≤   i 694 297 ≥

3 Write the next ten numbers.
   a 483 058   b 674 294   c 239 184
   d 856 921   e 470 365   f 561 596

Refresher

1 Put each set of numbers in ascending order.

a
85 353
62 354
84 287
92 351
35 627

b
28 365
28 148
28 654
28 307
28 749

c
17 268
71 395
17 215
17 521
71 591

d Choose one number from each set and write it out in words.

2 Copy and complete the statements.

a 68 354 <
b 38 214 >
c 72 351 >

d 82 155 <
e 30 024 <
f 14 625 >

g 72 391 >
h 61 320 <
i 96 200 >

j 10 323 >
k 36 487 >
l 46 020 <

3 Write the next ten numbers.

a 30 562
b 41 210
c 54 368

d 15 266
e 63 788
f 42 307

Challenge
Reach the target

You need:
- a sheet of paper each
- a pencil each

What to do

Work in twos, threes or fours.

1 Write one of these numbers at the top of your paper. Each player must choose a different number.

285 635   285 641   285 653   285 658

The target number is 285 700.

2 Next to the number write the number that comes next. Then give your paper to the player sitting next to you.

3 Write the next number. Give your paper to the next player.

4 Keep going until somebody writes 285 700. They are the winner.

Variation

Play again with these numbers.
547 109
547 115
547 123
547 127
The target number is 547 150.

Ten times bigger, ten times smaller

Practice

1 Copy and complete the tables.

a

Number	×10	×10
287	2870	28 700
165		
8911		
5126		
3864		

b

Number	×100	×100
8	800	80 000
2		
28		
59		
81		

c

Number	÷10	÷10
400	40	4
2700		
31 900		
4320		
5610		

d

Number	÷100	÷100
5000	50	0·5
620 000		
217 000		
14 000		
38 000		

2 Copy the calculations filling in the missing numbers.

a 99   × ▢ = 9900

b 120   × ▢ = 1200

c 4500   × ▢ = 45 000

d 260   × ▢ = 26 000

e 1680   × ▢ = 168 000

f 217   × ▢ = 2170

g 5600   × ▢ = 560 000

h 2729   × ▢ = 27 290

i 9243   × ▢ = 92 430

j 6831   × ▢ = 683 100

k 500   ÷ ▢ = 50

l 270   ÷ ▢ = 27

m 25 800 ÷ ▢ = 258

n 41 300 ÷ ▢ = 4130

o 57 200 ÷ ▢ = 572

p 19 500 ÷ ▢ = 195

q 41 320 ÷ ▢ = 4132

r 12 960 ÷ ▢ = 1296

s 812 300 ÷ ▢ = 8123

t 729 400 ÷ ▢ = 7294

Refresher

1 Multiply the numbers by 10. Write the answers as a calculation.

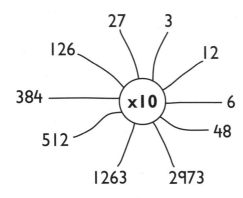

2 Divide the numbers by 10. Write the answers as a calculation.

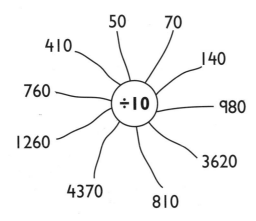

Challenge

Answer these questions using your knowledge of multiplying and dividing by 10 and 100. Show all your working.

  a How many times larger is 3700 than 37?

  b How many £10 notes in £360?

  c A bar of chocolate costs 39p. How much would ten bars cost?

  d How many times larger is 4900 than 4·9?

  e 100 packets of biscuits cost £48. How much does one packet cost?

7

Constantly counting

Practice

1 Write these numbers out in descending order.

a −4, −3, −8, −1, 0, −9

b 6, −7, 1, −2, 3, −6

c 0, 10, −1, 4, 7, −7

d 7, −4, 6, −8, 5, 1

e −3, 2, 0, −11, −8, 5

f −2, −8, −6, 5, 8, 12

2 Copy and complete the number line.

3 Use the constant function on your calculator to count. Press the equals key ten times. Write down all the numbers the calculator displays.

a Starting at **0** count forwards in **8** s.

b Starting at **3** count forwards in **2** s.

c Starting at **5** **0** count backwards in **5** s.

d Starting at **2** count backwards in **1** s.

e Starting at **0** count backwards in **2** s.

f Starting at **1** **0** **0** count backwards in **3** s.

g Starting at **7** **1** count backwards in **2** s.

h Starting at **7** count forwards in **5** s.

i Starting at **8** **1** count backwards in **9** s.

j Starting at **1** count forwards in **1** **1** s.

Refresher

1 Copy and complete the number lines.

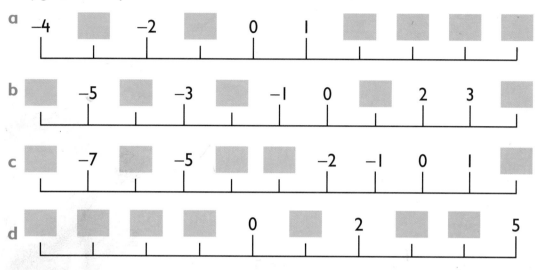

a −4 ▢ −2 ▢ 0 1 ▢ ▢ ▢ ▢

b ▢ −5 ▢ −3 ▢ −1 0 ▢ 2 3 ▢

c ▢ −7 ▢ −5 ▢ ▢ −2 −1 0 1 ▢

d ▢ ▢ ▢ ▢ 0 ▢ 2 ▢ ▢ 5

2 Use the constant function on your calculator to count. Press the equals key ten times. Write down all the numbers the calculator displays.

a Starting at **0** count forwards in **2**s. b Starting at **0** count forwards in **1**s.

c Starting at **0** count forwards in **3**s. d Starting at **40** count backwards in **4**s.

Challenge

Up and down

You need:
- a pencil
- a sheet of paper
- a calculator

What to do

You can do this on your own or with a partner.
1 Write the numbers 1 to 9 on your sheet of paper.
2 Choose a number and decide whether to add or subtract it. Keep going until you have used all the numbers. Cross them out as you use them.
3 The aim is to reach −10 exactly.

Multiplication and division facts

Practice

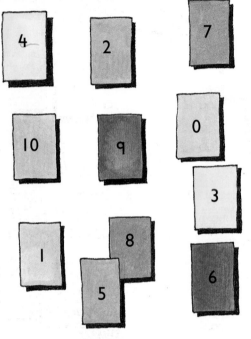

1 Use the numbers 0 – 10 to find the answers.

  a If I multiply the number by 3, the answer is 18.

> **Example**
> $3 \times 6 = 18$.
> The number is 6.

  b If I multiply the number by itself, the answer is 49.
  c If I multiply the number by 9, the answer is 72.
  d If I multiply the number by 6, the answer is 24.
  e Double the number to get an answer of 16.
  f Multiply the number by any number to get an answer of 0.

2 Use these number cards and the cards from question 1 to write 20 division calculations.

> **Example**
> $40 \div 4 = 10$

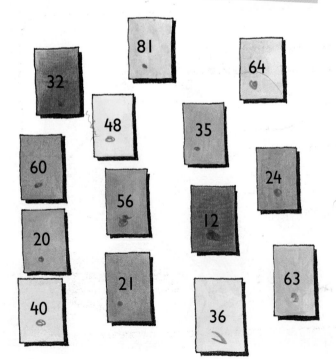

3 Use the words in the boxes and the numbers from questions 1 and 2 to make 20 sentences about numbers. Use each word at least once.

> **Example**
> The product of 9 and 3 is 27.

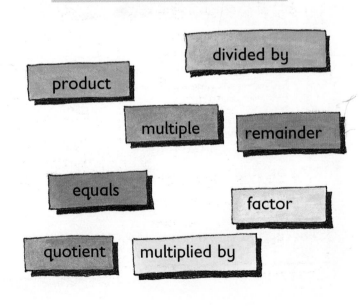

Refresher

1 Use each set of cards to make three multiplication facts.

Example

2 × 7 = 14
2 × 5 = 10
7 × 5 = 35

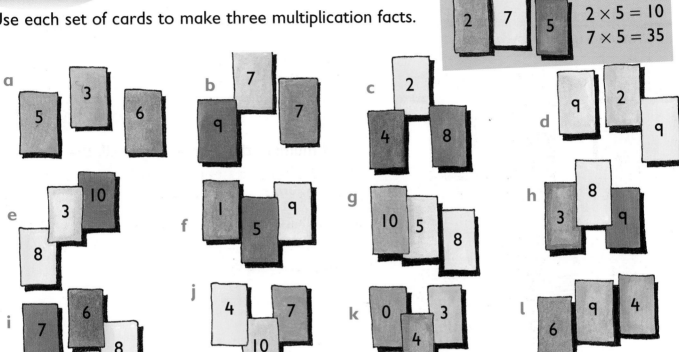

a 5 3 6

b 7 9 7

c 2 4 8

d 9 2 9

e 3 10 8

f 1 5 9

g 10 5 8

h 3 8 9

i 7 6 8

j 4 7 10

k 0 3 4

l 6 9 4

Challenge

Find 5

You need:

1	2	3	4	5	6	7	8	9	10
11	12	13	14	15	16	17	18	19	20
21	22	23	24	25	26	27	28	29	30
31	32	33	34	35	36	37	38	39	40
41	42	43	44	45	46	47	48	49	50
51	52	53	54	55	56	57	58	59	60
61	62	63	64	65	66	67	68	69	70
71	72	73	74	75	76	77	78	79	80
81	82	83	84	85	86	87	88	89	90
91	92	93	94	95	96	97	98	99	100

per pair

● 24 counters each
  (1 colour per person)

●   per pair

What to do

(For 2 players)

1 Take turns to throw the two dice.
2 Multiply the two numbers together.
3 Place a counter over the answer.
4 The first person to get five
  counters in a row, horizontal,
  vertical or diagonal, is
  the winner.

Doubling and halving multiples of 100

Practice

I Find the multiples of 100. Double them.
   Record your answer as a multiplication number sentence.

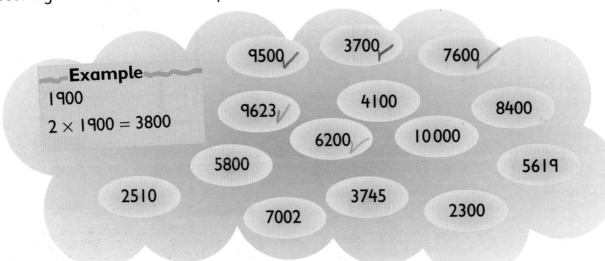

Example
1900
2 × 1900 = 3800

9500 ✓   3700 ✓   7600 ✓
9623 ✓   4100   8400
6200 ✓   10 000
5800   5619
2510   3745   2300
7002

2 Find the multiples of 100. Halve them.
   Record your answer as a division number sentence.

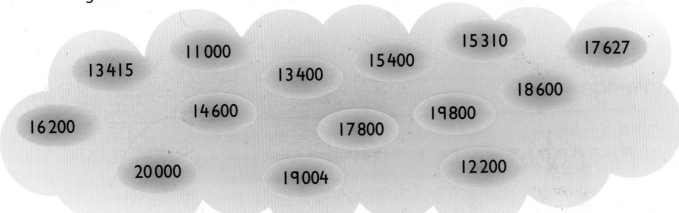

11 000   15 310   17 627
13 415   13 400   15 400   18 600
16 200   14 600   17 800   19 800   19 004   12 200
20 000

3 Halve each of these numbers in your head. Draw a diagram to show your answer.
   Check your answer is correct by performing the inverse operation on your calculator.
   Complete the diagram.

Example
÷ 2
6500   3250
× 2

a 8700   b 11 200   c 14 900
d 20 600   e 16 300   f 10 400
g 9700   h 13 500   i 18 900
j 15 800   k 12 500   l 17 400

Refresher

1 Double each number.

a 18   **Example**   b 86   c 46   d 75
e 54 $18 \times 2 = 36$ f 84   g 37   h 95
i 29   j 39   k 63   l 92

2 Halve each number.

a 92   **Example**   b 30   c 66   d 28
e 54 $92 \div 2 = 46$ f 72   g 46   h 74
i 90   j 82   k 8   l. 34

Challenge

Doubles

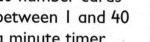

You need:
- paper and pencil
- 20 number cards between 1 and 40
- a minute timer

What to do

(For 2 players)
1 Place the number cards face down in a pile.
2 Turn over the top card.
3 Both players write the number.
4 Start the minute timer.
5 Double the number and keep doubling your answer until the minute is up.
6 Compare your answers. The person with the most correct numbers scores 1 point. The first person to reach 10 points is the winner.

Order of operations

Practice

Class 5 worked out how many different answers they could get from the number sentence.

$2 + 8 \times 4 + 5 = \boxed{}$

$2 + (8 \times 4) + 5 = 2 + 32 + 5 = 39$
$(2 + 8) \times 4 + 5 = 10 \times 4 + 5 = 45$
$2 + 8 \times (4 + 5) = 2 + 72 = 74$
$(2 + 8) \times (4 + 5) = 10 \times 9 = 90$

1 How many different answers can you get from these calculations?
(You can put brackets around any calculation – remember to calculate what is inside the brackets first!)

a $36 \div 6 \times 2 + 1$

b $7 \times 8 \div 4 \times 2$

c $3 \times 4 \div 2 + 4$

d $15 - 5 \times 4 + 6$

e $10 + 10 - 5 \times 3$

f $6 \times 4 - 3 \times 6$

g $10 + 15 - 5 \times 3$

h $7 \times 4 + 2 \times 3$

i $40 \div 4 + 4 \times 6$

j $8 \times 4 + 2 \times 3$

k $32 \div 8 \times 4 + 5$

l $9 \times 5 + 15 \div 3$

2 Draw a table like the one below.

Number sentence	First calculation	Second calculation	Next calculation	Answer
$(20 \div 4) \times 3 - 5$	$20 \div 4 = 5$	$5 \times 3 = 15$	$15 - 5 = 10$	10

● Write the number sentence in the first column.
● Decide which order to complete the calculations.
● Write the calculations in the order you do them.
● Write the answer.

a $2 \times 5 + 3 \times 9$ b $72 \div 9 + 4 \times 3$ c $56 \div (8 - 1) \times 7$ d $(33 + 3) \div 4 - 3$

e $9 \times 9 - 10 \times 3$ f $(9 \times 9) - 10 + 1$ g $(48 - 8) \div 4 \times 2$ h $48 - (8 \div 4) \times 2$

i $48 - 8 + (4 \times 2)$ j $16 + (5 \times 2) \times 6$ k $6 \times 4 + 8 \times 7$ l $36 \div (16 - 7) - 4$

Refresher

Remember

Always divide or multiply before you add or subtract unless there are (BRACKETS). If there are brackets, do what is inside the brackets FIRST!

- Draw a table like the one below.
- Write the number sentence in the first column.
- Decide which order to complete the calculations.
- Write the calculations in the order you do them.
- Write the answer.

Number sentence	First calculation	Next calculation	Answer
$3 + 6 \times 5$	$6 \times 5 = 30$	$30 + 3 = 33$	33

a $4 \times (3 + 5)$

b $4 \times 3 + 5$

c $12 + 16 \div 4$

d $(25 \div 5) \times 3$

3 $(32 - 8) \div 3$

f $10 + 30 \div 3$

g $3 \times 3 \times 2$

h $(18 \div 2) \times 7$

i $36 \div (6 \times 2)$

j $36 \div 6 \times 2$

Challenge

1 Copy and complete these number sentences.

a $(3 \times 4) + \boxed{} = 27$

b $(5 \times 5) - \boxed{} = 14$

c $4 \times 3 \times 2 + \boxed{} = 25$

d $5 \times \boxed{} + 2 \times 3 = 36$

e $24 \div \boxed{} \times 4 \times 2 = 24$

f $16 \times \boxed{} \div 4 + 4 = 8$

g $(25 - \boxed{}) \times 3 \times 2 = 120$

h $42 \div (\boxed{} \times 3) \times 12 = 24$

i $3 \times 9 + 6 \times \boxed{} = 81$

j $\boxed{} \div 5 + 7 \times 9 = 70$

2 Use any combinations of these symbols to make the number sentences below true.

a $16 \boxed{} 4 \boxed{} 3 \boxed{} 4 = 16$

b $24 \boxed{} 2 \boxed{} 6 \boxed{} 3 = 24$

c $8 \boxed{} 4 \boxed{} 2 \boxed{} 1 = 1$

d $(6 \boxed{} 3) \boxed{} (6 \boxed{} 3) = 18$

e $(15 \boxed{} 9) \boxed{} (15 \boxed{} 9) = 36$

f $(12 \boxed{} 2 \boxed{} 2) \boxed{} 6 = 8$

g $(8 \boxed{} 7) \boxed{} 3 \boxed{} 9 = 5$

h $(8 \boxed{} 6 \boxed{} 4) \boxed{} 8 = 4$

Using factors

Practice

1 Find as many ways as you can to split these calculations using factors to help you.

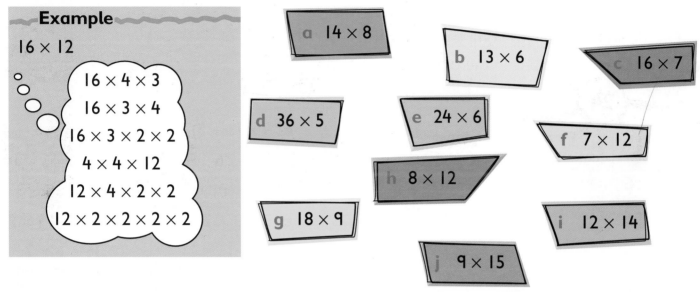

Example

16 × 12

16 × 4 × 3
16 × 3 × 4
16 × 3 × 2 × 2
4 × 4 × 12
12 × 4 × 2 × 2
12 × 2 × 2 × 2 × 2

a 14 × 8

b 13 × 6

c 16 × 7

d 36 × 5

e 24 × 6

f 7 × 12

h 8 × 12

g 18 × 9

i 12 × 14

j 9 × 15

2 a For each calculation above, circle the calculation made
   using factors that you find easiest to work out.

  b Write the answer to the calculation.

3 Find as many ways as you can to split these calculations using factors to help you.

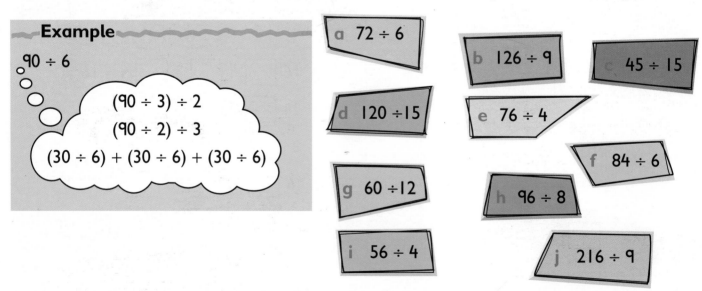

Example

90 ÷ 6

(90 ÷ 3) ÷ 2
(90 ÷ 2) ÷ 3
(30 ÷ 6) + (30 ÷ 6) + (30 ÷ 6)

a 72 ÷ 6

b 126 ÷ 9

c 45 ÷ 15

d 120 ÷ 15

e 76 ÷ 4

f 84 ÷ 6

g 60 ÷ 12

h 96 ÷ 8

i 56 ÷ 4

j 216 ÷ 9

4 a For each calculation above, circle the calculation
   made using factors that you find easiest to work out.

  b Write the answer to the calculation.

Refresher

1 Find the factors of these numbers.

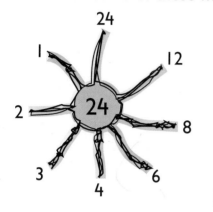

24

1

12

2

24

8

3   6

4

 b 42

 c 9

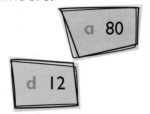 a 80

 d 12

 e 32

 f 20

 g 30

 i 60

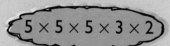 h 18

j 21

k 48

Challenge

1 Make your own "two-digit by two-digit" multiplication calculations.
How many different calculations can you make for each number sentence?

Example

$5 \times 5 \times 5 \times 3 \times 2$

→ 25×30 $(5 \times 5) \times (5 \times 3 \times 2)$
→ 50×15 $(5 \times 5 \times 2) \times (5 \times 3)$
→ 75×10 $(5 \times 5 \times 3) \times (5 \times 2)$

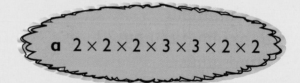 a $2 \times 2 \times 2 \times 3 \times 3 \times 2 \times 2$

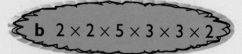 b $2 \times 2 \times 5 \times 3 \times 3 \times 2$

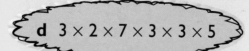 d $3 \times 2 \times 7 \times 3 \times 3 \times 5$

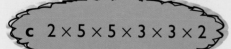 c $2 \times 5 \times 5 \times 3 \times 3 \times 2$

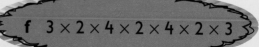 f $3 \times 2 \times 4 \times 2 \times 4 \times 2 \times 3$

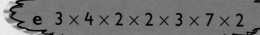 e $3 \times 4 \times 2 \times 2 \times 3 \times 7 \times 2$

17

Terrific twenty

Practice

1 Calculate the answers to these. Show your working.

    a 8 × 19   **b** 6 × 19

    c 17 × 19   **d** 13 × 19

    e 15 × 19   **f** 23 × 19

    g 18 × 19   **h** 35 × 19

    i 48 × 19   **j** 67 × 19

Example

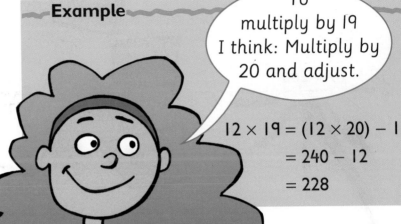

To multiply by 19 I think: Multiply by 20 and adjust.

$$12 \times 19 = (12 \times 20) - 12$$
$$= 240 - 12$$
$$= 228$$

2 Calculate the answers to these. Show your working.

    a 9 × 21   **b** 14 × 21

    c 18 × 21   **d** 25 × 21

    e 27 × 21   **f** 36 × 21

    g 39 × 21   **h** 43 × 21

    i 52 × 21   **j** 68 × 21

Example

To multiply by 21 I think: Multiply by 20 and adjust.

$$13 \times 21 = (13 \times 20) + 13$$
$$= 260 + 13$$
$$= 273$$

Refresher

1 Multiply each of the numbers below by 20.

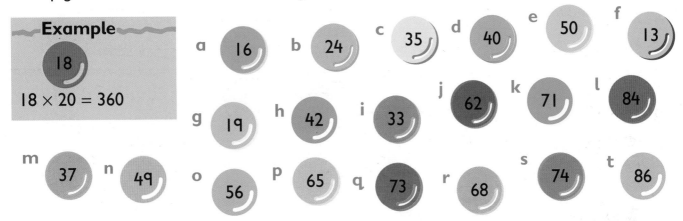

Example

18

$18 \times 20 = 360$

a 16   b 24   c 35   d 40   e 50   f 13

g 19   h 42   i 33   j 62   k 71   l 84

m 37   n 49   o 56   p 65   q 73   r 68   s 74   t 86

Challenge

Mr and Mrs Oldham bought new tiles for the centre of their kitchen floor.

Tile prices

Y   £19   W   £21

Gr   £20   Bl   £9

Prepare an invoice showing:

- the total cost for each colour tile
- the total cost for tiling the floor

INVOICE

TILES
YELLOW
WHITE
GREEN
BLUE

TOTAL

Multiplying by 12

Practice

1 Partition 12 into 10 and 2 to work out the answers. Show your working.

a 12 × 9

b 12 × 15

c 12 × 6

d 12 × 8

e 12 × 13

f 12 × 16

g 12 × 22

h 12 × 25

i 12 × 31

j 12 × 28

k 12 × 40

l 12 × 50

m 12 × 35

Remember

A quick way to multiply by 12 is:

$12 \times 7 = (10 \times 7) + (2 \times 7)$
$= 70 + 14$
$= 84$

2 Read each story about 12.
Choose an appropriate method of calculating your answer.
- mental
- mental with jottings (use the partition method)

Remember

1 dozen = 12

a Eggs are packed in boxes of 12. How many eggs are in 14 boxes?

b The florist sold 23 dozen red roses. How many roses altogether?

c For the school picnic, cook ordered 36 dozen bread rolls. How many rolls?

d The supermarket had family packs of crisps on sale. Mum bought nine packs. There were 12 small packs inside. How many small packs of crisps were there altogether?

e Orange juice is packed in cartons of 12. The junior teachers bought 28 cartons. How many children could have orange juice in the junior school?

f The corner shop had 32 dozen eggs on the shelf. Half of them were broken. How many eggs could be sold?

Refresher

1 Multiply each of the numbers below by 10. Write the new number.

e 38

f 14

g 23

h 35

a 8
b 12
c 19
d 42

46

j 27

2 Multiply each of the numbers below by 2. Write the new number.

d 36

f 28

e 43

g 19

a 8

h 29

b 14

i 58

c 12

j 46

Challenge

The 12s game

You need:
- a stopwatch

or:
- a clock

What to do

(For 2 players)
1 Copy the grid below.
2 Start the timer.
3 Multiply the number cards by 12 to find the matching answer.
4 Write the number from the number card above the correct number on the grid.
5 The first player to complete the grid is the winner.

12

132	168	540	396
720	348	264	612
456	204	528	780

60
44
14
45
65
22
33
17
51
11
29
38

6 How long did you take to complete the game?

Division methods

Practice

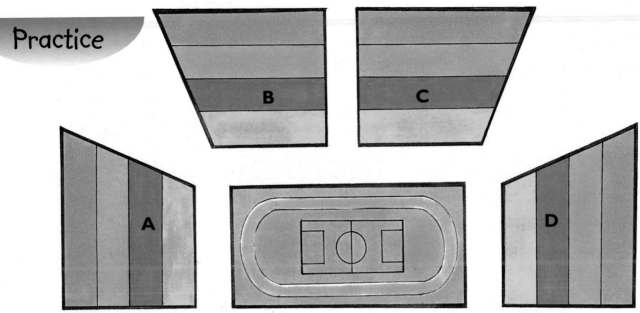

The sports stadium organises its seating in blocks A, B, C, D. Each block consists of rows of different numbers of seats. Find out how many rows of seats were filled in each block during one sports match.

Copy the tables.

Approximate your answer first.

Record your working using a standard written method of division.

 6 seats per row

 7 seats per row

a

Block	Total number of seats	Total number of rows
A	336	
B	384	
C	282	
D	474	

b

Block	Total number of seats	Total number of rows
A	406	
B	483	
C	357	
D	574	

8 seats per row

9 seats per row

c

Block	Total number of seats	Total number of rows
A	424	
B	472	
C	360	
D	592	

d

Block	Total number of seats	Total number of rows
A	558	
B	657	
C	522	
D	774	

Refresher

Write multiplication facts for each bag.

a ×5
20
70
60 30
40

b ×8
50 90
80 60
30

c ×6
20
40
50
60
90

d ×9
30
70
20 60
80

e ×7
70 30
40 60
80

Challenge

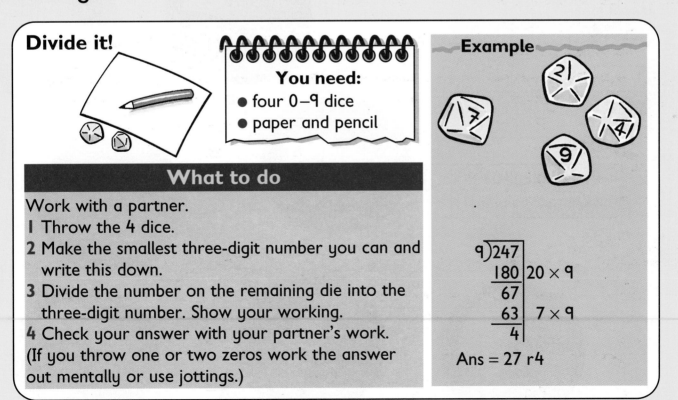

Divide it!

You need:
- four 0–9 dice
- paper and pencil

Example

What to do

Work with a partner.
1 Throw the 4 dice.
2 Make the smallest three-digit number you can and write this down.
3 Divide the number on the remaining die into the three-digit number. Show your working.
4 Check your answer with your partner's work.
(If you throw one or two zeros work the answer out mentally or use jottings.)

```
  9)247
     180  20 × 9
      67
      63   7 × 9
       4
```

Ans = 27 r4

Division methods

Practice

Approximate your answer first.
Choose a standard written method of recording to
work out the answer to each calculation.

Example

$686 \div 8 \rightarrow (640 \div 8 = 80)$

```
8)686
   640  (80 × 8)
    46
    40  (5 × 8)
     6
```

Answer 85 r6

or

$686 \div 8 \rightarrow (640 \div 8 = 80)$

```
     85 r6
8)686
   64
   46
   40
    6
```

Remember

Keep the numbers in
the correct columns!

a $386 \div 7$

b $269 \div 5$

c $863 \div 9$

d $452 \div 6$

e $285 \div 3$

f $498 \div 8$

g $627 \div 7$

h $376 \div 7$

i $207 \div 8$

j $398 \div 9$

Refresher

Approximate the answer to each calculation. The first one is done for you.

Example

a $346 \div 6 \rightarrow 60$ $(360 \div 6 = 60)$

b $248 \div 5$

c $332 \div 4$

d $496 \div 5$

e $256 \div 3$

f $275 \div 3$

g $456 \div 6$

h $362 \div 8$

i $576 \div 8$

j $389 \div 6$

k $156 \div 4$

l $378 \div 9$

m $467 \div 7$

n $283 \div 9$

o $627 \div 9$

p $562 \div 4$

Challenge

1 Five answers total 55.
Can you find them?

a $495 \div 9$

b $270 \div 6$

c $360 \div 8$

d $275 \div 5$

e $385 \div 7$

f $330 \div 6$

g $455 \div 7$

h $175 \div 5$

i $440 \div 8$

j $585 \div 9$

2 Five answers total 79.
Can you find them?

a $356 \div 4$

b $474 \div 6$

c $316 \div 4$

d $712 \div 8$

e $632 \div 8$

f $801 \div 9$

g $623 \div 7$

h $553 \div 7$

i $711 \div 9$

j $534 \div 6$

Exchange rates

Practice

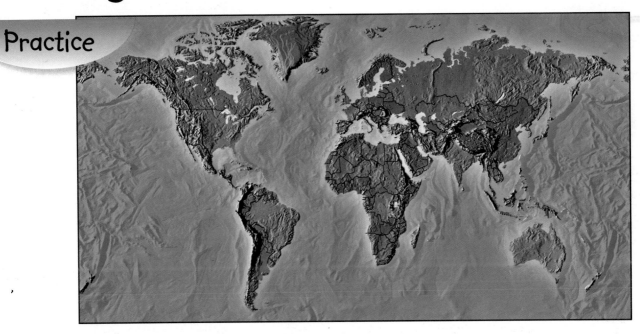

1 Answer these questions about exchange rates.

   a Why are exchange rates also referred to as "tourist rates"?

   b What information does the tourist rate give us?

   c Why does the tourist rate appear in the newspaper on a daily basis?

   d What are the main reasons people need to know how much the pound is worth in other currencies?

   e What does an exchange rate of 10·42 mean?

2 The Phillips family are deciding where to go on holiday. Copy and complete the table to find out how much of each currency they would receive if they exchanged £5, £10 or £20. Use the tourist rates shown in the Refresher activity.

Country	Currency	Exchange Rate	Round to the nearest whole number	£5 =	£10 =	£20 =
a Australia						
b Belgium						
c Denmark						
d Finland						
e India						
f Mexico						
g South Africa						
h Thailand						

Refresher

Tourist rates

Australia ($)	2·57	Malaysia (ringgits)	5·72
Austria (schillings)	22·95	Malta (lira)	0·66
Belgium (francs)	67·46	Mexico (nuevo peso)	13·42
Canada ($)	2·25	Netherlands (guilders)	3·67
Cyprus (pounds)	0·95	New Zealand ($)	3·09
Denmark (kroner)	12·49	Norway (kroner)	13·61
Finland (markka)	9·98	Portugal (escudos)	333·18
France (francs)	10·92	Saudi Arabia (rials)	5·72
Germany (marks)	3·28	Singapore ($)	2·55
Greece (drachma)	562·90	South Africa (rands)	10·31
Hong Kong ($)	11·80	Spain (pesetas)	276·95
Ireland (punts)	1·31	Sweden (kronor)	13·67
India (rupees)	61·55	Switzerland (francs)	2·63
Israel (shekels)	5·84	Thailand (bahts)	54·92
Italy (lira)	3249	Turkey (lirasi)	930029
Japan (yen)	165·21	USA ($)	1·52

1 What currency is used in:
   a Spain
   b Thailand
   c France
   d Ireland
   e Australia

2 Which countries use:
   a dollars
   b francs
   c lira

3 Which country uses the currency:
   a rupees
   b yen
   c escudos
   d shekels
   e kroner

4 What is the exchange rate for the:
   a Italian lira
   b German mark
   c Spanish peseta
   d US dollar
   e New Zealand dollar

Challenge

The Phillips family bought some items on their round-the-world holiday. Use the exchange rates above to work out the cost of each item in English pounds. Round each currency to the nearest whole number.

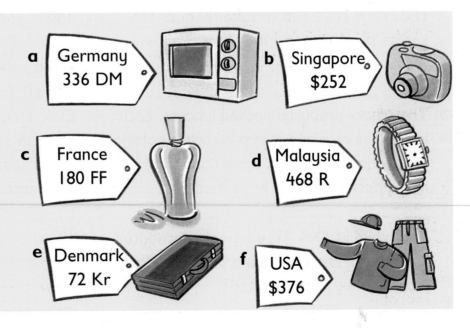

a Germany 336 DM
b Singapore $252
c France 180 FF
d Malaysia 468 R
e Denmark 72 Kr
f USA $376

Solving word problems

Practice

Read the story problems. Choose an appropriate method of calculating your answer.

- mental
- mental with jottings
- paper and pencil

a Oak Tree School has 486 pupils. Nine coaches were hired to take them to the sports stadium. How many children were there on each coach?	**d** From each class, 21 children entered the 100 m sprint races. There are 14 classes in Oak Tree School. How many children ran a sprint race?
b The school prepared packed lunches. Each packed lunch was put into a carton holding 19 lunches. 18 cartons were required. How many packed lunches were made?	**e** Oak Tree School sat in Stand A. There are 525 seats in Stand A. Each row has seven seats. How many rows of seats altogether?
c Each child at Oak Tree school contributed £2 towards the cost of the coaches. How much money was collected?	**f** 12 schools competed in the relay races. Each team had four runners. How many children were there altogether in the relays?

Refresher

1 For each story, decide which operation you will use to answer the question.

(+) (−) (×) (÷)

a French fries cost ⬜. Jim buys ⬜. How much does he spend?

b It cost ⬜ for ⬜ burgers. How much do they cost?

c Samuel buys a hot dog, a can of drink and an ice-cream. How much does he spend?

d A carton of drink cans costs ⬜. Each can costs ⬜. How many cans in a carton?

e Mrs Joseph has ⬜. She pays ⬜ for her food. How much change does she get?

f Hot dogs cost ⬜ each. How much does it cost for ⬜?

Challenge

1 Use the pictures and information on both pages to write your own word problems for these calculations.

2 Approximate the answer first (if necessary).

3 Calculate the answer using the most appropriate method.

a 486 × 4   b 525 − 486   c 14 × 12

d 486 ÷ 6   e 256 × 9   f 400 × 3

29

Fractions in order

Practice

1 Which of these fractions is more than $\frac{1}{2}$?

   a $\frac{7}{8}$ b $\frac{2}{10}$ c $\frac{5}{6}$ d $\frac{3}{20}$

   e $\frac{51}{100}$ f $\frac{3}{4}$ g $\frac{1}{12}$

2 Order these fractions.

   a $\frac{1}{2}$ $\frac{1}{4}$ $\frac{3}{4}$ $\frac{9}{10}$ $\frac{1}{8}$ b $\frac{3}{20}$ $\frac{5}{10}$ $\frac{7}{8}$ $\frac{4}{6}$ $\frac{4}{10}$

   c $\frac{2}{3}$ $\frac{5}{6}$ $\frac{1}{3}$ $\frac{1}{6}$ $\frac{8}{9}$ d $\frac{96}{100}$ $\frac{25}{50}$ $\frac{5}{20}$ $\frac{6}{10}$ $\frac{4}{100}$

3 Copy the number lines and write the numbers on them in the correct order.

   a $2\frac{1}{2}$, $1\frac{1}{2}$, $1\frac{1}{4}$, $1\frac{3}{4}$

   b $3\frac{1}{3}$, $2\frac{2}{3}$, $1\frac{1}{2}$, $2\frac{1}{2}$

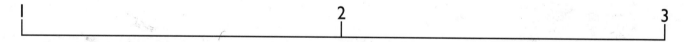

   c $1\frac{4}{10}$, $2\frac{8}{10}$, $2\frac{1}{10}$, $1\frac{3}{4}$

   d $1\frac{3}{10}$, $3\frac{1}{2}$, $2\frac{1}{4}$, $1\frac{8}{10}$

   e $3\frac{1}{5}$, $4\frac{2}{5}$, $3\frac{4}{5}$, $2\frac{1}{2}$

Refresher

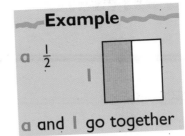
I Match the fractions to the amount shaded on each shape.

a $\frac{1}{2}$

    b $\frac{3}{8}$

c $\frac{3}{4}$

    d $\frac{6}{10}$

e $\frac{2}{3}$

    f $\frac{1}{6}$

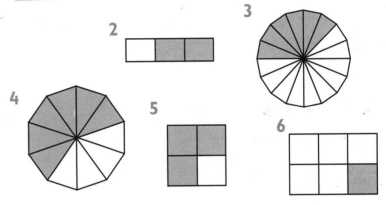

2   3   4   5   6

2 Now put them in order from smallest to largest.

3 Which ones are more than half?

4 Copy the number lines and put the numbers in the right places.

a $1\frac{1}{2}$, $2\frac{1}{4}$, $3\frac{3}{4}$

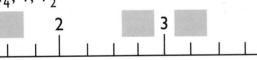

1 ⬜ 2 ⬜ 3 ⬜ 4

b $1\frac{1}{4}$, $2\frac{1}{2}$, 2, $3\frac{1}{2}$

1 ⬜ ⬜ ⬜ 3 ⬜ 4

c $3\frac{1}{4}$, $2\frac{3}{4}$, 1, $1\frac{1}{2}$

⬜ ⬜ 2 ⬜ 3 ⬜ 4

d 0, $2\frac{1}{4}$, $1\frac{3}{4}$, $3\frac{3}{4}$

⬜ 1 ⬜ 2 ⬜ 3 ⬜ 4

e $\frac{1}{4}$, $\frac{1}{2}$, $\frac{3}{4}$, 0, 1

⬜ ⬜ ⬜ ⬜ ⬜

Challenge

I Draw a number line from 0 to 1 and put the fractions from question 1 in the Practice section on it.

2 How many of each fraction would be equal to a half?

3 How many more of each fraction would make a whole?

Fractions and division

Practice

Remember
You can use division to find fractions.

1 Copy and complete the statements.

a To find halves you divide by ☐ .

b To find thirds you divide by ☐ .

c To find eighths you divide by ☐ .

d To find tenths you divide by ☐ .

e To find hundredths you divide by ☐ .

2 Work out the fractions of these numbers or quantities.

a $\frac{1}{2}$ of 16

b half of 60 kg

c $\frac{1}{2}$ of 84

d half of £5

e third of 90

f $\frac{1}{3}$ of 27 g

g quarter of £1

h $\frac{1}{4}$ of 240?

i fifth of 500 ml

j $\frac{1}{5}$ of £1.50

k $\frac{1}{6}$ of an hour

l sixth of 54

m $\frac{1}{7}$ of 140

n seventh of 77

o $\frac{1}{8}$ of 8000

p an eighth of 32 minutes

q $\frac{1}{9}$ of 900 km

r ninth of 18 hours

s $\frac{1}{10}$ of 700

t tenth of 420 ml

u $\frac{1}{100}$ of 6700

v hundredth of 12 300

Refresher

Remember
To find **half** of a number you divide by **2**.

1 Find half of these numbers and amounts.

a 14   b 26   c 48   d 100   e 140

f 500 g   g 60 minutes   h 208 km   i £700   j 90 cm

Remember
To find a **quarter** of a number you divide by **4**.

2 Find a quarter of these numbers and amounts.

a 40   b 16   c 24   d 100

e 84   f 400 m   g £36   h 60 g   i 800 km   j 200 cm

Remember
To find **thirds** you divide by **3**.

3 Find a third of these numbers and quantities.

a 30   b 15   c 21

d 90   e 300   f 9 kg   g 600 km   h £27

i 3000 m   j 3 minutes

Challenge

1 What is:

a half of £7

b half of £10·50?

c a tenth of 56 km?

d a tenth of 386 m?

e a hundredth of £480?

f a hundredth of 720?

g a quarter of £17?

h a quarter of 33 km?

i a fifth of £101?

j a fifth of 256 litres?

Skittle fractions

Practice

1 Find the fractions of these numbers.

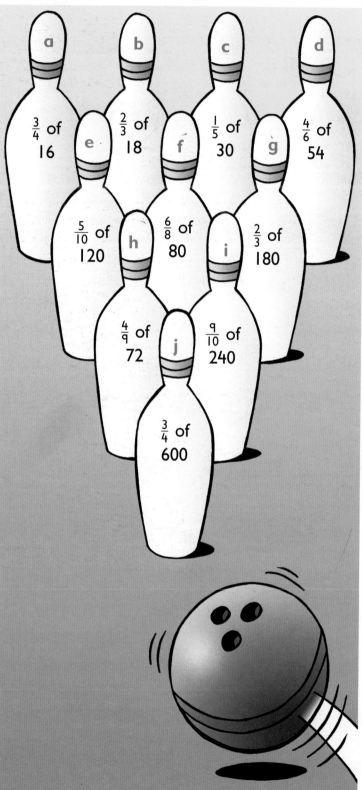

a. $\frac{3}{4}$ of 16

b. $\frac{2}{3}$ of 18

c. $\frac{1}{5}$ of 30

d. $\frac{4}{6}$ of 54

e. $\frac{5}{10}$ of 120

f. $\frac{6}{8}$ of 80

g. $\frac{2}{3}$ of 180

h. $\frac{4}{9}$ of 72

i. $\frac{9}{10}$ of 240

j. $\frac{3}{4}$ of 600

2 Find the fractions of these quantities.

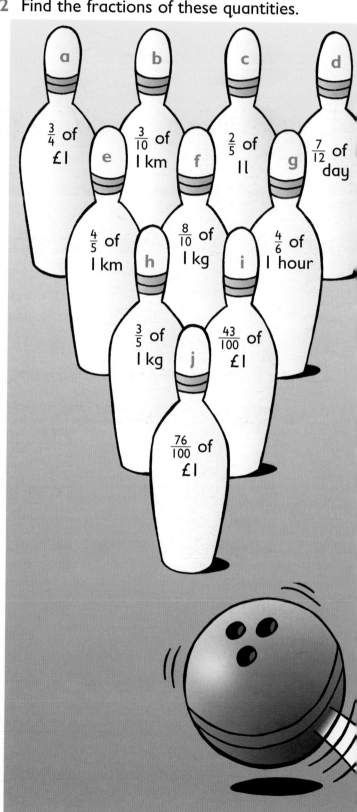

a. $\frac{3}{4}$ of £1

b. $\frac{3}{10}$ of 1 km

c. $\frac{2}{5}$ of 1 l

d. $\frac{7}{12}$ of day

e. $\frac{4}{5}$ of 1 km

f. $\frac{8}{10}$ of 1 kg

g. $\frac{4}{6}$ of 1 hour

h. $\frac{3}{5}$ of 1 kg

i. $\frac{43}{100}$ of £1

j. $\frac{76}{100}$ of £1

First I need to find $\frac{1}{4}$, then I can work out $\frac{3}{4}$.

Refresher

Work out these fractions. The first one is done for you.

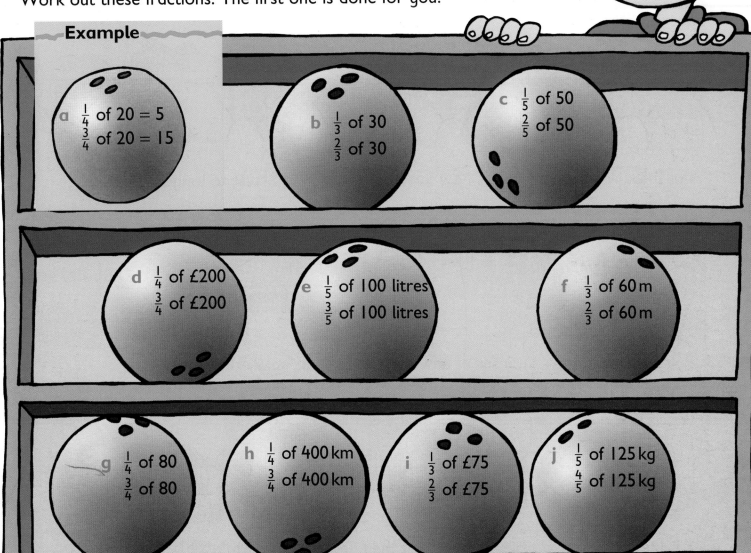

Example

a $\frac{1}{4}$ of 20 = 5
$\frac{3}{4}$ of 20 = 15

b $\frac{1}{3}$ of 30
$\frac{2}{3}$ of 30

c $\frac{1}{5}$ of 50
$\frac{2}{5}$ of 50

d $\frac{1}{4}$ of £200
$\frac{3}{4}$ of £200

e $\frac{1}{5}$ of 100 litres
$\frac{3}{5}$ of 100 litres

f $\frac{1}{3}$ of 60 m
$\frac{2}{3}$ of 60 m

g $\frac{1}{4}$ of 80
$\frac{3}{4}$ of 80

h $\frac{1}{4}$ of 400 km
$\frac{3}{4}$ of 400 km

i $\frac{1}{3}$ of £75
$\frac{2}{3}$ of £75

j $\frac{1}{5}$ of 125 kg
$\frac{4}{5}$ of 125 kg

Challenge

What fraction?

a What fraction of £1 is 70p?
b What fraction of 1 km is 750 m?
c What fraction of 1 litre is 200 ml?
d What fraction of a day is 16 hours?
e What fraction of an hour is 10 minutes?
f What fraction of 1 m is 70 cm?
g What fraction of £1 is 45p?
h What fraction of 1 kg is 800 g?
i What fraction of a minute is 40 seconds?
j What fraction of 1 km is 400 m?

35

Ordering decimals

Practice

1 Put these parcels in order of weight, lightest to heaviest.

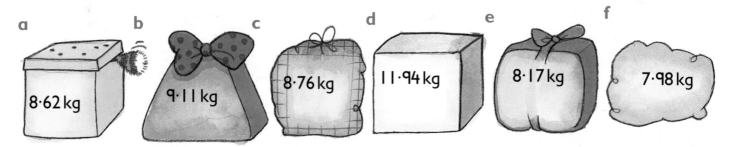

a 8·62 kg   b 9·11 kg   c 8·76 kg   d 11·94 kg   e 8·17 kg   f 7·98 kg

2 Put these runners in order of how far they have run, shortest to longest distance.

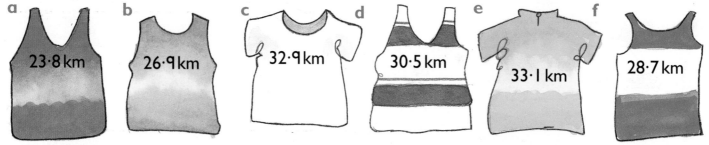

a 23·8 km   b 26·9 km   c 32·9 km   d 30·5 km   e 33·1 km   f 28·7 km

3 Put these containers in order of how much they hold, smallest to largest.

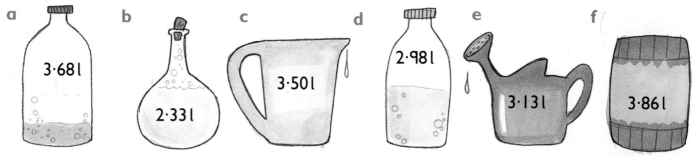

a 3·68 l   b 2·33 l   c 3·50 l   d 2·98 l   e 3·13 l   f 3·86 l

4 Put these children in order of how long they held their breath for – longest time to shortest time.

a 8·21 s   b 8·38 s   c 9·22 s   d 8·76 s   e 9·46 s

5 Now round all the above quantities to the nearest whole number.

Example
8·62 kg rounds up to 9 kg

36

Refresher

1 Copy out the number lines and put the decimal numbers in the correct place on them.

a 4·6 4·8 4·7 4·2

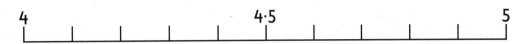

b 8·8 8·1 8·3 8·9

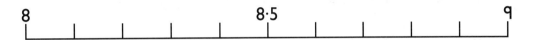

c 2·6 2·9 2·2 2·4

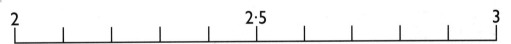

d 6·7 6·3 6·1 6·8

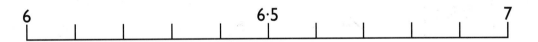

2 Now round each decimal number to the nearest whole number.
Use their place on the number line to help you.

Challenge

These numbers are a mixture of one- and two-place decimals. Order each group.

a 14·31 14·4 14·8 14·76 14·01   b 26·5 26·52 26·87 26·9 26·2

c 178·01 178·1 178·12 178·26 178·6   d 86·99 86·09 86·9 86·19 86·1

e 362·5 362·05 362·4 362·14 362·1   f 54·3 54·13 54·03 54·31 54·1

Funfair fractions and decimals

Practice

1 Work out these fractions using a calculator.
Write the division calculation.

a $\frac{2}{3}$ of 111

b $\frac{3}{4}$ of 172

c $\frac{1}{4}$ of 96

d $\frac{4}{6}$ of 234

e $\frac{3}{10}$ of 270

f $\frac{4}{7}$ of 301

g $\frac{5}{8}$ of 424

h $\frac{9}{10}$ of 530

i $\frac{4}{5}$ of 605

2 Convert these fractions to decimals using a calculator. Write the division calculation.

a $\frac{1}{2}$

b $\frac{1}{4}$

c $\frac{1}{10}$

d $\frac{1}{5}$

e $\frac{1}{100}$

f $\frac{3}{4}$

Refresher

1 Find these fractions using the calculator.

Example
$\frac{1}{4}$ of 76 = 19
76 ÷ 4 = 19

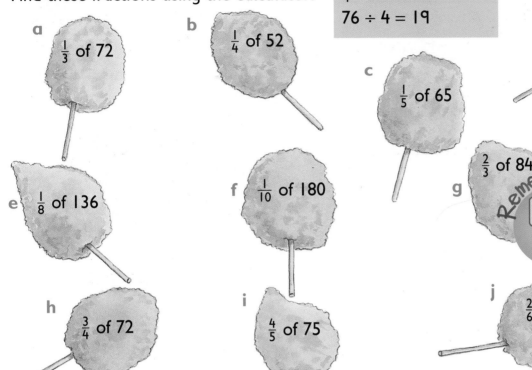
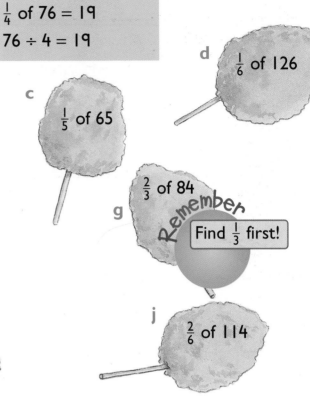

a $\frac{1}{3}$ of 72

b $\frac{1}{4}$ of 52

c $\frac{1}{5}$ of 65

d $\frac{1}{6}$ of 126

e $\frac{1}{8}$ of 136

f $\frac{1}{10}$ of 180

g $\frac{2}{3}$ of 84

Remember
Find $\frac{1}{3}$ first!

h $\frac{3}{4}$ of 72

i $\frac{4}{5}$ of 75

j $\frac{2}{6}$ of 114

Challenge

1 Use the calculator to convert these fractions to decimals.
Write the division calculation.

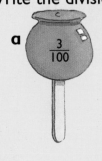

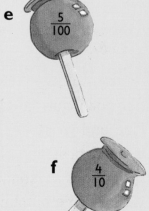

a $\frac{3}{100}$

b $\frac{75}{100}$

c $\frac{9}{10}$

d $\frac{2}{5}$

e $\frac{5}{100}$

f $\frac{4}{10}$

2 Which two fractions convert to the same decimal?
Explain why this is.

Solid sorts

Practice

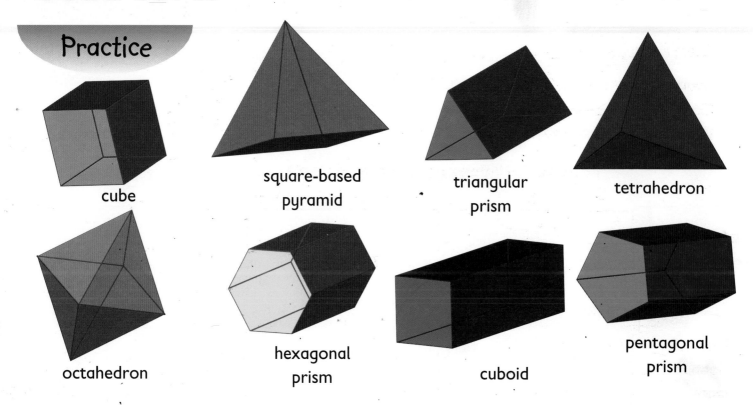

cube

square-based
pyramid

triangular
prism

tetrahedron

octahedron

hexagonal
prism

cuboid

pentagonal
prism

1 For each question, write in which region, 1, 2 or 3, you would sort these shapes.

a cuboid, octahedron, cube,
triangular prism

All faces congruent	At least 1 right-angled face

1   2   3

b tetrahedron, square-based pyramid,
hexagonal prism, pentagonal prism

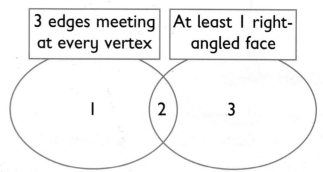

3 edges meeting at every vertex	At least 1 right-angled face

1   2   3

2 For each clue, choose from the 8 solids shown above.
Find and write the name of the solid which has:

a 8 vertices and all right-angled faces congruent to each other.

b 4 edges meeting at every vertex and all faces are triangular.

c the same number of right-angled vertices as a cube, but edges of different lengths.

d 4 more vertices than a cube and the 2 identical end faces are regular.

e one right-angled face and 4 edges meeting at one of the vertices.

3 Write your own clues for these solids.

a tetrahedron

b hexagonal prism

40

Refresher

1 Look at the 8 shapes on page 40.
  Copy and complete this table.
  Write the name of the shape in the correct region.

Number of edges meeting at a vertex

	3	more than 3
Has at least 1 right-angled face		
Has no right-angled faces		

Challenge

In the 18th century a Swiss mathematician, Leonard Euler (pronounced Oiler) said:

> ❝The sum of the number of faces and vertices is always equal to the number of edges plus two. ❞

1 Is Euler's claim true or false?
  Copy and complete this table for each of the 8 shapes on the opposite page.

Name of solid	Faces	Vertices	Edges
cuboid	6	8	12

2 Does Euler's rule, $F + V = E + 2$, work for a cone?

Visualising 3D shapes

Practice

1 Work out the least number of unit cubes you need to turn each shape into a cuboid.

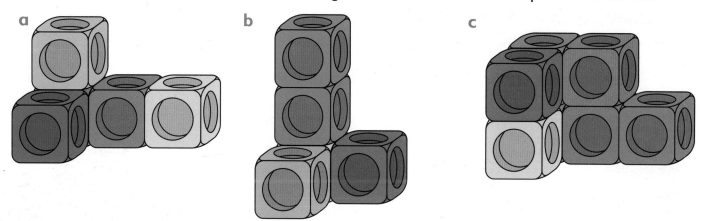

a   b   c

2 Simon is a supermarket shelf-stacker.
He fills the spaces on the shelves and makes a cuboid display of each type of packet.
The diagrams show how many packets are on each shelf.
Work out the least number of cartons Simon must add to make each display a cuboid.

a

b

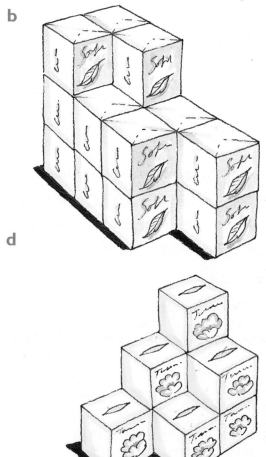

c

d

Refresher

You need:
- about 12 interlocking cubes in two colours

1 Make each of these shapes, in turn, with interlocking cubes of the same colour.

2 Work out the least number of cubes needed to turn each shape into a cuboid.

3 Now add that amount of cubes, in the second colour, to the shape to check that you are correct.

a
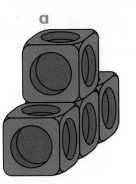

b
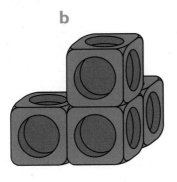

c
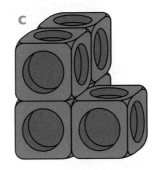

d
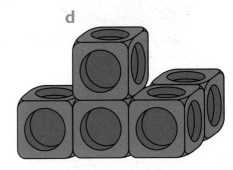

Challenge

Work with a partner.
You need a supply of cubes in two colours.

1 Build each of the 3 towers with cubes of the same colour.

2 Work out the least number of cubes you need to turn the first tower into a cube. Take that number of cubes in the second colour and complete the cube.

3 Repeat for the other towers.

4 Copy and complete.

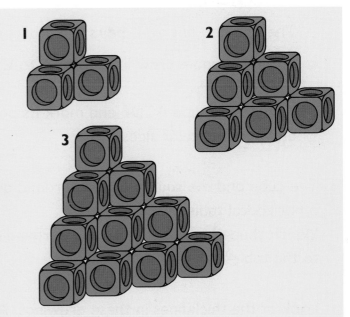

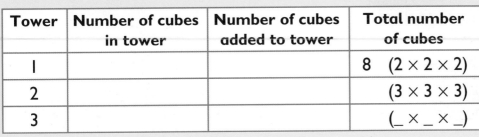

Tower	Number of cubes in tower	Number of cubes added to tower	Total number of cubes
1			8 $(2 \times 2 \times 2)$
2			$(3 \times 3 \times 3)$
3			$(\_ \times \_ \times \_)$

Perpendicular and parallel lines

Practice

1 This is a drawing of a football pitch.
   The corners are marked A, B, C and D.
   Copy and complete.

   a Line AB is parallel to line ☐.

   b Line AD is parallel to line ☐.

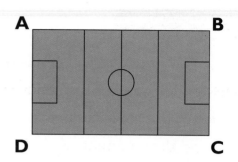

2 Helen made a drawing of her house.

   a Name 2 pairs of perpendicular lines.
   b Name 1 pair of parallel lines.

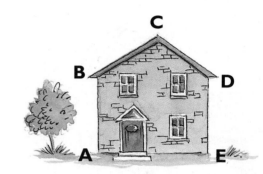

3 Draw these shapes on squared paper.

   a Mark all the parallel lines in both shapes.
   b Copy and complete.

      The hexagon has ☐ pairs of parallel lines.

      The octagon has ☐ pairs of parallel lines.

   c In the hexagon, draw lines from A to C and
      from F to D.
      Name the shape ACDF and mark its parallel
      and perpendicular sides.

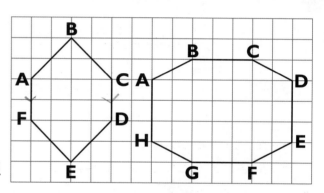

4 The cube and the square-based pyramid are on
   a horizontal table.
   Which shape has sides which are perpendicular
   to the table?

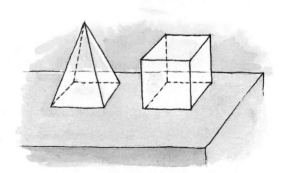

5 Look at the thick lines in these drawings. Are
   the lines parallel? Check with a ruler.

   a

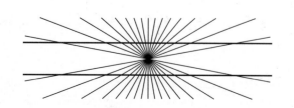

   b

Refresher

1 For each arrow, decide whether the **thick** lines are perpendicular or parallel.

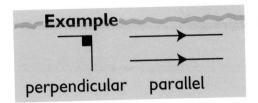

Example

perpendicular   parallel

2 Refer to the picture.
Name one more pair of parallel lines and one more pair of perpendicular lines.

Challenge

During the American Civil War, Union soldiers used the pig pen code to send secret messages.

ABC	DEF	GHI
JKL	MNO	PQR
STU	VWX	YZ

1 Use the code to work out this message.

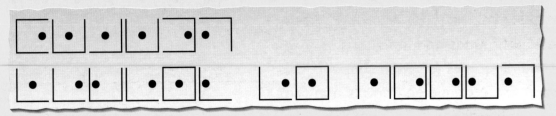

2 Using the pig pen code, write a message to a friend.

45

Diagonal lines

Practice

Remember

Remember to use a ruler.

1 a Copy these diagonals on to dot squared paper.
   b Join the vertices in order to complete each shape.
   c Find the matching shape at the top of the page
      and write its letter.

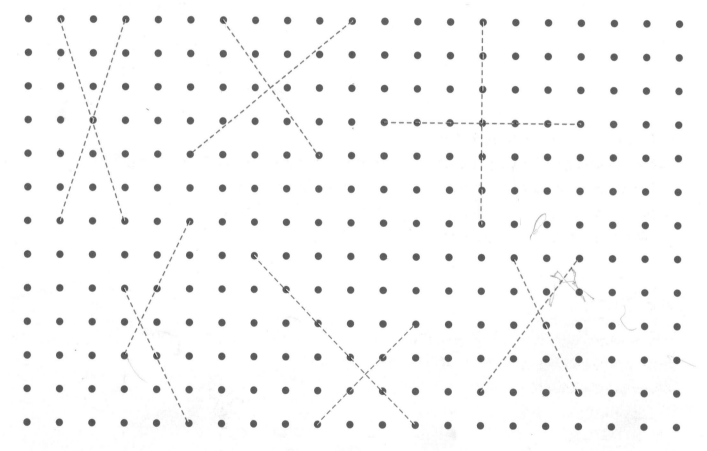

2 a Copy these pentagons and hexagons.
   b Draw all the diagonals for each shape.
   c Draw two more concave pentagons and two
      more concave hexagons.
   d Count the diagonals in each polygon and write
      what you notice.

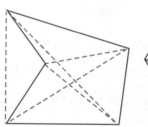
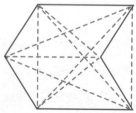

46

Remember

Remember to use a ruler.

Refresher

Five children are standing in a circle to practise throwing and catching a ball.
They throw the ball to each other in this order.
A throws to C
C throws to E
E throws to B
B throws to D
D throws to A

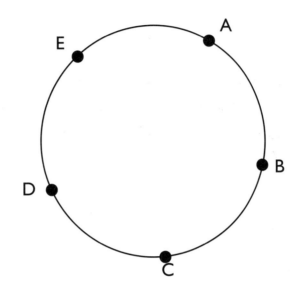

1 a Draw round a circle template.
  b Mark five points on the circumference and label them A, B, C, D and E.
  c Draw straight lines to show the throws the children made.
  d Next, join the points in order : A to B to C to D to E to A.
  e Name the shape you have made.

Challenge

1 How many diagonals can you draw, without them crossing each other, in
  a a quadrilateral
  b a pentagon
  c a hexagon
  d a heptagon
  e an octagon?

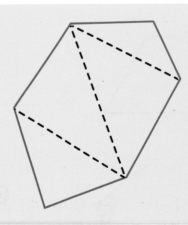

2 Make a table of your results and write about any patterns you notice.

3 What if you had a nine-sided shape? Can you predict the number of diagonals there will be which do not cross each other?

Naming angles

Practice

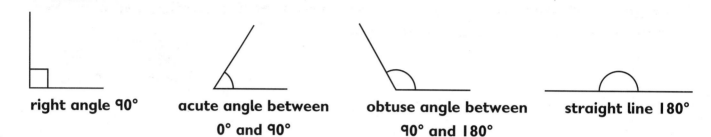

right angle 90°   acute angle between   obtuse angle between   straight line 180°
                         0° and 90°   90° and 180°

1   Estimate whether each sector has an acute, obtuse or right angle.
    Use your right angle measurer to check.
    Write the acute angles in order, beginning with the smallest angle.

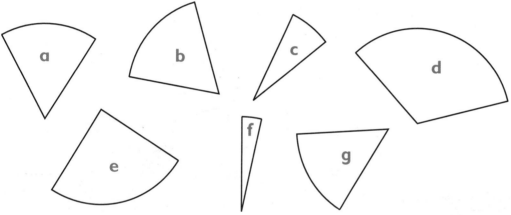

2   Name the marked angle in each of these shapes.

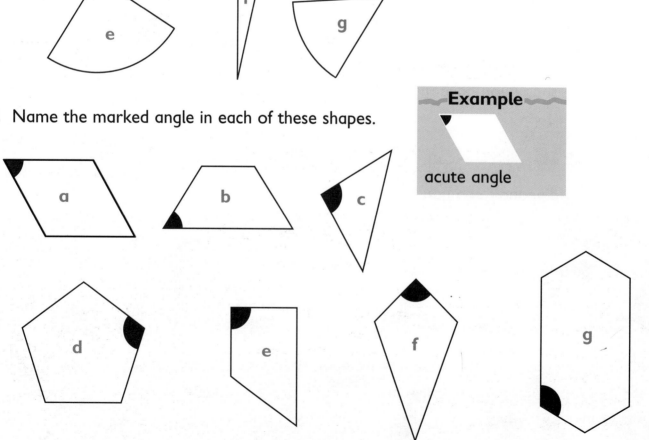

Example

acute angle

48

Refresher

1 Use your right angle measurer to help you decide whether these angles are acute, obtuse or right angles.

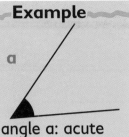
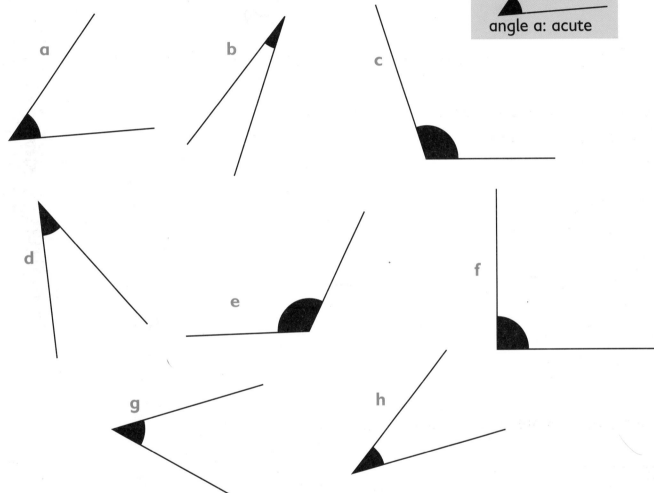

a

b

c

d

e

f

g

h

Challenge

Draw these polygons:

a 3 sides and 1 right angle

b 4 sides and 1 obtuse angle

c 5 sides and 1 acute angle

d 6 sides and 2 acute angles

e 3 sides and 1 obtuse angle

f 4 sides and 2 obtuse angles

You need:
• a ruler
• a right angle measurer or set square

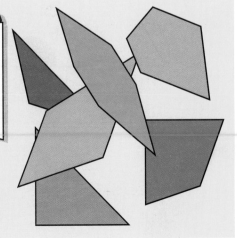

Measuring angles

Practice

1 Measure these angles to the nearest 5°.

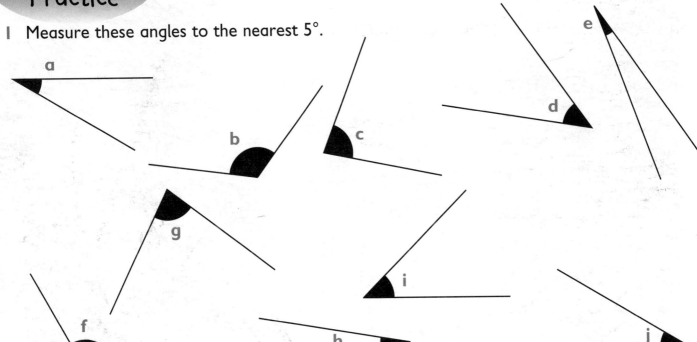

2 List the pairs of angles above of the same size.

3 a Measure the marked angles in these shapes. Write the number of degrees.

 b Write what you notice about your answers.

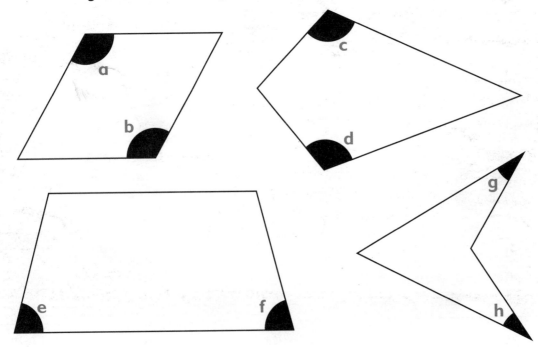

Refresher

Measure these angles. Write the number of degrees.

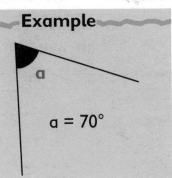

Example

a = 70°

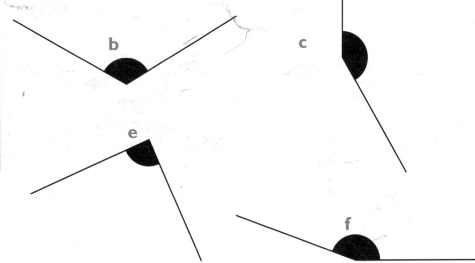

Challenge

Angles in an octagon

What to do

(For 2 players)
- Draw round the octagon template.
- Draw the 5 diagonals from one vertex.
- Choose an angle. Each player estimates the size of the angle to the nearest 5°.
- Measure the angle.
- Repeat 7 more times for the remaining vertices.
- The player with the higher score wins.

Scoring
Exactly right .... 5 points
Within 5° of the angle size .... 3 points
Within 10° of the angle size ...... 1 point

You need:
- a plastic octagon template
- a ruler
- a protractor

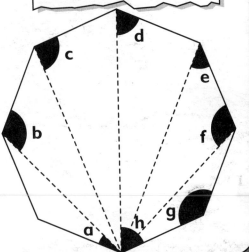

Drawing angles

Practice

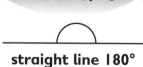

straight line 180°

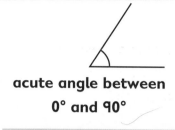

right angle 90°

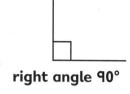

acute angle between
0° and 90°

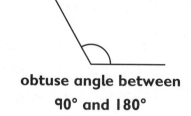

obtuse angle between
90° and 180°

1　Draw and label these acute angles.

　　a　50°　　　　　b　70°

　　c　25°　　　　　d　55°

　　e　85°　　　　　f　20°

Example

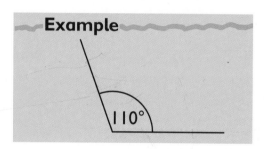

2　Draw and label two right angles.

3　Draw and label these obtuse angles.

　　a　120°　　　　b　160°

　　c　135°　　　　d　95°

　　e　105°　　　　f　170°

Example

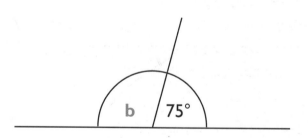

4　Copy these diagrams.
　　Calculate the size of angles a to d.
　　Check with your protractor.

Example

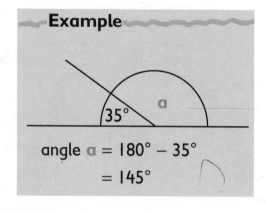

angle a = 180° − 35°
　　　　　= 145°

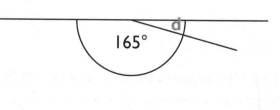

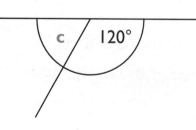

Refresher

1 Use your protractor to draw these right angles in your exercise book. Mark the right angle each time.

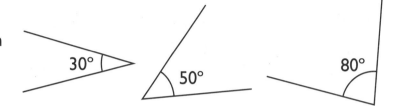

2 Draw these acute angles. Mark each angle with an arc and write its size.

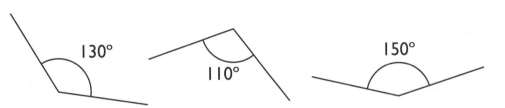

30°   50°   80°

3 In the same way, draw these obtuse angles.

130°   110°   150°

Challenge

Angles in a clock face

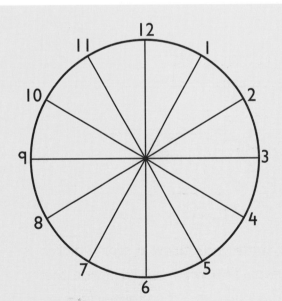

1 Find a way to draw this clock face.

You can begin by:
   drawing round a large plastic circle or using a pair of compasses to draw the circle.

Mark the centre of the circle.

Draw angle arms to each of the hours.

Number the hours 1 to 12.

2 Calculate the obtuse angle between the hands at: **a** 4 o'clock **b** 5 o'clock.

3 At the half hour, the hour hand is halfway between the hours.
Draw and measure:
   a the acute angle at 3:30   **b** the obtuse angle at 9:30.

4 Work out the size of the remaining 10 acute or obtuse angles for the half hour times between 1:30 and 12:30.

Rotating shapes

Practice

You need:
● a protractor, compasses or a large plastic circle
● ruler
● eraser
● felt-tip pens

Remember
Draw lightly in pencil.

1 **a** Draw round a circle template or draw a circle with a radius of 4·5 cm

b Mark the centre of the circle. Use the circular protractor to divide the circumference into 4 equal parts.

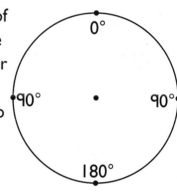

c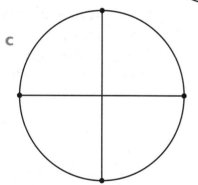

Join the opposite points.

d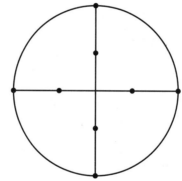

On each radius, put a dot 2 cm from the centre.

e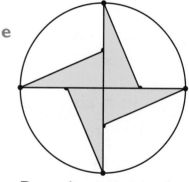

Draw lines to join the points. Erase the circles. Colour your star.

2 In the same way, draw a star which has six points. You will need to divide the circumference into 6 equal parts so mark the circumference in multiples of 60°.

3 Design a star which has 8 points. You will have to make angles of 45° at the centre of the circle.

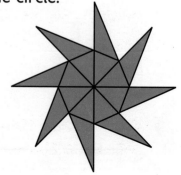

Refresher

1 Draw round a large square template.

2 Draw the diagonals with your ruler.

3 Place the right angle of the triangle on the right angle made by the diagonals.

4 Draw round the triangle.

5 Repeat 3 more times.

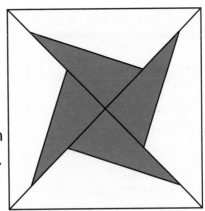

You need:
- a large plastic square
- a small plastic right-angled triangle
- a ruler

Challenge

Car wheel patterns

1 Using your protractor and intervals of 45°, draw 8 equally spaced angles.

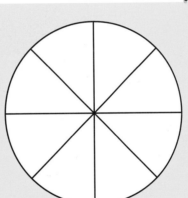

You need:
- a protractor
- compasses
- a square of card
- scissors
- a felt-tip pen

2 Take your square of card and cut out a shape.

3 Place a corner of the card at the centre of the grid, and the opposite corner on one of the lines.

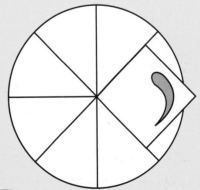

4 Rotate the card and draw 8 outlines of your shape, one on each line.

5 Repeat several times to create different patterns.

55

Calculating areas

Practice

1 Find the areas of these rectangles.

a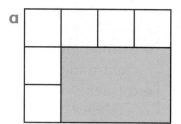

b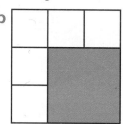

c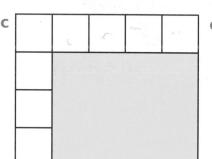

d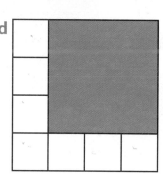

e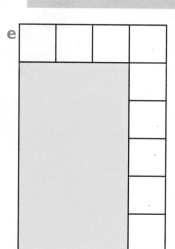

f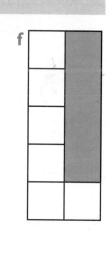

2 Ellen made a collage with her holiday photographs.

a Find the area of each picture.

b List the pictures in order. Begin with the smallest area.

56

Refresher

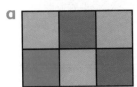

1 Find the area of these rectangles.

a   b

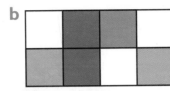

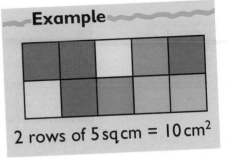

Example

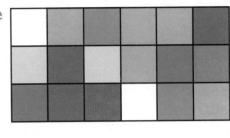

2 rows of 5 sq cm = 10 cm²

c   d   e

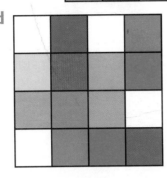

2 List the rectangles in order, smallest to largest.

Challenge

You have 9 rectangular cards measuring 10 cm × 5 cm.

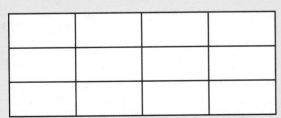

1 Using all the cards each time, make 3 different rectangles.

2 Find the area of each rectangle.

3 You have another 3 cards also measuring 10 cm × 5 cm.
You make these rectangles with the 12 cards.

a   b

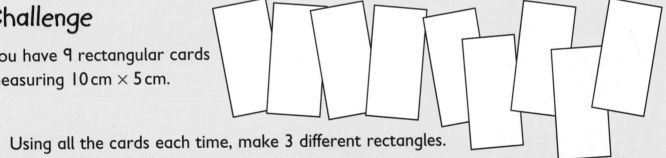

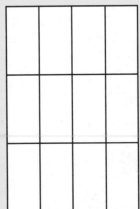

Find the area and the perimeter of each rectangle.

57

Using square units

Practice

Size of square	
I square millimetre	I mm²
I square centimetre	I cm²
I square metre	I m²

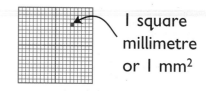
I square millimetre or I mm²

1 Write which size of square you would use to measure the area of:
   a the front cover of your textbook
   b the board
   c a petal of a daisy
   d a football pitch
   e a computer key
   f a slice of bread
   g your thumbnail
   h the assembly hall

2 Find the area of each of these.
   Remember to answer in square units.

a
60 mm
90 mm
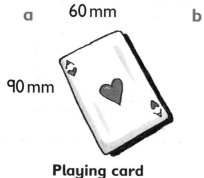
Playing card

b
8 mm
8 mm
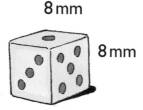
Top of die

Example
40 mm
20 mm
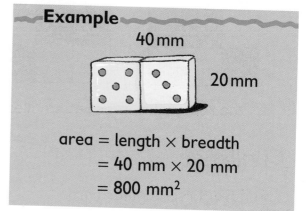
area = length × breadth
     = 40 mm × 20 mm
     = 800 mm²

c
60 mm
60 mm
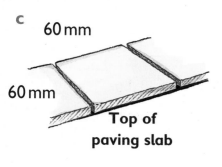
Top of paving slab

d
6 cm
18 cm
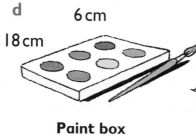
Paint box

e
120 m
80 m
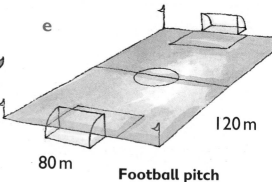
Football pitch

3 Write the approximate area of each rectangle.

a
4·6 cm
1·9 cm
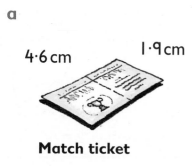
Match ticket

b
1·8 m
0·2 m
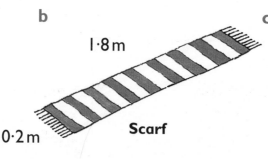
Scarf

c
2·5 m
7 m
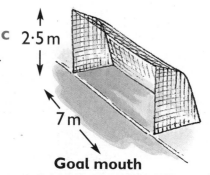
Goal mouth

58

Refresher

1 Draw these rectangles on 1 cm squared paper.
Find the area of each rectangle.

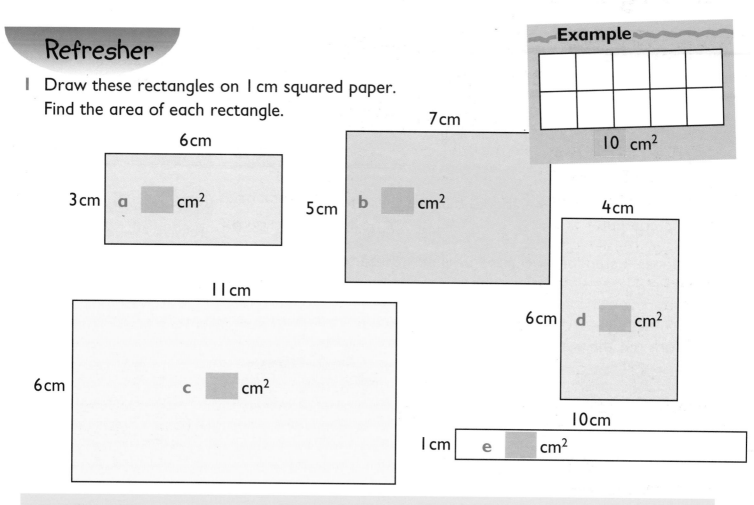

Example

10 cm²

6cm

3cm | a | cm²

7cm

5cm | b | cm²

4cm

6cm | d | cm²

11 cm

6cm | c | cm²

10cm

1cm | e | cm²

Challenge

Work in a small group.

1 Choose two of the following objects, or some other object if you prefer.

2 Estimate then measure the area of each object, using the most suitable units.

3 Prepare a report for the class.

Desktop

Tennis court

Door

Stamp

Credit card

Envelope

Window

Using standard weights

Practice

 10 g 20 g  50 g  100 g  200 g  500 g  1000 g

1 Choose 3 standard weights to balance these totals.

   a 650 g   **b** 710 g   **c** 260 g   **d** 1550 g

> **Example**
> (500 + 20 + 10) g = 530 g

2 Choose 4 standard weights to balance these totals.

   a 1350 g   **b** 1130 g   **c** 820 g   **d** 730 g   **e** 580 g

3 The table below shows which standard weights were used to weigh each object. Work out the weight of each object.

  a hand basin   **b** dictionary   **c** sports bag   **d** pair of trainers

Object	Standard weights used						
	1000 g	500 g	200 g	100 g	50 g	20 g	10 g
a	5	-	1	1	1	-	1
b	-	-	2	-	1	2	-
c	2	1	-	3	-	4	-
d	-	3	2	-	2	-	4

4 Look at the weights at the top of the page.
   Make the pans balance by adding the fewest number of weights.

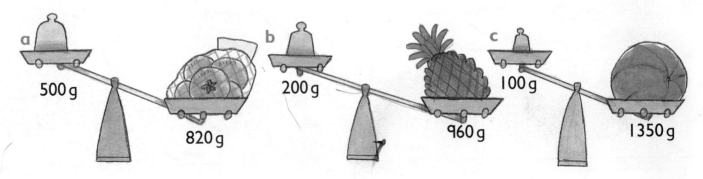

a 500 g   820 g   b 200 g   960 g   c 100 g   1350 g

Refresher

1 Write these weights in grams.

Example
$2\frac{1}{2}$ kg = 2000 g + 500 g = 2500 g

a $3\frac{1}{2}$ kg   b $4\frac{1}{4}$ kg   c $5\frac{3}{4}$ kg   d $6\frac{1}{10}$ kg   e $4\frac{3}{4}$ kg

2 Write these weights in kilograms and grams.

a 7470 g   b 3860 g   c 7070 g

Example
2240 g = 2000 g + 240 g = 2 kg + 240 g

d 3060 g   e 7400 g   f 3600 g

3 a Write 3 ways to balance 1 kg.

use 2 weights 1 kg = 500 g + ⬜

use 4 weights 1 kg = 200 g + ⬜

use 5 weights 1 kg = 100 g + ⬜

b Write 3 ways to balance 100 g.

use 2 weights 100 g = 50 g + ⬜

use 4 weights 100 g = 20 g + ⬜

use 5 weights 100 g = 10 g + ⬜

Challenge

Look at the weights on the balance scales.
Work out the weight of each piece of fruit.

a

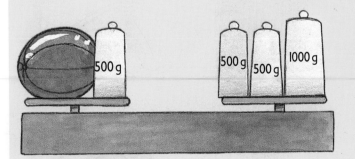

b

c

d

Using scales

Practice

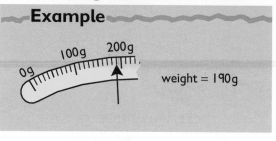
1 Write the weight in grams shown by each scale.

a
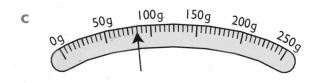

b
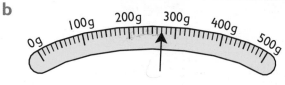

c
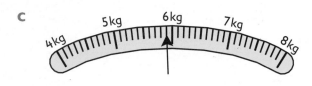

d
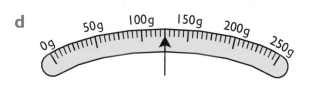

2 Write the weight in kilograms and grams shown by each scale.

a
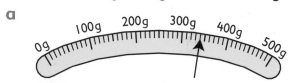

b
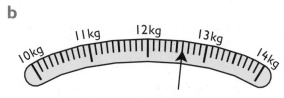

c
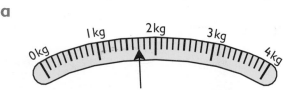

d
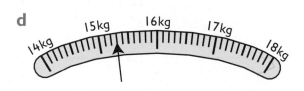

3 For each object, state whether you would use grams or kilograms to record its weight.

a   b   c   d

e   f   g   h

Refresher

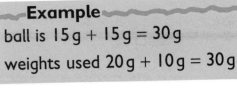

Example
ball is 15 g + 15 g = 30 g
weights used 20 g + 10 g = 30 g

   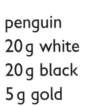 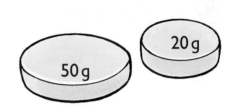

ball	kitten	poodle	penguin
15 g blue	30 g black	25 g white	20 g white
15 g white	5 g blue	25 g black	20 g black
			5 g gold

1 Write the weights you would use to balance the scales for these soft toys.
Use the least number of weights each time.

2 List the soft toys in order of weight beginning with the lightest.

Challenge

You need:
● some small objects
● one each of these weights: 10 g, 20 g and 50 g
● balance scales

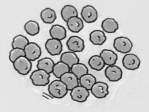

drawing pins

plastic counters

dried peas

paper clips

1 Choose one of the above sets of objects for weighing.
Find a way to work out about how many of your object will balance 1 kg.

2 Write down what you did.

3 Repeat for a second set of small objects.

Shopping in kilograms

Practice

pasta – 500 g

bread – 800 g

potatoes – 2600 g

apples – 900 g

flour – 1500 g

cereal – 750 g

butter – 250 g

tin soup – 400 g

sugar – 1000 g

Example

flour   1500 g = 1·5 kg

soup   400 g = 0·4 kg

_____

1900 g = 1·9 kg

1   Change each weight from grams to kilograms. Record in decimal form. Total the weights. Write the answer in decimal form.

a   soup   b   sugar
    pasta   bread

c   apples   d   flour
    butter   pasta

e   cereal   f   bread
    flour   potatoes

g   cereal   h   sugar
    potatoes   flour

2   Find the two items which together weigh:

a   1·0 kg   b   1·55 kg   c   2·4 kg   d   4·1 kg

3   Find the total weight of two loaves of bread and two tins of soup.

Refresher

1 Copy and complete.

Grams	Kilograms and grams	Fraction	Decimal
100 g	0 kg 100 g	$\frac{1}{10}$ kg	0·1 kg
200 g	▢ kg ▢ g	$\frac{2}{10}$ kg	0·2 kg
400 g	▢ kg ▢ g	▢ kg	▢ kg
▢ g	0 kg 500 g	▢ kg	▢ kg
250 g	▢ kg ▢ g	▢ kg	▢ kg
▢ g	0 kg 750 g	▢ kg	▢ kg
▢ g	▢ kg ▢ g	▢ kg	1·0 kg

2 Write these weights in three different ways.

a 1200 g   b 2500 g   c 3250 g

Challenge

3-fruit salads

apples
300 g

pears
250 g

cherries
200 g

bananas
400 g

1 Each 3-fruit salad must have apples and two other fruits. How many different 3-fruit salads can you make with the above fruits?

2 Work out the total weight of each 3-fruit salad.

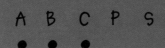

Hint: Make a list and mark each fruit you use with a dot.

A B C P S
● ● ●

strawberries
250 g

65

Rounding weights

Practice

1 Use the digits 4, 6 and 8.
Place them in the boxes to make six different weights.

| 4 | 6 | 8 |

☐ . ☐ ☐ kg

Example
6 . 4 8 kg

2 Copy and complete this table.
Using the 6 different weights from
question 1, round each weight
  a to the nearest tenth of a kilogram
  b to the nearest whole kilogram

Weight	Rounded to nearest	
	tenth of a kg	whole kg
6·48	6·5 kg	6 kg

3 Each of these scales shows the weight of a pack of ten books.

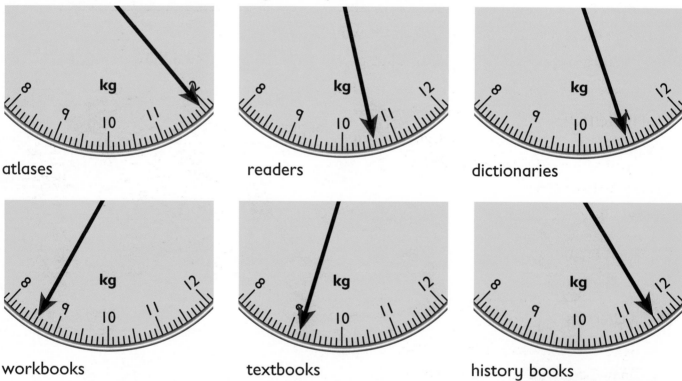

atlases   readers   dictionaries

workbooks   textbooks   history books

  a Round the weight of each pack to the nearest whole kilogram.
  b For each pack, find the weight of 1 book.
  c What is the total weight of the pack of atlases and readers?
  d How much heavier is the pack of history books than the text books?
  e Collins Street Primary has ordered 30 dictionaries.
    What is the total weight of their order?

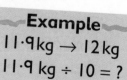

Example
11·9 kg → 12 kg
11·9 kg ÷ 10 = ?

Refresher

Round these weights to the nearest whole kilogram.
Copy and complete the table.

	Weight	Rounded to nearest whole kg
	5·7 kg	6 kg
a	2·4 kg	▢ kg
b	2·8 kg	▢ kg
c	4·2 kg	▢ kg
d	4·8 kg	▢ kg
e	8·2 kg	▢ kg
f	8·4 kg	▢ kg

Challenge

1 A boy and his sister took it in turns to stand on a weighing machine with their pet dog.
 The brother and sister together weighed 85 kg.
 The boy and the dog weighed 60·5 kg.
 The girl and the dog weighed 49·5 kg.
 Find the weight in kilograms of
 a the brother
 b the sister
 c their pet dog

2 Three collie puppies together weigh 8·6 kg.
 Harris is 0·3 kg heavier than Jura.
 Jura is 100 g heavier than Lewis.
 What does each puppy weigh?

Cooking up problems

Practice

1 5 oranges weigh 1·25 kg. Simon eats one of them.
4 oranges weigh 0·95 kg.
What is the weight of the orange which he ate?

2 One egg weighs 70 g.
What is the weight of a box of six eggs?

3 Gran is making her special soup.
Here is her recipe.

Here is her shopping.

$\frac{1}{4}$ head of celery
1 green pepper
$\frac{1}{2}$ bag of carrots
2 onions
1 tin plum tomatoes
50 g mini pasta shells

600 g
450 g
320 g
1 kg
400 g

a Work out the weight of each vegetable which she uses.
b Find the total weight of vegetables which go into her soup.

4 Kenny has built this display of tins of dog food.
a What weight of dog food is in the display?
b He adds a fifth row of five cans.
What does the food in the display now weigh?

450 g
450 g 450 g
450 g 450 g 450 g
450 g 450 g 450 g 450 g

5 Carol's cat and its kitten weigh 2·6 kg.
The cat weighs 1600 g more than its kitten.
What is the weight of the kitten?

Refresher

1 Work out the weight of food in each bag.

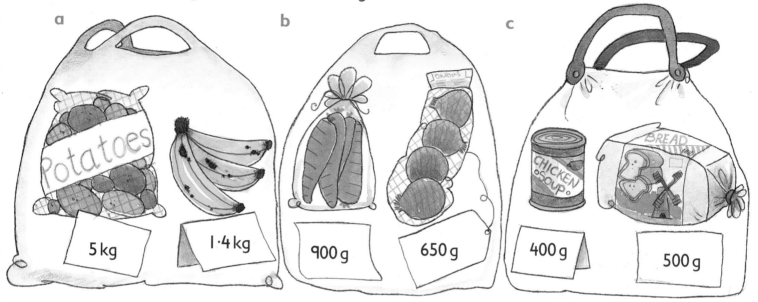

a   5 kg   1·4 kg

b   900 g   650 g

c   400 g   500 g

2 How much heavier is the bag of potatoes than the bag of carrots?

3 What is the approximate weight of one onion?

Challenge

Strong plastic

You need:
- a spring balance or a measuring scale
- standard metric weights
- about 5 plastic shopping bags from different supermarkets and stores

What to do
- Set up and carry out a test to see which shopping bag is the strongest. Make sure the test is fair.
- Write a report of what you did.

Temperature line graphs

You need:
● squared paper
● a ruler

Practice

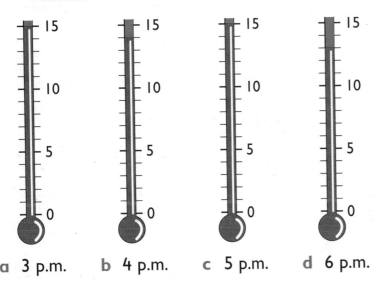

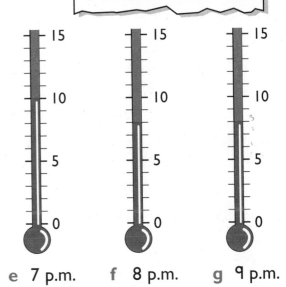

a 3 p.m.   **b** 4 p.m.   **c** 5 p.m.   **d** 6 p.m.   **e** 7 p.m.   **f** 8 p.m.   **g** 9 p.m.

Sally read the thermometer outside every hour.

1 Copy and complete her table.

2 Copy and complete the line graph.

Time	Temperature (°C)
3 p.m.	15

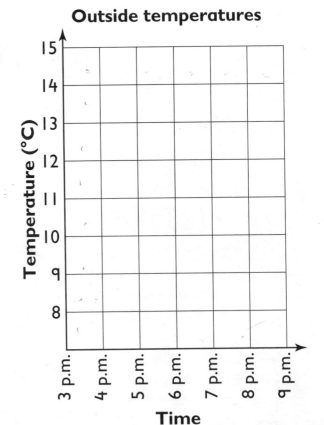

3 **a** When was it coldest outside?

   b What was the temperature at 5:00 p.m.?

   c At what other time of day was the temperature the same as at 5:00 p.m.?

   d How did the temperature change between 5:00 p.m. and 6:00 p.m.?

   e When was it colder than 12°C?

70

Refresher

The graph shows the temperature in Gerald's bedroom one evening.

1 a What was the temperature at 10:00 p.m.?
   b When was the temperature 19°C?
   c What was the lowest temperature?
   d When was it hottest?
   e When did the temperature fall?
   f Why do you think the temperature fell then?

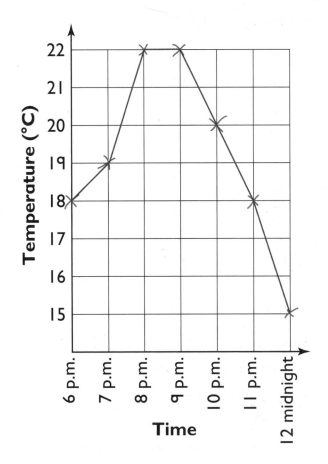

2 Copy and complete the table.

Time	Temperature (°C)
6 p.m.	
7 p.m.	
8 p.m.	
9 p.m.	
10 p.m.	
11 p.m.	
12 midnight	

Challenge

The table shows the temperature in Fay's kitchen in one day.

Copy and complete the line graph. Use a scale of 1 cm to 2°C on the temperature axis.

You need:
● squared paper
● a ruler

Time	Temperature (°C)
10 a.m.	12
11 a.m.	13
12 noon	12
1 p.m.	27
2 p.m.	29
3 p.m.	22
4 p.m.	17

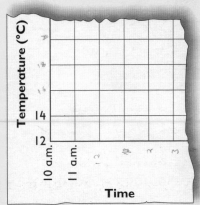

2 a When was the kitchen coldest?
   b When do you think Fay did some cooking? Explain your answer.
   c When was the temperature below 20°C?

71

Cost line graphs

Practice

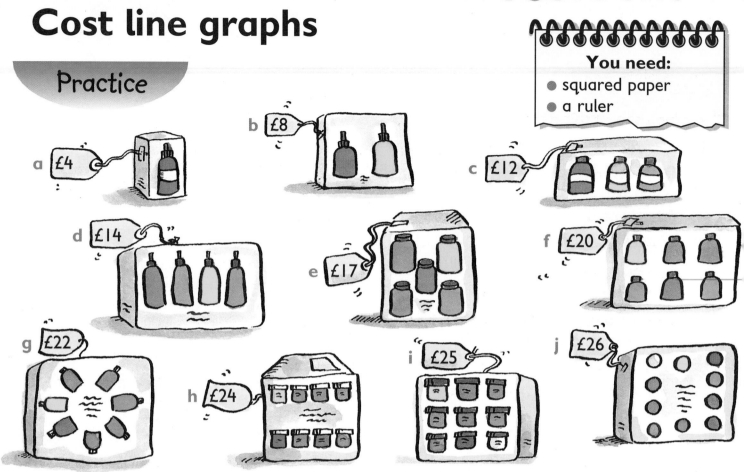

a £4

b £8

c £12

d £14

e £17

f £20

g £22

h £24

i £25

j £26

1 Copy and complete the table of prices.

2 Copy and complete the line graph. Use a scale of 1 cm to £2 on the Cost axis.

Number	Cost
0	
1	
2	

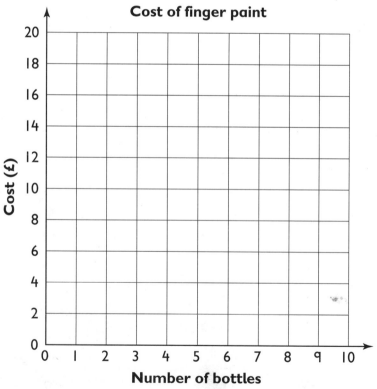

Cost of finger paint

Cost (£)

Number of bottles

3 a Meera buys two pots of paint. How much does each cost?

b Vera buys eight pots of paint. How much does each cost?

c How much more does Meera pay for each pot of paint?

d Anton buys ten pots of paint. How much does each cost? How much more expensive is it to buy just one pot?

Refresher

The table shows the prices of paint brushes.

1 Copy and complete the line graph.

2 a Liam buys two brushes. How much does he pay altogether?

b How much does one of his brushes cost?

c Liam buys another two brushes. How much has he spent altogether?

d Liam could have bought all four brushes at once. How much would he have saved?

e What is the most expensive way of buying four brushes? How much would they cost altogether?

Number of brushes	Cost (£)
1	3
2	5
3	7
4	8
5	9
6	10

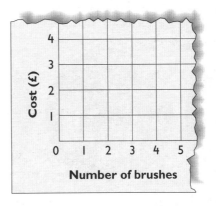

Challenge

Number of rolls	Cost (£)
1	8
2	15
3	22
4	29
5	35
6	41
7	47
8	52
9	57
10	62

1 Copy and complete the line graph. Use a scale of 2 cm to £10 on the Cost axis.

2 a How much would you charge for two rolls of wallpaper?

b Jason has £32 for wallpaper. How many rolls does he buy?

c He needs another roll. How much will it cost?

d He could have bought all five rolls together. How much would he have saved?

e What is the lowest price of a roll of wallpaper? Explain your answer.

You need:
● squared paper
● a ruler

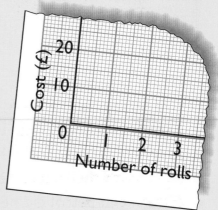

73

Liquid line graphs

Practice

Daniel went on a ten-hour trip. The petrol gauges show the petrol in his car.

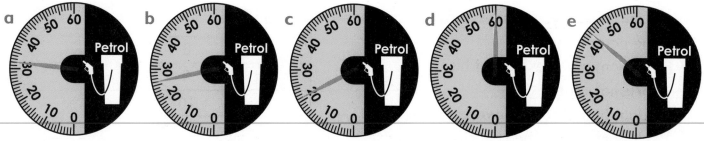

Time: 0 hours   Time: 1 hour   Time: 2 hours   Time: 3 hours   Time: 5 hours

  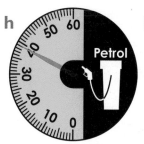 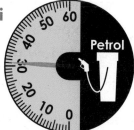 

Time: 6 hours   Time: 7 hours   Time: 8 hours   Time: 9 hours   Time: 10 hours

1 Copy and complete the table below.

2 Copy and complete the line graph. Use a scale of 2 cm to 10 litres on the Petrol axis.

Time (hours)	Petrol (litres)
0	
1	
2	
3	

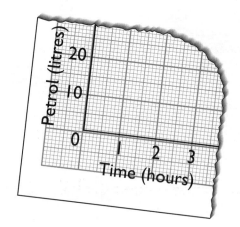

3 Daniel always fills his tank at the petrol station.
  a Which times did he fill it?
  b How much petrol does his tank hold?
  c What was the smallest amount of petrol in his tank?
  d How much petrol did he use during the first hour of his trip?
  e When do you think Daniel stopped for lunch? Explain your answer.

You need:
- squared paper
- a ruler

Refresher

The table shows the water in a fish pond as Maria filled it.

1 Copy and complete the line graph.

Time (minutes)	Water (litres)
5	10
10	15
15	30
20	30
25	30
30	50
35	65
40	70

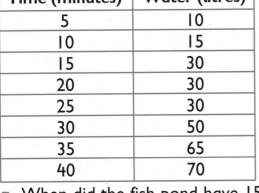

2 a When did the fish pond have 15 litres of water?

   b How much water did it take to fill the fish pond?

   c How long did it take Maria to fill the pond?

3 Maria took a break after 15 minutes.

   a How much water was in the pond then?

   b After how many minutes did her break end?

Challenge

The table shows the water in a kettle during the afternoon.

You need:
- graph paper
- a ruler

1 Copy and complete the line graph.

2 a When was the kettle empty?

   b When do you think the kettle was full?

   c When did the kettle hold less than 300 ml of water?

   d How much water was used between 4:00 p.m. and 4:15 p.m.?

   e How much water was used between 3:00 p.m. and 3:15 p.m.?

Time (p.m.)	Water (ml)
2:00	200
2:15	0
2:30	0
2:45	600
3:00	350
3:15	120
3:30	120
3:45	600
4:00	390
4:15	0

75

Flying kites

Practice

1 Write ten addition and ten subtraction calculations using these numbers. Work them out in your head and then record your method as a calculation.

68 + 81
I added 60 and 80,
then 8 and 1.

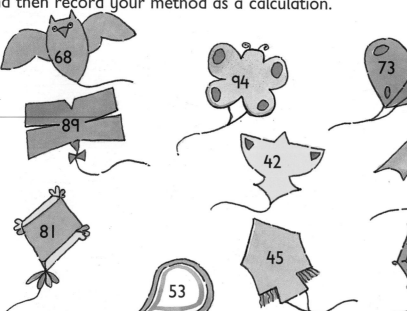

2 Add these three numbers together. Then add them again in the reverse order. Check that both of your ways get the same answer.

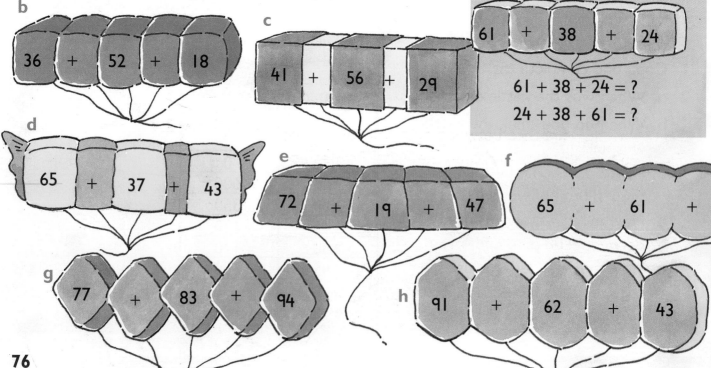

Example

a

61 + 38 + 24

61 + 38 + 24 = ?

24 + 38 + 61 = ?

b

36 + 52 + 18

c

41 + 56 + 29

d

65 + 37 + 43

e

72 + 19 + 47

f

65 + 61 +

g

77 + 83 + 94

h

91 + 62 + 43

Refresher

1 Add each pair of numbers together. First add the tens and then the units. Record your method as a calculation.

Example

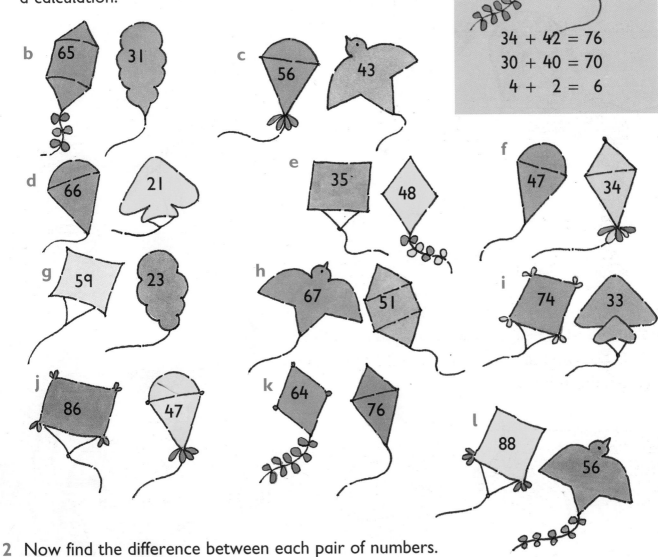

a

34   42

34 + 42 = 76
30 + 40 = 70
4 + 2 = 6

b 65   31

c 56   43

d 66   21

e 35   48

f 47   34

g 59   23

h 67   51

i 74   33

j 86   47

k 64   76

l 88   56

2 Now find the difference between each pair of numbers. First subtract the tens and then the units. Record your method as a calculation.

Challenge

1 Find as many ways as you can to add three two-digit numbers together with a total of 100.

Fishy calculations

Practice

1 Copy the calculations from each octopus. Work them out by adding
  and subtracting multiples of 10 or 100 and adjusting the answer.

a **158**: −201, +201, −198, +198, −79, +79, −81, +81

b **272**: −302, +302, −299, +299, −91, +91, −69, +69

c **346**: +397, −397, +202, −202, +89, −89, +61, −61

d **417**: −92, +92, −78, +78, −502, +502, −401, +401

Refresher

1 Copy out the numbers and write the nearest multiple of 10.

a  31
b 19
c  49
d 52
e  28

f 39
g 51
h 69
i 61
j 82

2 Add and subtract these near multiples of 10.

a  124 +31 −31

b  107 +41 −41

c  136 +29 −29

d 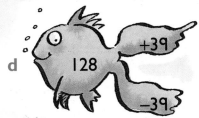 128 +39 −39

e  132 +51 −51

f  164 +61 −61

g  173 +59 −59

h 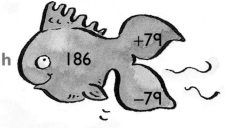 186 +79 −79

i 237 +42 −42

j  251 +28 −28

Challenge

1 For each of the calculations in the Practice section write the inverse operations. The first one is done for you.

Example
158 + 81 = 239
239 − 81 = 158

79

Make 1

Practice

1 Copy out the decimal numbers and write
   in the decimal that goes with it to equal 1.

a 0.4 ?

| 0 | 0·1 | 0·2 | 0·3 | 0·4 | 0·5 | 0·6 | 0·7 | 0·8 | 0·9 | 1 |

b 0.8 ?

| 0 | 0·1 | 0·2 | 0·3 | 0·4 | 0·5 | 0·6 | 0·7 | 0·8 | 0·9 | 1 |

c 0.5 ?

| 0 | 0·1 | 0·2 | 0·3 | 0·4 | 0·5 | 0·6 | 0·7 | 0·8 | 0·9 | 1 |

d 0.1 ?

| 0 | 0·1 | 0·2 | 0·3 | 0·4 | 0·5 | 0·6 | 0·7 | 0·8 | 0·9 | 1 |

e 0.3 ?

| 0 | 0·1 | 0·2 | 0·3 | 0·4 | 0·5 | 0·6 | 0·7 | 0·8 | 0·9 | 1 |

f 0.7 ?

| 0 | 0·1 | 0·2 | 0·3 | 0·4 | 0·5 | 0·6 | 0·7 | 0·8 | 0·9 | 1 |

g 0.2 ?

| 0 | 0·1 | 0·2 | 0·3 | 0·4 | 0·5 | 0·6 | 0·7 | 0·8 | 0·9 | 1 |

h 0.6 ?

| 0 | 0·1 | 0·2 | 0·3 | 0·4 | 0·5 | 0·6 | 0·7 | 0·8 | 0·9 | 1 |

i 0.9 ?

| 0 | 0·1 | 0·2 | 0·3 | 0·4 | 0·5 | 0·6 | 0·7 | 0·8 | 0·9 | 1 |

2 Work with a partner. One of you says a decimal and the other has
   to reply with the number that would equal 1. Take it in turns.

3 Now test yourself and see if you can write out all the pairs of
   decimals that equal 1.

Refresher

1 Use the number lines to work out the missing decimal.

a 0.9 + ☐ = 1   0   0.1   0.2   0.3   0.4   0.5   0.6   0.7   0.8   0.9   1

b 0.1 + ☐ = 1   0   0.1   0.2   0.3   0.4   0.5   0.6   0.7   0.8   0.9   1

c 0.6 + ☐ = 1   0   0.1   0.2   0.3   0.4   0.5   0.6   0.7   0.8   0.9   1

d 0.4 + ☐ = 1   0   0.1   0.2   0.3   0.4   0.5   0.6   0.7   0.8   0.9   1

e 0.7 + ☐ = 1   0   0.1   0.2   0.3   0.4   0.5   0.6   0.7   0.8   0.9   1

f 0.5 + ☐ = 1   0   0.1   0.2   0.3   0.4   0.5   0.6   0.7   0.8   0.9   1

g 0.2 + ☐ = 1   0   0.1   0.2   0.3   0.4   0.5   0.6   0.7   0.8   0.9   1

h 0.8 + ☐ = 1   0   0.1   0.2   0.3   0.4   0.5   0.6   0.7   0.8   0.9   1

i 0.3 + ☐ = 1   0   0.1   0.2   0.3   0.4   0.5   0.6   0.7   0.8   0.9   1

Challenge

1 Work out the number that goes with these decimals to equal 1.

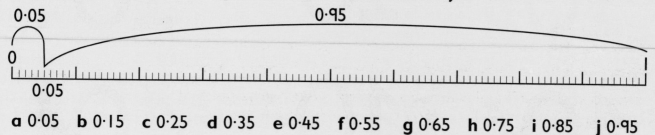

0.05   0.95

0

0.05

a 0.05   b 0.15   c 0.25   d 0.35   e 0.45   f 0.55   g 0.65   h 0.75   i 0.85   j 0.95

Make 10

Practice

1 Copy out the numbers and write in the number that goes with each one to equal 10.

a 2·4 10 ?
b 6·7 10 ?
c 8·1 10 ?

d 9·6 10 ?
e 7·6 10 ?
f 1·8 10 ?

g 7·5 10 ?
h 3·2 10 ?
i 4·9 10 ?

j 5·3 10 ?
k 8·6 10 ?
l 3·5 10 ?

m 1·7 10 ?
n 6·9 10 ?
o 5·8 10 ?

p 2·3 10 ?
q 6·1 10 ?
r 7·2 10 ?

Refresher

1 Work out how many tenths to the next whole number.

a 3·3 + ▢ = 4

b 5·6 + ▢ = 6

c 7·1 + ▢ = 8

d 1·3 + ▢ = 2

e 3·9 + ▢ = 4

f 8·2 + ▢ = 9

g 9·5 + ▢ = 10

h 2·4 + ▢ = 3

i 6·7 + ▢ = 7

j 4·6 + ▢ = 5

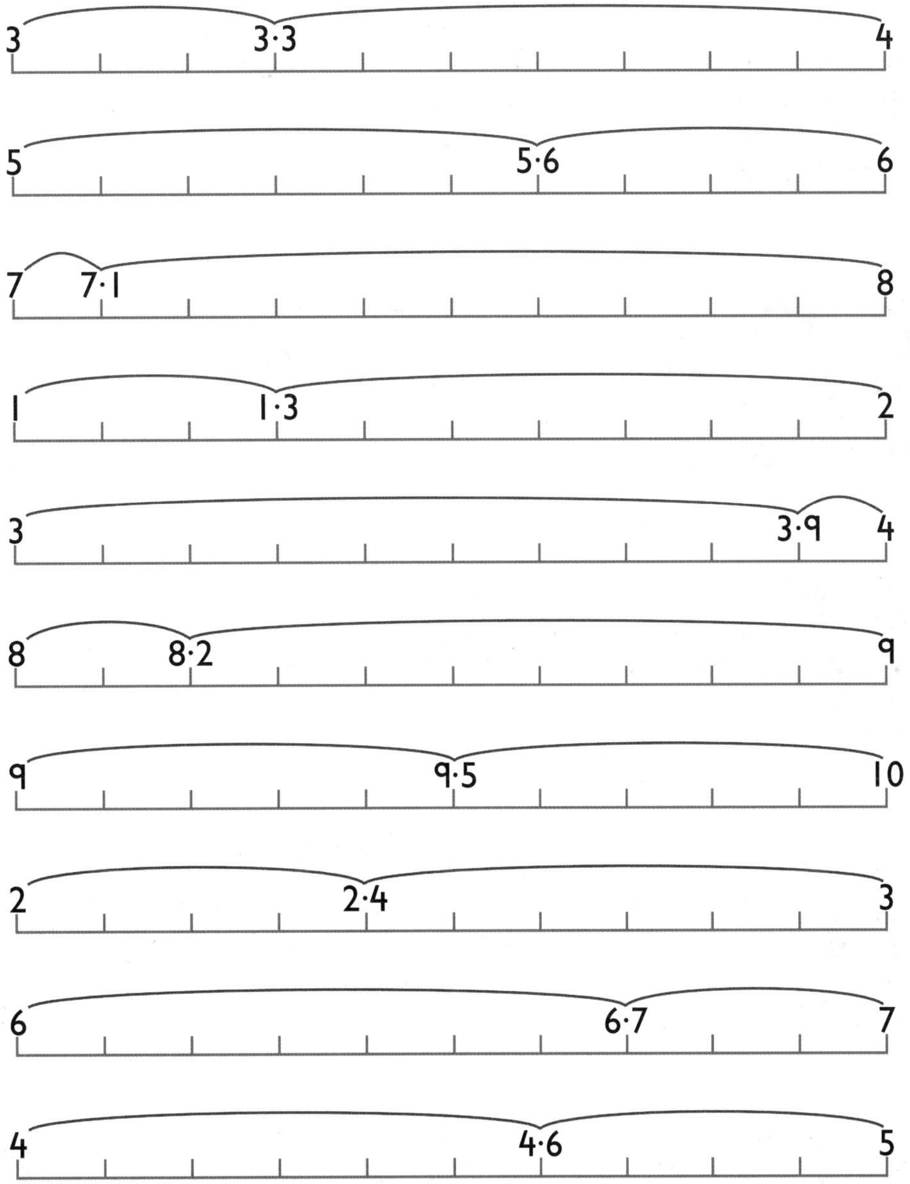

Challenge

6 3 8 4

Example

3·4, 6·8

1 Using these digits make up 16 single-digit numbers with one decimal place. Order them and write the number that goes with each one to equal 10.

Rocky near doubles

Practice

Work out these near doubles. Write the double that helped you.

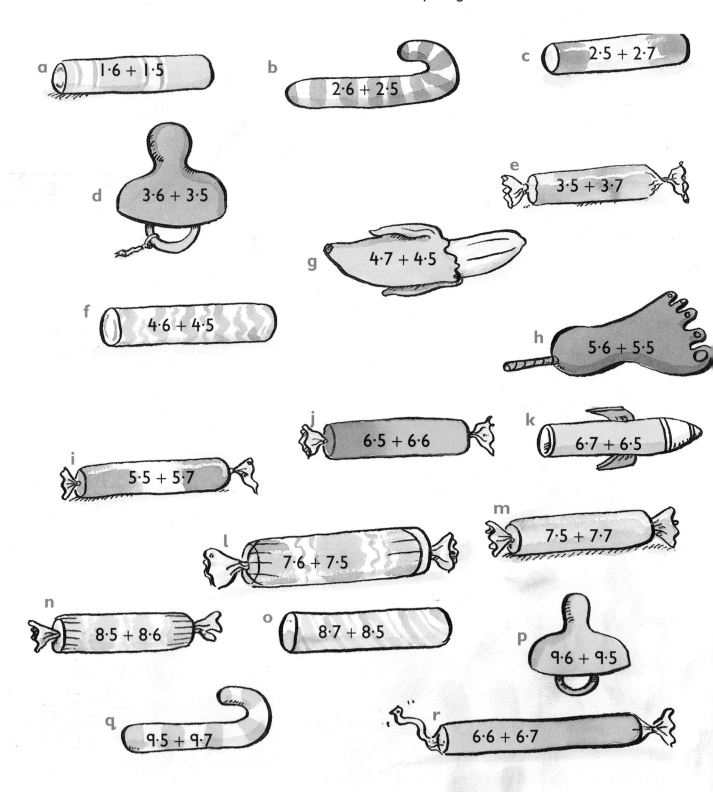

a 1·6 + 1·5

b 2·6 + 2·5

c 2·5 + 2·7

d 3·6 + 3·5

e 3·5 + 3·7

g 4·7 + 4·5

f 4·6 + 4·5

h 5·6 + 5·5

j 6·5 + 6·6

k 6·7 + 6·5

i 5·5 + 5·7

l 7·6 + 7·5

m 7·5 + 7·7

n 8·5 + 8·6

o 8·7 + 8·5

p 9·6 + 9·5

q 9·5 + 9·7

r 6·6 + 6·7

84

Refresher

Work out these doubles. First add the whole numbers and then the decimals.

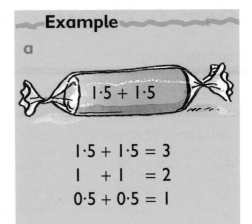

a

$$1 \cdot 5 + 1 \cdot 5 = 3$$
$$1 \quad + 1 \quad = 2$$
$$0 \cdot 5 + 0 \cdot 5 = 1$$

b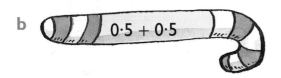

0·5 + 0·5

c

4·5 + 4·5

d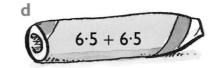

6·5 + 6·5

e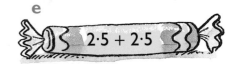

2·5 + 2·5

f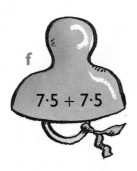

7·5 + 7·5

g

3·5 + 3·5

h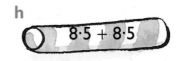

8·5 + 8·5

i

5·5 + 5·5

j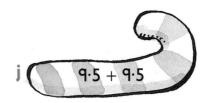

9·5 + 9·5

Challenge

Work out these doubles.

a 1·6 + 1·6	**e** 3·7 + 3·7	**i** 2·8 + 2·8
b 2·6 + 2·6	**f** 4·7 + 4·7	**j** 3·8 + 3·8
c 3·6 + 3·6	**g** 5·7 + 5·7	**k** 4·8 + 4·8
d 4·6 + 4·6	**h** 6·7 + 6·7	**l** 6·8 + 6·8

Under a thousand

Practice

Copy out these calculations vertically and then work out the answers. The first one is done for you.

a 4662 + 2104 + 1415

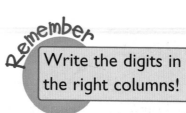

Example

a
```
  4 6 6 2
  2 1 0 4
+ 1 4 1 5
---------
  8 1 8 1
    1   1
```

b 3748 + 6052 + 2131
c 2462 + 1670 + 2543
d 5036 + 6427 + 7205
e 2451 + 7260 + 3191
f 4683 + 2832 + 1950
g 6804 + 3832 + 4941
h 7284 + 1357 + 1263
i 4623 + 1738 + 2206
j 8921 + 5302 + 9745
k 7062 + 9242 + 9341
l 8219 + 5254 + 6123

Remember

Write the digits in the right columns!

Refresher

1 Copy out these calculations vertically and then work out the answers. The first one is done for you.

a 2638 + 1125

Example

```
 a 2 6 3 8
 + 1 1 2 5
   3 7 6 3
       1
```

b 3672 + 1135

c 2067 + 3492

d 3721 + 2554

e 2162 + 3753

f 3047 + 8532

g 4215 + 9206

h 3263 + 4819

i 4127 + 8391

j 5621 + 2639

Challenge

Add them up

What to do

Play this game in twos or threes.

1 Take turns to roll the die four times and make a four-digit number.

2 Each player writes down the two (if two players) or three (if three players) numbers and adds them together.

3 After everyone has finished adding, use a calculator to check the answers.

4 The first player to get the correct answer scores 1 point. The winner is the first player to collect 5 points.

You need:
- a 1–6 die
- paper and pencil each
- calculator

87

How much? How far? How heavy?

Practice

Remember

The decimal points must go underneath each other.

1 Add these quantities together using the vertical method.

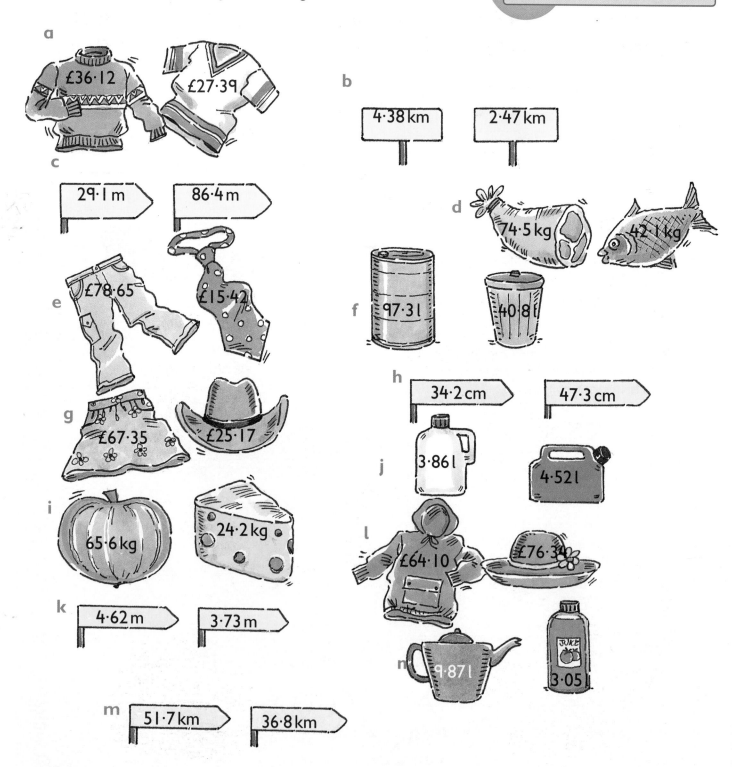

a £36·12   £27·39

b 4·38 km   2·47 km

c 29·1 m   86·4 m

d 74·5 kg   42·1 kg

e £78·65   £15·42

f 97·3 l   40·8 l

g £67·35   £25·17

h 34·2 cm   47·3 cm

i 65·6 kg   24·2 kg

j 3·86 l   4·52 l

k 4·62 m   3·73 m

l £64·10   £76·34

m 51·7 km   36·8 km

n 9·87 l   3·05 l

Refresher

I Add these amounts together using the vertical method.

a   £6·37
  + £5·21
  ‾‾‾‾‾‾‾

b   £7·76
  + £2·19
  ‾‾‾‾‾‾‾

c   £4·62
  + £2·91
  ‾‾‾‾‾‾‾

d   £3·05
  + £6·46
  ‾‾‾‾‾‾‾

e   £8·72
  + £1·34
  ‾‾‾‾‾‾‾

f   £5·62
  + £3·74
  ‾‾‾‾‾‾‾

g   £16·86
  + £21·32
  ‾‾‾‾‾‾‾

h   £24·36
  + £17·21
  ‾‾‾‾‾‾‾

i   £36·24
  + £37·23
  ‾‾‾‾‾‾‾

j   £42·72
  + £33·51
  ‾‾‾‾‾‾‾

Challenge

I How many different totals can you make using these prices?

£78·63

£24·38

£35·76

£52·91

What's the difference?

Practice

Subtract these quantities from each other to find the difference. Use the vertical method.

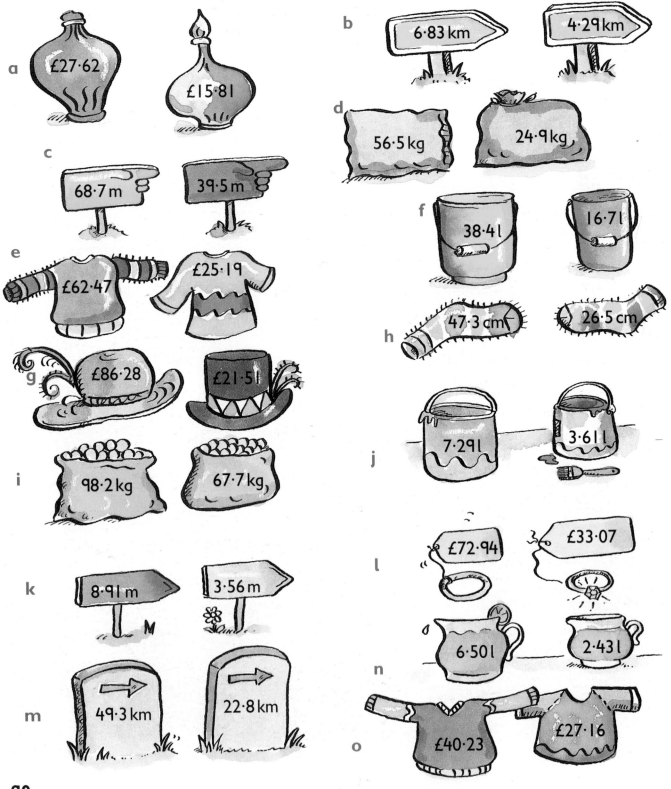

a £27·62   £15·81

b 6·83 km   4·29 km

c 68·7 m   39·5 m

d 56·5 kg   24·9 kg

e £62·47   £25·19

f 38·4 l   16·7 l

g £86·28   £21·51

h 47·3 cm   26·5 cm

i 98·2 kg   67·7 kg

j 7·29 l   3·61 l

k 8·91 m   3·56 m

l £72·94   £33·07

m 49·3 km   22·8 km

n 6·50 l   2·43 l

o £40·23   £27·16

90

Refresher

Subtract these quantities from each other to find the difference.

a £8·72
− £6·25

b £6·38
− £3·72

c £5·73
− £2·04

d £9·74
− £6·29

e £7·24
− £3·52

f £8·36
− £4·82

g £14·72
− £12·16

h £25·39
− £17·10

i £34·62
− £22·47

j £37·63
− £19·28

Challenge

I go shopping with my friend. I start with £98·26. I buy a jacket
that costs £23·51. I buy two tickets for the cinema. They cost
£6·70 each. Then I buy lunch and this costs me £4·81.
My friend borrows £45·79 to buy some shoes. I see a great
shirt that costs £14·65. Do I have enough money left?
If I do, what will I have left after I buy the shirt?
If I don't, how much more will I need?

91

At the cinema

Practice

1 Work out the answers to these problems about the cinema.

a The cinema can seat 1860 people. It is full for three films. How many people saw these films?

b In a week, 1472 chocolate, 2642 vanilla and 3108 strawberry ice-creams were sold. How many ice-creams were sold that week?

c The total spent on popcorn on Monday came to £68·24, and £29·38 on Tuesday. How much was spent altogether? What was the difference between the two amounts?

d The total spent on fizzy drinks on Monday was £96·17 and £74·83 on Tuesday. What was the difference between the two totals?
What was the total spent altogether?

e At the end of a film everyone was asked if they had enjoyed it. 486 said yes, 572 said it was OK and 194 said no. How many people saw the film?

f On Tuesday 76·5 litres of orangeade was drunk, and 57·9 litres of cherryade. How much was drunk altogether?

g 2467 people wanted to buy tickets for the first showing of a film. The cinema holds 1860 people. How many people couldn't buy tickets?

2 Now check your answers using a calculator.

Refresher

1 Work out these problems.

a My ticket to get into the cinema costs £5·40 and my drink and ice-cream costs £2·62. How much did I spend altogether?

b 372 people went to the 3 o'clock showing of the film and 594 went to the 6 o'clock. How many people went altogether?

c 1265 people went to the cinema on Monday and 1782 went on Tuesday. How many people went altogether?

d I went to the cinema with £8·60. I spent £6·43. How much do I have left?

e At one film, 864 ice-creams were sold. 371 were chocolate. How many were strawberry?

f At one film 28·6 litres of orange juice was drunk and 16·9 litres of water. How much was drunk altogether?

Challenge

Make up four word problems for a friend to work out:

- one adding money
- one subtracting money
- one adding three four-digit numbers
- one with kilograms

In your head

Practice

1 Work out these problems in your head. Make jottings if you need to.

a I am thinking of a number. If I subtract 57 and then subtract 38 I am left with 27. What was the number?

b I have £78. I spend £25 in one shop and some more money in another shop. I have £17 left. How much did I spend in the second shop?

c I am thinking of a number. If I add 36 to it and then 48 and I get 97. What number did I start with?

d Three buses arrive at the museum. At the bus stop 259 people get off the three buses. There were 89 on the first bus and 97 on the second bus. How many on the third bus?

e I am thinking of a number. I subtract 198 and then add 51 and I get 99. What number am I thinking of?

f Steve has just got the results of his three maths tests. His total score was 86. He scored 24 in the first test and his scores in the other two tests had a difference of 2. What did he score in the other two tests?

g I am thinking of a number. If I add 62 and 39, then subtract 17 I get 96. What number was I thinking of?

h The school has raised £271. The parents raised £102. The Y5 sponsored silence raised £64. The rest came from the school fair. How much was raised at the fair?

Refresher

Now answer these problems.

a I spent £21 on some shoes and £36 on a jacket. How much did I spend altogether?

b We picked 83 apples from our tree. We gave 37 to our neighbours. How many apples did we have left?

c 158 people bought books from the book shop on Saturday. Credit cards were used by 79 of them and the rest paid cash. How many people paid with cash?

d I went to the market with £24. I came back with £13. How much did I spend?

e I weigh 37 kg and my dad weighs 82 kg. What is our total weight?

f The car park has 271 cars. At midday 72 more arrive. How many cars are there altogether?

Challenge

What two consecutive two-digit numbers have been added together to make these totals?

a 47	b 77	c 93	d 131	e 137
f 165	g 187	h 171	i 189	j 153

Counting in 25s

Practice

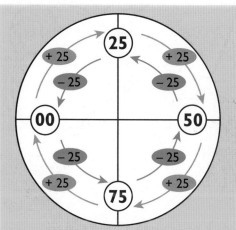

Multiples of 25 end in the repeated pattern 25, 50, 75, 00

Look at the cycle.
- Start anywhere on the cycle.
- Follow the arrows around the number of 25s you need.
- Your answer will always have one of the endings shown on the cycle.

Adding multiples of 25 to multiples of 25 is EASY!

Example
■ Start at 225
  Add 50 (two lots of 25)
  Finish at 275

■ Start at 475
  Add 75 (three lots of 25)
  Finish at 550

1 Copy and complete the table using the cycle to help you.

	Start	Add/subtract	Finish	Number sentence
a	175	+ 50	225	175 + 50 = 225
b	525	+ two lots of 25		
c	700	+ 75		
d	975	+ 25		
e	−250	+ three lots of 25		
f	825	− 50		
g	−475	+ 75		
h	300	− 25		
i	250	− 75		
j		+ 50	−325	
k		− 25	450	
l		− 75	225	
m		+ 100	−325	

2 Answer these.

a 675 + 50 =

b −150 + 75 =

c 925 − 50 =

d −350 + 25 =

e 725 + 75 =

f −600 + 25 =

g 500 − 75 =

h −475 + 50 =

i 1000 − 75 =

Refresher

1 Find your way up or down each set of stairs by counting in 25s.

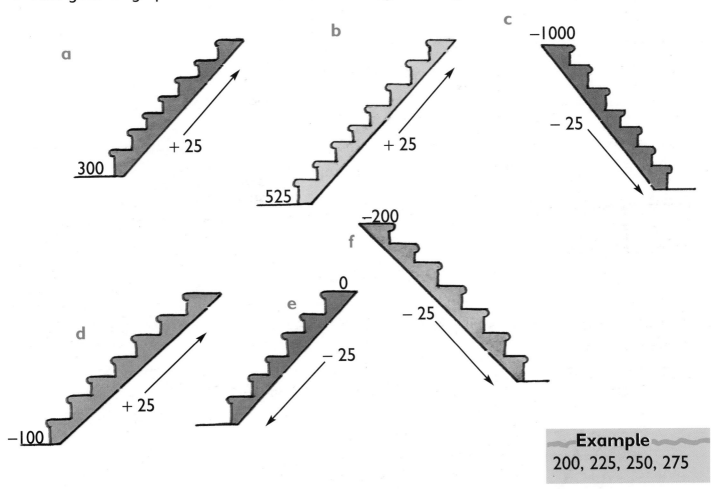

a

300   + 25

b   + 25

525

c   −1000

− 25

d   + 25

−100

e   0   − 25

f   −200   − 25

Example
200, 225, 250, 275

Challenge

1 Copy and complete each table.

	+50	−25	+100	−75
675				
925				
−375				
700				
−550				
−875				

	+25	−50	+75	−100
−950				
−1000				
1000				
475				
−850				

Multiples of 6, 7, 8, 9

Practice

1 Copy and complete the first ten multiples of each sequence.

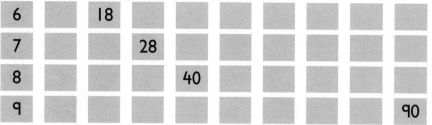

6		18							
7			28						
8				40					
9									90

2 The numbers have escaped! Find the multiples of 6, 7, 8 and 9.
Write a multiplication fact for each multiple you find.

Example
$2 \times 6 = 12$

Refresher

1 Use a hundred square.
   a Mark the multiples of 6.
   b Mark the multiples of 7.

2 Practise counting in multiples of each number.

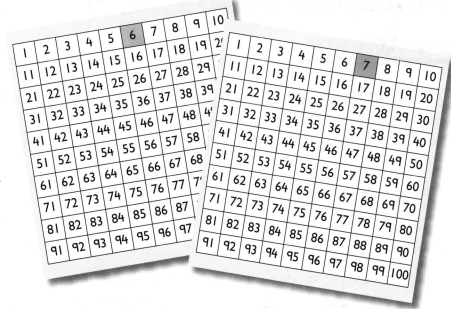

Challenge

1 Find your way through the obstacle course by following the correct sequence.

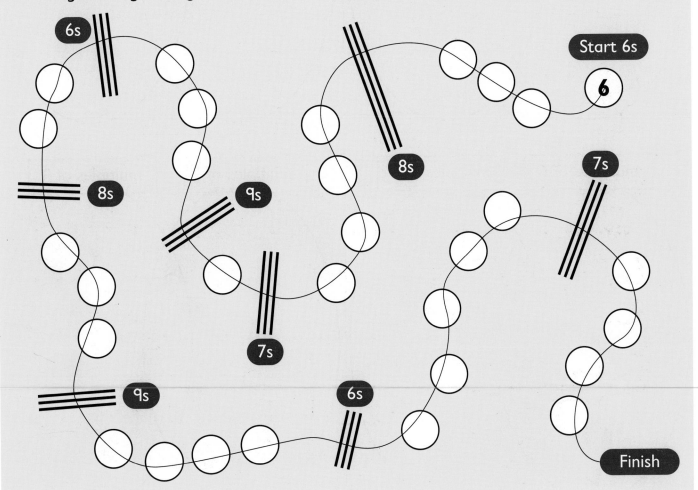

Finding multiples of 6, 7, 8, 9

Practice

Draw your own Venn diagrams like the ones below.

Sort the numbers 1 to 90 to match the labels.

Write any numbers that belong in both sets in the (middle) intersecting set.

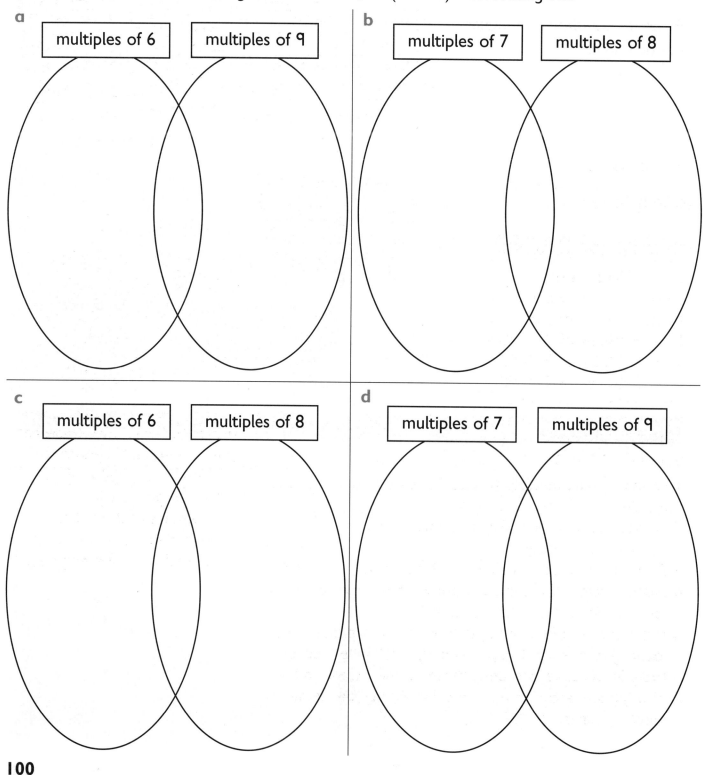

a

| multiples of 6 | multiples of 9 |

b

| multiples of 7 | multiples of 8 |

c

| multiples of 6 | multiples of 8 |

d

| multiples of 7 | multiples of 9 |

Refresher

1 Use a hundred square.
   a Mark the multiples of 8.
   b Mark the multiples of 9.

2 Practise counting in multiples of each number.

Challenge

Multiple snap

You need:
- a set of 1–60 cards
- number cards for
  - multiples of 7: 1–70
  - multiples of 8: 1–80
  - multiples of 9: 1–90

What to do

(For 2–3 players)

1 Decide which number to use, for example 6. Find the multiples of 6 during the game.
2 Shuffle the number cards and divide them evenly between the players.
3 Each player places their cards face down on the table.
4 Players select the top card one at a time. Place them face up on to the centre pile.
5 If the top card is a multiple of 6, the first player to identify and touch the pile calling out "Snap!" collects the pile of cards and adds these to their existing pile.
6 The game continues until one player has all of the number cards.

Variation

1 Use a different number. Choose from 7, 8 or 9.
2 Play the game using:
- multiples of 2 numbers
- multiples of 3 numbers
- multiples of all 4 numbers.

Sorting numbers by divisibility

Practice

Sort the numbers into the correct box.
Use the "divisible by" labels to help you.
(Some numbers may go into more than 1 box.)

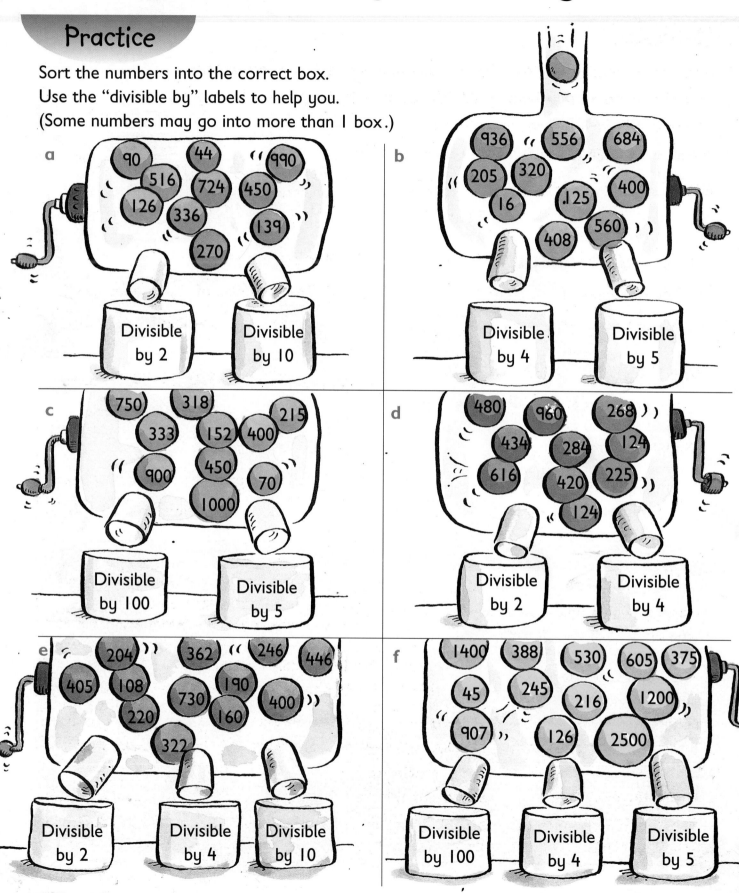

a 90, 44, 990, 516, 724, 450, 126, 336, 139, 270

Divisible by 2   Divisible by 10

b 936, 556, 684, 205, 320, 400, 16, 125, 408, 560

Divisible by 4   Divisible by 5

c 750, 318, 215, 333, 152, 400, 900, 450, 70, 1000

Divisible by 100   Divisible by 5

d 480, 960, 268, 434, 284, 124, 616, 420, 225, 124

Divisible by 2   Divisible by 4

e 204, 362, 246, 446, 405, 108, 190, 730, 400, 220, 160, 322

Divisible by 2   Divisible by 4   Divisible by 10

f 1400, 388, 530, 605, 375, 45, 245, 216, 1200, 907, 126, 2500

Divisible by 100   Divisible by 4   Divisible by 5

Refresher

In each set of multiples below, there is one number that does not belong.

1 Find the numbers that belong. Which set of multiples do they belong to?

2 Write a rule for each set of multiples.

3 Write a divisibility rule for each set of numbers.

600   2900   900   4500   1700   740   265   4150   1395

450   3100   8200   675   626   435   520

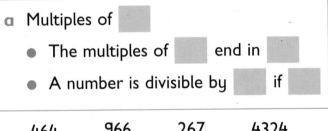

a Multiples of ☐
  ● The multiples of ☐ end in ☐
  ● A number is divisible by ☐ if ☐

b Multiples of ☐
  ● The multiples of ☐ end in ☐
  ● A number is divisible by ☐ if ☐

464   966   267   4324   330   720   4570   1490   3260

1208   7850   5712   384   5620   141   480

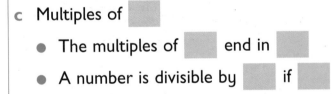

c Multiples of ☐
  ● The multiples of ☐ end in ☐
  ● A number is divisible by ☐ if ☐

d Multiples of ☐
  ● The multiples of ☐ end in ☐
  ● A number is divisible by ☐ if ☐

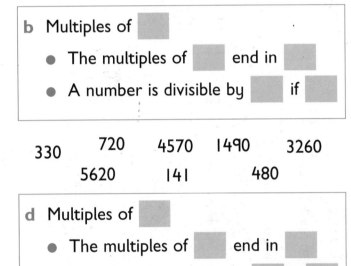

Challenge

1 Use your knowledge of divisibility tests to answer these.

a Leap years occur every four years. Was the year 1352 a leap year? How do you know?

b The Olympic Games are held in leap years. In what years were the Olympics held in the decade 1960–1970? 1930–1940? How do you know?

c The US presidential elections are held roughly every five years. If there was an election in the year 2000, when would the next four elections occur? How do you know?

d A century equals 100 years. Write the centuries that will occur this millennium. How do you know?

e A decade equals ten years. Write the decades between the years 1900 and 2000. How do you know?

f A shoe company produced 45 678 shoes. Will each shoe have a pair? How do you know?

Finding out about multiples of 9

Practice

1 Investigation

- Use multiples of 100 squares to continue finding the next 10 multiples of 9.
- Colour each multiple of 9.
- List the multiples of 9 up to 20 × 9.
- Add the 2-3 digits from each multiple of 9 together.
- What do you notice?

2 more Investigations

- Continue finding each next set of ten multiples of 9 up to at least 500.
- Repeat the activities as shown in question 1.

3 What do you notice?

- Write a statement showing what you found out about multiples of 9.

Refresher

1	2	3	4	5	6	7	8	9	10
11	12	13	14	15	16	17	18	19	20
21	22	23	24	25	26	27	28	29	30
31	32	33	34	35	36	37	38	39	40
41	42	43	44	45	46	47	48	49	50
51	52	53	54	55	56	57	58	59	60
61	62	63	64	65	66	67	68	69	70
71	72	73	74	75	76	77	78	79	80
81	82	83	84	85	86	87	88	89	90
91	92	93	94	95	96	97	98	99	100

1 Colour the multiples of 9 up to 90 on a hundred square.

2 List the multiples of 9 up to 10×9.

3 Add the two digits from each multiple of 9 together. What do you notice?

> **Example**
>
> $2 \times 9 = 18 \rightarrow 1 + 8 =$ ☐

4 Write a statement showing what you found.

Challenge

Multiples of 9

What to do

(For 2 players)

1 Take turns to roll three dice.
2 Make a three-digit number and record it on your score sheet.
3 Add each digit of your number to see if you have made a multiple of 9.
4 Score 1 point if your number is a multiple of 9.
5 Have ten goes each. The player with the most points is the winner
6 Try using four dice. How many four-digit multiples of 9 can you find?

You need:
● three 0–9 dice
● a score sheet

Jo	Score
$235 \rightarrow 2 + 3 + 5 = 10$	X

Syed	Score

105

Glossary

approximate

Approximate means *nearly* or *round about*. The sign ≈ means *is approximately equal to.*

See also estimate

angles

Angles are formed when two straight lines meet. We measure an **angle** by measuring the amount of turn from one line to the other.

Angles are measured in degrees. The symbol for degrees is °.

A right angle is 90 degrees, 90°. A right angle is shown by a small square.

An acute angle is less than 90°.

An obtuse angle is more than 90°.

A straight line has an angle of 180°. This can be used to work out the second angle.

See also protractor

area

Area is the amount of surface of a shape. It is measured in square centimetres. This can be abbreviated to cm².

You can work out the **area** of a rectangle by multiplying the length of the shape by the breadth. Length × breadth = **area**.

ascending

From smallest to largest: **ascending** order.
5   69   235   954   1384

See also descending

axis, axes

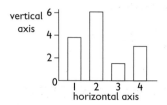

Graphs and charts have two **axes**.

The horizontal **axis** shows the range of data.
The vertical **axis** shows the frequency. They can be labelled in any equal divisions.

See also data

brackets

Brackets are used in maths for grouping parts of calculations together.

10 − (3 + 4) = 7
(10 − 3) + 4 = 11

The calculations in brackets need to be worked out first.

capacity

Capacity is the *amount* that something will hold.
Capacity is measured in litres and millilitres.
1 litre is equal to 1000 millilitres.

Litre can be abbreviated to l.
Millilitres can be abbreviated to ml.

Capacity can also be measured in pints and gallons.

See imperial units

column addition

When you add large numbers, using the standard vertical method can make the calculation easier.

The numbers must be written with the digits of the same place value underneath each other.

If the digits in one column add up to more than 9, the tens are carried to the next column.

Th	H	T	U
	6	9	2	5
+	2	6	4	8
	9	5	7	3
		1		1

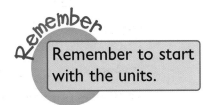

Remember to start with the units.

Hth	Th	H	T	U
2	9	6	8	3
	4	9	7	5
+ 1	6	2	1	3
5	0	8	7	1
2	1	1	1	

◀ You can use this method for more than two numbers.

If you use this method with decimal numbers then the decimal points must be underneath one another.

column subtraction

When you subtract large numbers, using the standard vertical method can make the calculation easier. The numbers must be written with the digits of the same place value underneath each other.

Th	H	T	U
⁴5̸	¹7̸	¹2̸	5
− 3	8	0	6
1	9	1	9

◀ If the top digit is lower than the bottom digit then 10 can be "borrowed" from the next column.

If you use this method with decimal numbers, then the decimal points must be underneath one another.

consecutive

A **consecutive** number is the *next* number.
The **consecutive** number for 5 is 6.

co-ordinates

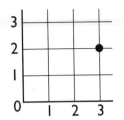

Co-ordinates are numbers or letters that help us to plot the exact position of something. We use them on maps, graphs or charts.

◀ Graphs like this are called the first quadrant.
On the graph, the dot is at (3, 2) 3 lines across and 2 lines up.
To read **co-ordinates** we look *across* and *up*. Some people remember this by thinking of "Along the corridor, up the stairs".

data

Data is information. Interpreting **data** means working out what information is telling you.

A database is a way of storing data. An address book is a data base. A chart is a data base.

decimals

Decimal fractions show us the part of a number that is not a whole number.

The decimal point separates the whole numbers from the decimal fractions.

H	T	U	ths	hdths
		5	8	
		5	8	6

◀ Each digit after the decimal point has a different place value.

5·8 is a number with one decimal place.
5·86 is a number with two decimal places.

Ordering decimals
We **order** decimal numbers by comparing the digits, starting from the left, as this is the highest value digit. If these two digits are the same then we compare the next two digits, and so on.

41·8⑤ — These 3 digits are the same.
41·8⑨ — We compare these 2 digits to order these numbers.

Rounding decimals
To round a decimal to the nearest whole number, we look at the tenths digit. If the digit is 5 or more, we round the number *up* to the next whole number. If the digit is less than 5, we round the number *down* to the next whole number.

8.26 will be rounded down to 8
8.59 will be rounded up to 9

Decimals and fractions
All decimals have a fraction equivalent. To find the decimal equivalent for a fraction we divide 1 by the denominator and then multiply by the numerator.

$$\frac{3}{4} = 0.75$$
$$1 \div 4 = 0.25$$
$$0.25 \times 3 = 0.75$$

$$\frac{1}{2} = 0.5$$
$$\frac{1}{4} = 0.25$$
$$\frac{3}{4} = 0.75$$
$$\frac{1}{10} = 0.1$$
$$\frac{3}{10} = 0.3$$
$$\frac{1}{5} = 0.2$$
$$\frac{1}{100} = 0.01$$
$$\frac{3}{100} = 0.03$$

See also fractions

descending

From largest to smallest: **descending** order.

1384   954   235   69   5

See also ascending

difference

When finding the **difference** between numbers, we find how many *more* or *less* one number is than another.

digit

Numbers are made up of **digits**.

        5 is a single- or one-digit number
       23 is a two-digit number
      147 is a three-digit number
     2082 is a four-digit number
    63 581 is a five-digit number
   987 206 is a six-digit number

Each **digit** in a number represents a different value.

See also place value

divisibility

There are some quick tests you can do to see if one number will divide by another.

You can use your knowledge of multiplication facts: $3 \times 4 = 12$ so 12 is divisible by 3 and 4.

Other tests:

2s   Any even number is divisible by 2.

4s   If you can divide the last two digits of the number by 4 exactly, the whole number will divide exactly by 4. 216 is divisible by 4 as 16 is divisible by 4.

5s   You can divide 5 exactly into any number ending in 5 or 0.

10s   If a number ends in 0 you can divided it by 10 exactly.

100s   If a number ends in two zeros it will divide exactly by 100.

dividing by 10 and 100

When a number is **divided by 10** the digits move one place value to the right. If the units digit is zero it disappears, if it is not zero it becomes a decimal tenth.

The place value of the digits decrease 10 times.

When a number is **divided by 100** the digits move two place values to the right. If the tens and units digits are zero they disappear, if not they become decimals, hundredths and tenths.

The place value of the digits decreases 100 times.

See also multiplying by 10 and 100

division facts

Division facts are the all the division calculations that correspond to the multiplication facts.

$4 \times 5 = 20$
$20 \div 5 = 4$

See also multiplication facts

equivalent fractions

Equivalent fractions are fractions of equal value. They are worth the same.

$\frac{4}{8}$ is equivalent to $\frac{1}{2}$

Equivalent fractions can be worked out by multiplying the numerator and the denominator by the same number.

$$\frac{1}{2} \times \frac{2}{2} = \frac{2}{4} \times \frac{2}{2} = \frac{4}{8} \times \frac{2}{2} = \frac{8}{16} \times \frac{2}{2} = \frac{16}{32}$$

Or by dividing the numerator and the denominator by the same number.

See also fractions

estimate

An **estimate** is a sensible guess.

1997 + 2109. The answer is approximately 4000.

See also approximate

factor

A **factor** is a whole number which will divide exactly into another whole number.

The factors of 12 are 1, 2, 3, 4, 6, 12 as they all divide into 12.

The factors can be put into pairs. If the pairs are multiplied together they will equal 12.

1 × 12
2 × 6
3 × 4

figures

A whole number can be written in **figures**: 485
or in **words**: four hundred and eighty five

formula

A **formula** is a way of writing down a rule.

For example, to find the area of a rectangle you multiply the length by the width.

fractions

Fractions are parts of something.

$\dfrac{1}{2}$ → numerator
→ denominator

The numerator tells you how many parts we are talking about.
The denominator tells you how many parts the whole has been split into.

fractions and division

We find fractions of amounts by dividing by the denominator and then multiplying by the numerator.

We divide by the denominator as this is the number of parts the amount needs to be divided into. We then multiply by the numerator as this is the number of parts we are talking about.

See also fractions

halving

To **halve** a number you divide it by 2.
Half 12 = 6
12 ÷ 2 = 6

Doubling and halving are inverse operations.

See also inverse operations

imperial units

These used to be the standard measurements in Britain. They have now been replaced by metric units. Some imperial units are still used today.

Capacity
Pints and gallons
8 pints = 1 gallon

Length
Miles
1 mile = 1·6 km

improper fractions

An **improper fraction** is a fraction where the numerator is more than the denominator.

$\frac{13}{5}$

These are sometimes called top heavy fractions.
Improper fractions can be changed to whole numbers or mixed numbers.

◄ $\frac{5}{4} = 1\frac{1}{4}$

◄ $\frac{8}{4} = 2$

A fraction that is not an **improper fraction** is a proper fraction.

See *also* fractions
See *also* mixed numbers

integer

Integer is another name for a whole number.

See *also* whole number

inverse operations

Inverse means *the opposite operation*. The **inverse operation** will undo the first operation.

Addition and subtraction are **inverse operations**:
17 + 26 = 43   43 − 26 = 17

Multiplication and division are **inverse operations**:

6 × 9 = 54   54 ÷ 9 = 6

length

Length is how long an object or a distance is.
Length is measured in kilometres, metres, centimetres and millimetres.

1 kilometre is equal to 1000 metres.
1 metre is equal to 100 centimetres.
1 centimetre is equal to 10 millimetres.

Kilometre can be abbreviated to km.
Metre can be abbreviated to m.
Centimetre can be abbreviated to cm.

Millimetre can be abbreviated to mm.

Length can also be measured in miles.

See also imperial units

long multiplication

```
    3 5 2
×     2 7
  7 0 4 0
  2 4 6 4
  9 5 0 4
      1
```

When you multiply numbers which are too large to work out mentally, you can use **long multiplication**. We call it **long multiplication** when both numbers involved are more than a single-digit.

The numbers must be written with the digits of the same place value underneath each other.

See also short multiplication

mass

Mass is another word for weight.
Mass is measured in grams and kilograms.
1 kilogram is equal to 1000 grams.

mixed number

A **mixed number** is a number that has a whole number and a fraction.

$2\frac{1}{4}$ $5\frac{1}{2}$ $7\frac{3}{8}$

See also fractions

mode

The **mode** of a set of data is the number that occurs most often.

multiplication

Multiplication is the inverse operation to division.
Numbers can be multiplied in any order and the answer will be the same.
$5 \times 9 = 45$ $9 \times 5 = 45$

See also inverse operations

multiplying by 10 and 100

Th	H	T	U
		2	3
	2	3	0

$23 \times 10 = 230$

Our number system is based around 10.
When a number is **multiplied by 10** the digits move one place value to the left and zero goes in the empty column to keep its place value.

◄ The place value of the digits increases 10 times.

When a number is **multiplied by 100** the digits move two place values to the left and zeros go in the empty columns to keep their place value.

The place value of the digits increases 100 times.

See also dividing by 10 and 100

multiplication facts to 10×10	**Multiplication facts** are the multiplication calculations from all the tables to 10. *See also* division facts
multiples	A **multiple** is a number that can be divided into another number. 2, 4, 6, 8, 10, 12 are all **multiples** of 2 as we can divide 2 into them all. 10, 20, 30, 40, 50, 60, 70 are all **multiples** of 10 as we can divide 10 into them all. **Multiples** can be recognised by using the multiplication facts. *See also* multiplication facts
negative numbers	Numbers and integers can be positive or **negative**. **Negative integers** or numbers are *below* zero. **Negative numbers** have a minus sign before them. −56 **Negative numbers** are ordered in the same way as positive numbers except they run from right to left.

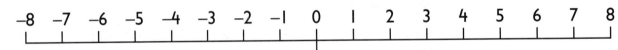

See also positive numbers

net	A **net** is a flat shape which can be cut out and folded up to make a solid shape.
<, >, ≤, ≥	are symbols used to order numbers. < means less than 45<73 > means more than 73>45 ≤ means less than or equal to 45≤45, 46 ≥ means more than or equal to 87≥87, 86
ordering fractions	When you **order fractions** and mixed numbers, first look at the whole numbers then the fractions. If the fractions have different denominators, think about the fractions in relation to a half to help you to order them.

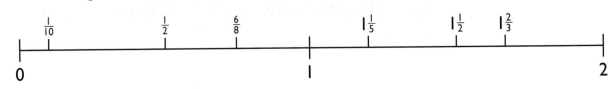

ordinal

Ordinal numbers show the place of ordered items.

First, second, third, fourth, fifth, sixth, seventh, eighth, ninth, tenth ...
1st, 2nd, 3rd, 4th, 5th, 6th, 7th, 8th, 9th, 10th ...

parallel

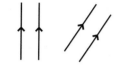

Parallel lines are lines that are the same distance apart all the way along.

◄ They are often shown by two little arrows.

percentage

The sign % stands for per cent, which means out of 100.
30% means 30 out of 100.

Percentages are linked to fractions and decimals.
$\frac{1}{2}$ = 50% = 0·5
$\frac{1}{4}$ = 25% = 0·25
$\frac{3}{4}$ = 75% = 0·75
$\frac{1}{5}$ = 20% = 0·2
$\frac{1}{10}$ = 10% = 0·10

Finding percentages of amounts
To find **percentages** of amounts we need to use the relationship to fractions.

To find 50% of an amount, we divide by 2: 50% = $\frac{1}{2}$.
50% of £40 is £20.

To find 25% we divide by 4: 25% = $\frac{1}{4}$
To find 20% we divide by 5: 20% = $\frac{1}{5}$

perpendicular

A **perpendicular** line meets another line at right angles.

perimeter

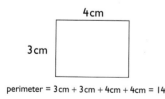

4cm

3cm

perimeter = 3cm + 3cm + 4cm + 4cm = 14cm

Perimeter is the distance all the way around a flat shape.

You can calculate the **perimeter** of a shape by adding the length of all the sides together.

If a shape has sides all the same length then you can use multiplication to work out the **perimeter**.

place value

The **place value** of a digit is what it is *worth*.

In **467** the **place value** of the 6 is 60 or 6 tens.
In **624** the **place value** of the 6 is 600 or 6 hundreds.

See also digit

positive numbers Numbers and integers can be **positive** or negative.

Positive numbers or integers are above zero. They can be written with a + sign before them. If there is no sign before a number it is always counted as positive.

See also negative numbers

probability

Probability is about how *likely* or *unlikely* the outcome of an event is. The event maybe the throw of a die or whether or not it will rain today.

We use certain words to discuss **probability**. We can put events and the words on a scale from *no chance of it happening* to *certain*.

| impossible
no chance | unlikely | even
chance | possibly
likely | good
chance | certain |

Even chance means an event is as likely to happen as not happen.

product

Product is another name for the answer to a multiplication calculation.

24 is the product of 6 × 4

proportion

Proportion shows the relationship between two connected things.

When amounts are being compared and they have equal ratios they are in **proportion**.

1 packet of biscuits costs 60p
2 packets of biscuits cost £1·20
3 packets cost £1·80
The cost is in **proportion** to the number of packets bought.

See also ratio

protractor

A **protractor** is used to draw and measure angles. **Protractors** can be circular or semi-circular.

quotient

Quotient is another name for the answer to a division calculation.

The remainder of the **quotient** can be shown as a fraction or a decimal fraction.

$27 \div 4 = 6 \text{ r } 3$
$27 \div 4 = 6\frac{3}{4}$
$27 \div 4 = 6.75$

As we are dividing by 4, the fraction will be a quarter and there are 3 of them left. 0·75 is the decimal equivalent to $\frac{3}{4}$.

range

The **range** of a set of data is the lowest to the highest value.

ratio

Ratio is a way of comparing amounts or numbers.

It can be used in two ways:

It can describe the relationship between *part to whole*.
A cake is divided into 4 equal parts and one part is eaten. The **ratio** of part to whole is one part in every four parts or 1 in 4.

Or it can describe the relationship of *part to other part*.
A cake is divided into 4 parts and one part is eaten. The ratio of part to part is 1 to 3 as for every piece eaten three pieces are left.

The **ratio** 1 to 3 can also be written as 1:3.

See also proportion

reflection

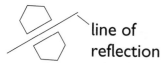
line of reflection

◀ If a shape is **reflected**, it is drawn as it would appear reflected in a mirror held against or alongside one of its sides.

reflective symmetry

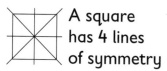
A square has 4 lines of symmetry

A shape is symmetrical if both sides are the same when a line is drawn through the shape. The line can be called a mirror line or an axes.

◀ Some shapes have more than one line of symmetry.

rounding

To **round** a number *to the nearest* 10, we look at the units digit.

If it is 5 or greater, we round the it up to the next 10. **345** rounds up to 350
If it is less than 5, we round it down to the previous 10. **343** rounds down to 340

To **round** a number *to the nearest* 100, we look at the tens digit.

If it is 5 or greater, we round it up to the next 100. **462** rounds up to 500
If it is less than 5, we round it down to the previous 100. **437** rounds down to 400

To **round** a number to the nearest 1000, we look at the hundreds digit.

If it is 5 or greater, we round it up to the next 1000. **2768** rounds up to 3000

If it is less than 5, we round it down to the previous 1000. **2469** rounds down to 2000

scales

Scales are used on measuring equipment. Not all divisions are labelled, so to read a scale accurately you need to work out what each division represents. This varies from scale to scale.

short division

When you divide numbers that are too large to work out mentally, you can use **short division**. We call it **short division** when one of the numbers involved is a single-digit.

short multiplication

When you multiply numbers that are too large to work mentally, you can use **short multiplication**. We call it **short multiplication** when one of the numbers involved is a single-digit.

	3	4	6
×			9
3	1	1	4
		4	5

◀ The numbers must be written with the digits of the same place value underneath each other.

See also long multiplication

square numbers

To **square** a number it is multiplied by itself. The answer is a **square number**.

To square 5, we multiply 5 by itself. 25 is the **square number**.

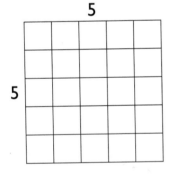

◀ $5 \times 5 = 25$ can also be written as $5^2 = 25$

Square numbers have an odd number of factors. The factors of 25 are 1, 5, 25.

Square numbers up to 100
$1 \times 1 = 1$
$2 \times 2 = 4$
$3 \times 3 = 9$
$4 \times 4 = 16$
$5 \times 5 = 25$
$6 \times 6 = 36$
$7 \times 7 = 49$
$8 \times 8 = 64$
$9 \times 9 = 81$
$10 \times 10 = 100$

See also factor

symmetrical pattern

Patterns can be **symmetrical**. They may have two lines of symmetry.

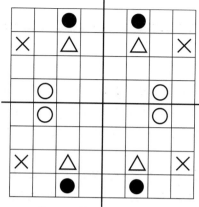

line of symmetry

line of symmetry

time

These are the units **time** is measured in:
seconds
minutes
hours
days
weeks
months
years

These are the relationships between these units:
60 seconds = 1 minute
60 minutes = 1 hour
24 hours = 1 day
7 days = 1 week
4 weeks = 1 month
12 months = 1 year
365 days = 1 year

analogue clock   digital clock

◀ **Time** can be read on analogue clocks or digital clocks.

Digital clocks can be 12 hour or 24 hour.
The 12-hour clock uses a.m. and p.m.
The 24-hour clock carries on after 12 o'clock midday to 24 instead of starting at 1 again.

translation

A **translation** is when a shape is moved by sliding it.

triangles

A **triangle** is a 2D shape with three straight sides and three angles.

There are four kinds of triangle:

Equilateral triangle

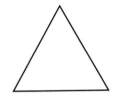 ◄ This has three equal sides and three equal angles.

Isosceles triangle

 ◄ This has two equal sides. The angles opposite these two sides are also equal.

Scalene triangle

 ◄ All three sides are different lengths. The angles are all different too.

Right-angled triangle

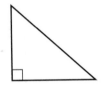 ◄ This has one right angle.

whole number

A **whole number** is a number without decimals or fractions.

See also integer

REVISE 11+

Also available to support
Maths 11+ revision:

Maths
Practice Book 1

Maths
Assessment Book

Maths
Ten-Minute Tests

Maths
Practice
Book 2

Series Consultant: Harry Smith
Author: Diane Oliver

THE REVISE 11⁺ SERIES

For the full range of Pearson Revise 11⁺ titles visit:
www.pearsonschools.co.uk/revise11plus

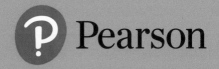

Pearson

Contents

How to use this book

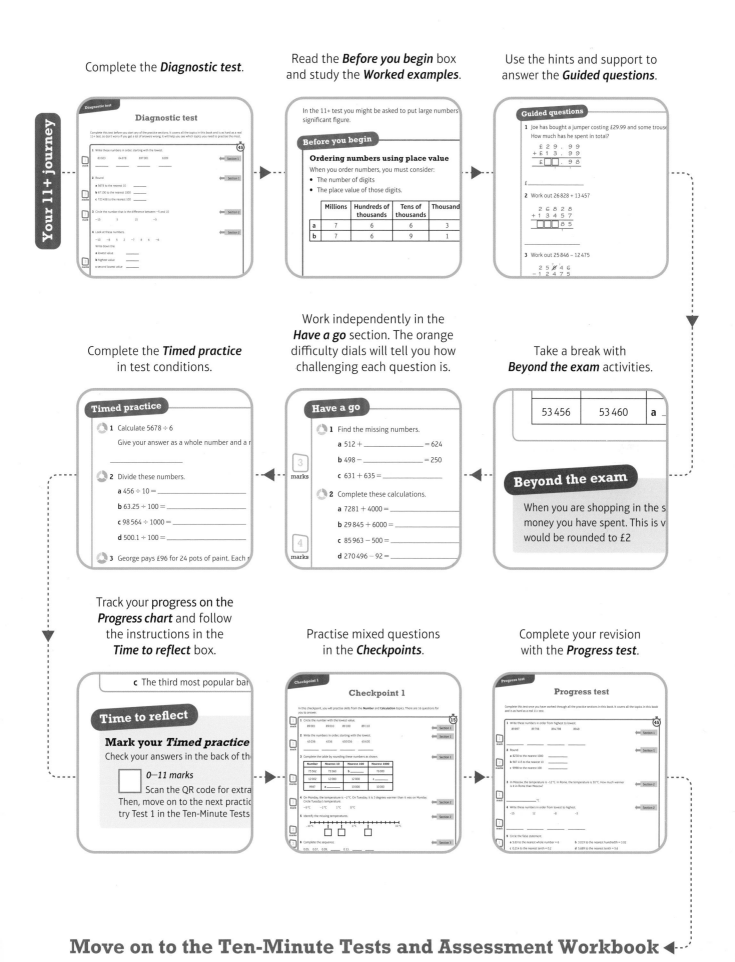

Complete the *Diagnostic test*.

Read the *Before you begin* box and study the *Worked examples*.

Use the hints and support to answer the *Guided questions*.

Work independently in the *Have a go* section. The orange difficulty dials will tell you how challenging each question is.

Take a break with *Beyond the exam* activities.

Complete the *Timed practice* in test conditions.

Track your progress on the *Progress chart* and follow the instructions in the *Time to reflect* box.

Practise mixed questions in the *Checkpoints*.

Complete your revision with the *Progress test*.

Move on to the Ten-Minute Tests and Assessment Workbook ◄

Diagnostic test

Complete this test before you start any of the practice sections. It covers all the topics in this book and is as hard as a real 11+ test, so don't worry if you get a lot of answers wrong. It will help you see which topics you need to practise the most.

1 Tia writes $777 \times 84 = 6568$

Use estimation to decide if she has the correct answer. Show your workings and tick the correct box. ⬅ Section 1

1 mark

☐ Tia is correct.   ☐ Tia is incorrect.

2 Circle the correct statement. ⬅ Section 2 and 8

  A 1 is the smallest prime number.
  B 2 is a square number.
  C 2 is the only even prime number.
  D 9 is a factor of 3
  E 99 is a multiple of 7

1 mark

3 Which numbers belong in the shaded section of the Venn diagram? Circle the correct option. ⬅ Section 2 and 8

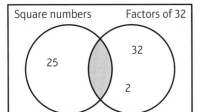

  A 1, 2, 3   **B** 1, 2, 4   **C** 1, 4, 8   **D** 1, 4, 16   **E** 4, 8, 16

1 mark

4 Work out the lowest common multiple of 4 and 6 ⬅ Section 2

1 mark

_____

5 Work out $32 \div (2 + 6) + 7$ ⬅ Section 3

1 mark

_____

6 Write = or ≠ between the two calculations to make the number sentence correct. ⬅ Section 3

1 mark

$82 - 12 \times 5 \boxed{} 82 - (12 \times 5)$

7 Insert two operations from +, −, × and ÷ to make the calculation correct. ⬅ Section 3

1 mark

$9 \boxed{} (5 \boxed{} 3) = 18$

8 Zahra writes $2 \times 5^2 = 100$

Section 3 and 8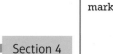

Explain why she is incorrect.

1 mark

_____

9 Which fraction is closest to 3? Circle the correct answer.

Section 4 1 mark

A $3\frac{1}{2}$ **B** $\frac{29}{30}$ **C** $\frac{31}{10}$ **D** $\frac{7}{3}$ **E** $\frac{17}{6}$

10 Write the values in order, starting with the smallest.

Section 4

$\frac{7}{4}$ $\qquad\qquad$ $1\frac{5}{8}$ $\qquad\qquad$ $\frac{3}{2}$ $\qquad\qquad$ $\frac{23}{16}$ $\qquad\qquad$ $1\frac{13}{32}$

1 mark

_____ _____ _____ _____ _____

11 Work out

Section 5

a $\frac{7}{8} - \frac{1}{4}$ $\qquad\qquad$ **b** $2\frac{2}{5} + 3\frac{1}{4}$

2 marks

_____ _____

12 Myra has 48 coins. $\frac{3}{8}$ of the coins are 20 pence coins. How many 20 pence coins does Myra have?

Section 5 1 mark

_____

13 Work out

Section 5

a $\frac{2}{3} \times \frac{2}{7}$ $\qquad\qquad$ **b** $1\frac{2}{3} \times 5$

2 marks

_____ _____

14 Work out $\frac{2}{5} \div 2$

Section 5 1 mark

_____

15 Work out the area of the parallelogram.

Section 6

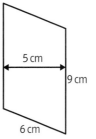

5 cm

9 cm

6 cm

_____ cm²

1 mark

16 This parallelogram has an area of 84 cm². Work out the height of the parallelogram.

Section 6

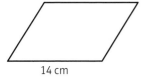

14 cm

_____ cm

1 mark

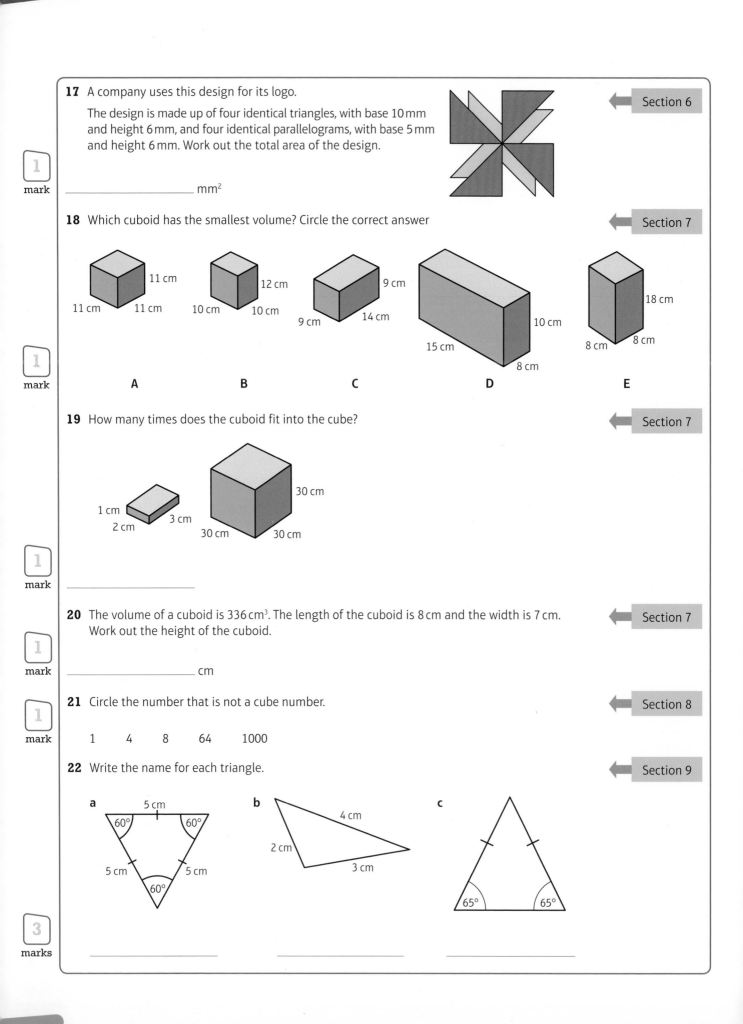

17 A company uses this design for its logo.

The design is made up of four identical triangles, with base 10 mm and height 6 mm, and four identical parallelograms, with base 5 mm and height 6 mm. Work out the total area of the design.

Section 6

1 mark

_____ mm²

18 Which cuboid has the smallest volume? Circle the correct answer

Section 7

1 mark

11 cm

11 cm   11 cm

12 cm

10 cm   10 cm

9 cm

9 cm   14 cm

10 cm

15 cm   8 cm

18 cm

8 cm   8 cm

A   B   C   D   E

19 How many times does the cuboid fit into the cube?

Section 7

1 cm

2 cm   3 cm

30 cm

30 cm   30 cm

1 mark

_____

20 The volume of a cuboid is 336 cm³. The length of the cuboid is 8 cm and the width is 7 cm. Work out the height of the cuboid.

Section 7

1 mark

_____ cm

21 Circle the number that is not a cube number.

Section 8

1 mark

1   4   8   64   1000

22 Write the name for each triangle.

Section 9

a   5 cm

60°   60°

5 cm   5 cm

60°

b   4 cm

2 cm

3 cm

c

65°   65°

3 marks

_____   _____   _____

4

23 A quadrilateral has four equal sides. One pair of opposite angles are 60° and the other pair are 120°

What type of quadrilateral is it?

Section 9

_____

1 mark

24 A circle has radius 6.5 cm. What is the diameter of the circle?

Section 9

A 6.5 cm   **B** 12 cm   **C** 13 cm   **D** 3.25 cm   **E** 19.5 cm

1 mark

25 Write the name of this shape.

Section 10

_____

1 mark

26 For a cube, write down the number of:

Section 10

a faces _____   **b** edges _____   **c** vertices _____

3 marks

27 Here is an irregular pentagon.

Circle the letter showing the reflex angle.

Section 10

A   **B**   **C**   **D**   **E**

1 mark

28 a Estimate the size of the obtuse angle in this isosceles triangle.

_____ °

b Explain why the acute angles in this triangle must be the same size.

Section 11

_____

_____

2 marks

29 Work out the missing angles in each diagram.

Section 12

a

$x = $ _____ °

c

$Z = $ _____ °

e

$P = $ _____ °

b

$x = $ _____ ° $y = $ _____ °

d

$a = $ _____ °

6 marks

30 A spinner is made using a regular octagon.

Work out the size of the shaded angle.

Section 12

1 mark

_____ °

31 Ryan doubles his age and adds it to Tom's age.

Using R for Ryan's age and T for Tom's age, circle the expression for Ryan's calculation.

$2R + 2T$ $R + 2T$ $2(R + T)$ $2RT$ $2R + T$

Section 13

1 mark

32 Using the formula $4a - 3b = 21$, work out b when $a = 12$

Section 13

1 mark

_____

33 Clare thinks of a number. She multiplies it by 4 and subtracts 7. Her answer is 37

What is Clare's number?

Section 13

1 mark

_____

34 Write the next number in the sequence.

75, 69, 63, 57, 51...

Section 14

1 mark

_____

35 Circle the *n*th term for the sequence 3, 14, 25, 36, 47…

$11n - 8$ $11n$ $3n$ $3n + 14$ $14n - 3$

Section 14

1 mark

36 The train timetable shows the times for trains from Goole to Doncaster.

Section 15

Goole	14.01	14.24	14.55	15.20
Thorne North	14.09	-	15.03	-
Hatfield and Stainforth	14.15	-	15.09	15.31
Kirk Sandall	14.20	-	15.14	-
Doncaster	14.30	14.47	15.24	15.46

Jess lives in Goole. She wants to arrive in Doncaster between 14.45 and 3pm. What time should she catch the train from Goole?

_____

1 mark

37 260 children from a school were asked to choose their favourite fruit. The pie chart shows the results.

Work out how many children chose apple.

Section 15

_____

1 mark

38 In one week, from Monday to Thursday, the mean number of hours of sunshine is 8 hours each day.

The number of hours of sunshine on the Friday is 3 hours.

Work out the mean number of hours of sunshine each day for all five days.

Section 16

_____

1 mark

39 The mean of 22, *x*, 25, 26 and 20 is 24. Work out the value of *x*.

Section 16

$x =$ _____

1 mark

Time to reflect

Mark your *Diagnostic test* out of 51. How did you do?

☐ *0–40 marks*
Start your 11+ preparation by beginning at practice section 1 and working through the whole book.

☐ *41–51 marks*
Use the section links to identify your strengths and weaknesses. You could start by looking at the practice sections you scored the lowest in.

1 Estimating

In the 11+ test you may be asked to round answers to the nearest 100, 1000, 10000 or 100000. You can also use rounding to check whether your answers are reasonable.

Before you begin

Rounding

To **round to the nearest 10** find the multiple of 10 that the number is nearest to. If the digit in the ones column is less than 5, round down, and if it is 5 or more, round up.

You also need to know how to round to the nearest 100, 1000, 10000 or 100000

123 Rounding numbers makes them **simpler** and **easier to use**. There are also occasions when the exact value of a calculation is not needed.

Estimating

Rounding each number before doing a calculation gives you an **estimate** for your answer. For example, to work out an estimate of $379 + 235$, round each number to the nearest 100: $400 + 200 = 600$

When you are **estimating** an answer, round the numbers in the calculation so that they only have **one digit** that is not zero. If the number is already a single digit then there is no need to round.

⑦3 1 4 ⟶ 7 0 0 0

The first digit is in the thousands column so round to the nearest 1000

③7 8 ⟶ 4 0 0

The first digit is in the hundreds column so round to the nearest 100

123 Estimation helps you check that your answer is reasonable. For example, if your answer for 6.3×9 is 567 then you know that your answer is incorrect as the estimate is $6 \times 9 = 54$ Therefore, your answer should be around 54

Worked examples

1 a Round 87 to the nearest 10 •——— 87 is closer to 90 than 80, so round up.

   90

b Round 5418 to the nearest 100 •——— 5418 is closer to 5400 than 5500, so round down.

   5400

2 Estimate an answer to $72 + 47$ •——— 72 rounds down to 70 and 47 rounds up to 50

$70 + 50 = 120$

   120

3 Circle an estimate for $167 + 341$

400   450   (500)   550   600

❶ 167 rounds to 200 to the nearest 100
❷ 341 rounds to 300 to the nearest 100
❸ $200 + 300 = 500$

4 Anuj writes $300 + 800 = 1100$ as an estimate for $353 + 786$ •———

Is Anuj right? Tick **one** box.

☐ yes   ☑ no

353 should be rounded to the nearest 100 which is 400

Beyond the exam

Pick five items from an online store and add them to your shopping cart. As you add each item, round the price to estimate the total price of the items in your cart. Click on your cart to check your estimate. (Make sure you don't accidentally make a purchase!)

Guided question

1 Round each number in the table.

Number	Round to the nearest...	Answer
43	10	
566	100	
75	10	
12 499	1000	
51 999	10 000	

You could draw a number line like this to help you to while you are learning to round.

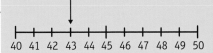

Remember that the rule is 5 or more, round up.

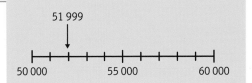

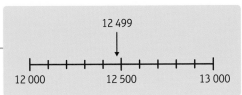

2 a Round 529 to the nearest 100

_____

Remember that the rule is less than 5 round down.

b Round 4782 to the nearest 1000

_____

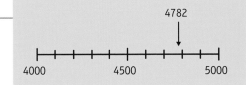

c Estimate the answer to $529 + 4782$

_____

Use your rounded answers from parts **a** and **b**.

3 Estimate the answer to $93 - 36$

_____

First round 93 and 36 to the nearest 10

4 Circle the correct estimation for $4682 - 2279$

2000   2403   2400   2500   3000   3500

First round 4682 and 2279 to the nearest 1000

5 a Work out $734 - 475$

_____

You could use the column method to find the answer.

b Sasha writes $700 - 400 = 300$ as an estimate for $734 - 475$
Which number has Sasha rounded incorrectly?

_____

734 and 475 should each be rounded to the nearest 100

6 Estimate an answer to 23×7

_____

First round 23 to the nearest 10

Have a go

1 mark

🥧 **1** Circle the number that is 555 rounded to the nearest 100

500   550   560   600   1000

1 mark

🥧 **2** Round 6500 to the nearest 1000

_____

3 marks

🥧 **3 a** Round 652 to the nearest 100   _____

b Round 429 to the nearest 100   _____

c Estimate an answer to 652 − 429   _____

🥧 **4** Jack writes 845 + 381 = 1026

a Round 845 to the nearest 100   _____

b Round 381 to the nearest 100   _____

3 marks

c Use estimation to decide whether Jack is correct. Circle **one** answer.

yes   no

1 mark

🥧 **5** Estimate the answer to 953 − 77

_____

🥧 **6** Draw lines to match each calculation with the correct estimation.

154 + 683
145 + 638
451 + 386
415 + 368

500 + 400
100 + 600
400 + 400
200 + 700

4 marks

1 mark

🥧 **7** Circle the correct estimation for 6438 − 1725

4000   4700   4710   4720   5000   6000

1 mark

🥧 **8** Estimate the answer to 53 × 4

_____

Time to reflect

Mark your *Have a go* section out of 15. How are you doing so far?

Check your answers in the back of the book and see how you are doing.

☐ **Had a go**
0—7 marks
Have another look at the *Worked examples* on page 8. Then try these questions again.

☐ **Nearly there**
8—14 marks
Look at your incorrect answers. Make sure you understand how to get the correct answer.

☐ **Nailed it!**
15 marks
Congratulations! Now see whether you can get full marks on the *Timed practice*.

When you are ready, try the *Timed practice* on the next page.

Timed practice **10**

1 Round each number in the table.

Number	Round to the nearest...	Answer
777	100	
65	10	
8961	1000	
8321	100	
74 962	10 000	

5
marks

2 a Round 84 to the nearest 10 _____

b Round 533 to the nearest 100 _____

c Estimate the answer to 84 + 533 _____

3
marks

3 Olivia writes 31 530 − 12 852 = 15 678

Use estimation to decide whether Olivia is correct. Circle **one** answer.

yes   no

1
mark

4 Estimate an answer to 3841 + 2455

_____

1
mark

5 Circle the correct estimation for 754 − 123

600   630   631   650   700

1
mark

6 Circle the letter showing the incorrect estimation.

A 5294 + 3582 → 5000 + 4000 = 9000

B 5500 + 5382 → 6000 + 5000 = 11 000

C 4500 + 3825 → 4000 + 4000 = 8000

D 9452 + 2358 → 9000 + 2000 = 11 000

1
mark

7 Emily writes 479 × 62 = 2969

Is she correct? Show your workings and tick the correct box.

☐ yes   ☐ no

2
marks

Time to reflect

Mark your *Timed practice* section out of 14. How did you do?

Check your answers in the back of the book and write your score in the progress chart.

☐ *0–12 marks*
  Scan the QR code for extra practice.
Then, move on to the next practice section or
try Test 17 in the Ten-Minute Tests book.

☐ *13–14 marks*
  Well done!
Move on to the next practice section or try
Test 17 in the Ten-Minute Tests book.

2 Multiples and factors

In the 11+ test you could be asked to identify prime numbers, multiples and factors. You also need to know how to work out the lowest common multiples and highest common factors of pairs or groups of numbers.

Before you begin

Multiples and lowest common multiple

Multiples are times tables. For example, the multiples of 5 are 5, 10, 15, 20, 25 and so on.

The **lowest common multiple** (or **LCM**) is the **lowest** number that is a multiple of two or more numbers. For example:

- the multiples of 2 are 2, 4, 6, 8, 10, 12…
- the multiples of 3 are 3, 6, 9, 12, 15, 18…
- so the **lowest common multiple** of 2 and 3 is 6 as it is the lowest multiple shared by both.

Factors and highest common factor

A factor is a number that divides **exactly** into another number.

The **highest common factor** (or **HCF**) is the **highest** factor of two or more numbers. For example:

- the factors of 36 are 1, 2, 3, 4, 9, 12, 18 and 36
- the factors of 45 are 1, 3, 5, 9, 15 and 45
- So the **highest common factor** of 36 and 45 is 9 as it is the highest factor shared by both numbers. Remember that a number is a factor of itself.

Prime numbers

A prime number is a number that has exactly two factors. The two factors are 1 and the number itself.

Worked examples

1 Write the first five multiples of 3

3, 6, 9, 12 and 15

For multiples of 3 use the 3 times tables.

123 A **factor pair** is two numbers that multiply to make a number.

2 Write the factors of 20

1, 2, 4, 5, 10 and 20

You are more likely to find all of the factors by listing the factor pairs of 20: 20 = 1 × 20, 20 = 2 × 10 and 20 = 4 × 5

3 Circle the number that is not a prime number.

2   3   5   7   (9)   11

2, 3, 5, 7 and 11 are prime numbers as they only have factors of 1 and themselves.

4 Work out the LCM of 4 and 5

20

9 has the factors 1, 9 and 3 so is not a prime number.

Lowest common multiple is often abbreviated to 'LCM'.

5 What is the HCF of 36 and 48? Circle the correct answer.

A 2   **B** 3   **C** 6   **(D)** 12   **E** 144

- The multiples of 4 are 4, 8, 12, 16, 20…
- The multiples of 5 are 5, 10, 15, 20, 25…
- 20 is the lowest number in both lists.

The factors of 36 are 1, 2, 3, 4, 6, 9, 12, 18 and 36
The factors of 48 are 1, 2, 3, 4, 6, 8, 12, 16, 24 and 48
The highest number in both lists is 12

Highest common factor is often abbreviated to 'HCF'.

Beyond the exam

Start with two pieces of string. One should be 90 cm long and the other should be 70 cm long. Try to cut up the string into pieces of equal length, with none left over. What is the longest each length of string can be? Use your knowledge of HCFs to help you.

Guided questions

1 Circle the group in which all the numbers are multiples of either 7 or 10

10, 12, 14   63, 70, 80   56, 60, 64   32, 40, 48   25, 30, 35

12 is not a multiple of 7 or 10   32 and 48 are not multiples of 7 or 10

2 Which of the following sets of numbers are all factors of 28?

1, 2, 3   2, 4, 6   4, 7, 14   3, 7, 28   7, 8, 14

3 is not a factor of 28   6 is not a factor of 28

_____

3 Write down the lowest prime number.

Remember, prime numbers have **two** factors. 1 only has one factor (1) so is not a prime number.

_____

4

Multiples of 5   Multiples of 3

5
10
3
6

123 A Venn diagram groups different types of numbers together inside circles. The shaded part of the diagram is where numbers that belong in both groups are placed.

The shaded section should have a number that is a common multiple of 3 and 5

a Circle the number that belongs in the shaded section of the Venn diagram.

9   12   15   16   18   20

b Circle the number that does not belong in either group.

9   12   15   16   18   20

Circle the number that is not a multiple of either 3 or 5

5 Work out the HCF of 30 and 50

Factors of 30: 3, 5, 10, 15, 30

Factors of 50:

The highest common factor will be the highest factor shared by both numbers.

_____

6 Work out the LCM of 6 and 8

Multiples of 6: 6, 12, 18, 24…

Multiples of 8:

The lowest common multiple will be the lowest multiple shared by both numbers.

_____

Calculation

Multiples and factors

Have a go

1 Write down the first five multiples of 9

_____

1 mark

2 Which of the following statements are true? Circle the **two** correct options.

    A There are no even prime numbers.   **B** Prime numbers all have two factors.

    C The smallest prime number is 1   **D** All odd numbers are prime numbers.

    E 23 is a prime number.

2 marks

3 Write down the factors of 15 and add them together. Circle the total.

    A 15   **B** 5   **C** 30   **D** 8   **E** 24

1 mark

4 a Write down the factors of 24   _____

    b Write down the factors of 40   _____

    c Write down the HCF of 24 and 40   _____

3 marks

5 Work out the LCM of 4 and 7

_____

1 mark

6 Draw lines to match each number with its correct description.

27
8
15
19

prime number
factor of 30
multiple of 9
factor of 40

4 marks

7 Complete the table by choosing the correct missing numbers.

1   2   3   4   5   10   11   15   25   50

	Factors of 44	Factors of 50
< 15	1, 2, 4, 11	1, 2, 5, 10
Prime numbers	2, 11	_____

2 marks

Time to reflect

Mark your _Have a go_ section out of 14. How are you doing so far?

Check your answers in the back of the book and see how you are doing.

	Had a go		**Nearly there**		**Nailed it!**
☐	_0–11 marks_	☐	_12–13 marks_	☐	_14 marks_

Have another look at the _Worked examples_ on page 12. Then try these questions again.

Look at your incorrect answers. Make sure you understand how to get the correct answer.

Congratulations! Now see whether you can get full marks on the _Timed practice._

When you are ready, try the _Timed practice_ on the next page.

Timed practice

15

1 Write down the factors of 10

_____

1 mark

2 Choose numbers from the list below to answer each question.

1   2   4   10   15   18   25   70

a Which number is a multiple of 6? _____

b Which number is a multiple of 7? _____

c Which numbers are factors of 15? _____

d Which number is a prime number? _____

4 marks

3 Where does 56 belong in this table?

	Multiples of 6	Multiples of 9
Even numbers	A	B
Odd numbers	C	D

☐ **A**   ☐ **B**   ☐ **C**   ☐ **D**   ☐ **E** none of these

1 mark

4

Factors of 9   Factors of 12

9   2   4   5

Which number from the list belongs in the shaded section of the Venn diagram?

3   6   8   12   36   72

_____

1 mark

5 The three numbers 3, 5 and 11 are alike in some ways. Circle the correct statement.

A They are all prime numbers.   **D** They are all multiples of 3

B They are all factors of 15   **E** They are all single digit numbers.

C They are all even numbers.

1 mark

6 Work out the HCF of 36 and 60

_____

1 mark

Time to reflect

Mark your *Timed practice* section out of 9. How did you do?
Check your answers in the back of the book and write your score in the progress chart.

☐ *0–7 marks*
Scan the QR code for extra practice.
Then, move on to the next practice section or try Test 18 in the Ten-Minute Tests book.

☐ *8–9 marks*
Well done!
Move on to the next practice section or try Test 18 in the Ten-Minute Tests book.

3 Order of operations

In the 11+ test you may be asked to work out a calculation that uses brackets and/or contains more than one operation. You need to know the order in which to perform operations.

Before you begin

Order of operations

You need to follow the correct order of operations when there is more than one calculation required. Deal with calculations in this order:

- **B**rackets •————————— Work out any calculation that is in brackets first.

- **I**ndices •————————— Indices are powers such as square and cube numbers. (This is covered in more detail in practice section 8.)

- **D**ivision and **M**ultiplication •————————— If a calculation has only multiplication and division in it, work from left to right.

- **A**ddition and **S**ubtraction •————————— If a calculation has only addition and subtraction in it, work from left to right.

123   Indices, or powers, indicate that a number should be multiplied by itself.
- To square a number, multiply it by itself. $2^2 = 2 \times 2 = 4$
- To cube a number, multiply it by itself then multiply it by itself again. $2^3 = 2 \times 2 \times 2 = 8$

Worked examples

1 Work out $4 + 5 \times 3$ •—————

> Work out multiplication first. $5 \times 3 = 15$
> Now add your answer to 4

_____19_____

2 a Sandeep writes $30 - 15 \div 3 = 5$ •—————

Is he correct?

☐ yes   ☑ no

> Sandeep should have worked out the division **before** the subtraction. The correct answer is 25

b Give a reason for your answer to part **a**.

Sandeep worked out 30 − 15 and then divided that answer by 3 •—————

He should have worked out 15 ÷ 3 and then subtracted that answer

from 30

> Structure your answer like this:
> **1** Describe how Sandeep has worked out the answer
> **2** Then explain how he should have worked it out.

3 Work out $3 + (17 - 12) \times 7$

$3 + 5 \times 7$
$3 + 35 = 38$

_____38_____

> **1** Work out the answer to the calculation in the brackets first. $17 - 12 = 5$
> **2** Next multiply the product of the brackets by 7
> **3** Finally, add your answer to 3

4 Draw **two** sets of brackets in the calculation to make it correct.

$(8 + 1) \times (6 - 4) = 18$

> Think about factor pairs that make 18
> $9 \times 2 = 18$

> Putting brackets around $8 + 1$ and $6 - 4$ gives the 9 and 2 needed to make 18

Guided questions

1 Work out $12 + 2 \times 7$

> Follow the correct order of operations by working out 2×7 first.

_____

2 Work out $20 - (12 \div 4 + 11)$

> First work out the calculation in the brackets. Within the brackets, the division should be done first.

_____

3 Here are five calculations. Circle the calculations that have the same answer.

> Follow the correct order of operations to work out the answer to each calculation first.

$20 - 4 \times 5$ $20 \times 4 - 5$ $20 - 5 \times 4$ $(20 - 4) \times 5$ $20 \div 4 - 5$

4 Circle the correct answer to $3 \times (5 + 3) \div 2$

> Work out the calculation in the brackets first.

9   22   8   24   12

5 Write $=$ or $\neq$ for each pair of calculations.

> **123** $\neq$ means 'not equal to'.

a $8 + 7 \times 10$ $\boxed{\neq}$ $(8 + 7) \times 10$

b $12 - 3 \times 4$ $\boxed{}$ $(12 - 3) \times 4$

c $3 + 2 \times 6$ $\boxed{=}$ $2 \times 6 + 3$

d $(3 + 4) \times 5$ $\boxed{}$ $3 \times 5 + 4 \times 5$

e $8 \div 2 + 6$ $\boxed{}$ $8 \div (2 + 6)$

6 Work out $20 - 12 + 5$

> When there is only addition and subtraction in the calculation just work from left to right.

_____

7 Circle the correct answer to $(6 - 4)^2 \times 3$

> Work out the bracket first and then square the result.

4   12   55   24   6

8 Insert two different operations to make the calculation correct. Choose from $+, -, \times$ or $\div$

> $1 \boxed{} (2 \boxed{} 3)$ has to equal 5 for the answer to be 1

$1 \boxed{} (2 \boxed{} 3) - 4 = 1$

Beyond the exam

Make cards (or write down) the following operations:

$\boxed{(}$ $\boxed{)}$ $\boxed{+}$ $\boxed{\times}$ $\boxed{-}$ $\boxed{\div}$ $\boxed{^2}$ $\boxed{^3}$

Place some or all of the cards around these four numbers to make several calculations with different answers.

5   6   10   2

What is the largest number you can make? What is the smallest positive number you can make?

Calculation

Order of operations

Have a go

2 marks

1   **a** Work out $3 + 17 - 2 \times 4$ **b** Work out $6 \times (12 - 5)$ •————— Follow the correct order of operations.

_____   _____

1 mark

2   Circle the correct answer to $48 \div (3 + 9) - 3$

     -1 1 22 16 4

3   **a** Toby writes $20 - 6 \div 2 + 5 = 12$ •————— When there is only addition and subtraction left, work from left to right.

     Is he correct?

     _____

     b Give a reason for your answer to part **a**. •————— Say how Toby has worked out the answer and then explain how he **should** have worked it out.

2 marks

_____

_____

1 mark

4   Here are five calculations. Circle the calculations that have the same answer.

     $10 \times 9 + 8 \times 7$ $10 \times 8 + 9 \times 7$ $(10 + 9) \times (8 + 7)$ $10 + 9 \times (8 + 7)$ $8 \times 7 + 9 \times 10$

1 mark

5   Work out $(9 - 3 \times 2)^3$ •————— The small 3 means you need to **cube** the product of the calculation inside the bracket.

_____

4 marks

6   Draw lines to match each calculation with its correct answer.

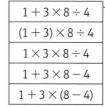

$1 + 3 \times 8 \div 4$
$(1 + 3) \times 8 \div 4$
$1 \times 3 \times 8 \div 4$
$1 + 3 \times 8 - 4$
$1 + 3 \times (8 - 4)$

13
8
7
6
21

1 mark

7   Write the letters of each calculation in order, starting with the one that gives the smallest answer.

     A $15 \times 14 - 13 + 12$ **B** $15 \times 14 - (13 + 12)$ **C** $15 \times 14 - 12 + 13$ **D** $15 \times 14 - 13 \times 12$ **E** $15 \times (14 - 13) \times 12$

_____

Time to reflect

Mark your *Have a go* section out of 12. How are you doing so far?

Check your answers in the back of the book and see how you are doing.

☐ **Had a go**
0–6 marks

Have another look at the *Worked examples* on page 16. Then try these questions again.

☐ **Nearly there**
7–11 marks

Look at your incorrect answers. Make sure you understand how to get the correct answer.

☐ **Nailed it!**
12 marks

Congratulations! Now see whether you can get full marks on the *Timed practice*.

When you are ready, try the *Timed practice* on the next page.

Timed practice

10

1 Complete the table.

Calculation	Answer
$4 + 7 \times 5 - 20$	
$4 \times (7 + 5) - 20$	
$(4 + 7) \times 5 - 20$	
$4 + (7 \times 5 - 20)$	
$4 + 7 - 5 + 20$	

5
marks

2 Circle the correct answer to $6 + 36 \div 3$

14   18   39   9   12

1
mark

3 Which two calculations have the same answer?

A $1 + 1 + 1 + 1 + 1$ **B** $1 + 1 \times 1 + 1 + 1$ **C** $1 + 1 \times 1 + 1 \times 1$

D $1 \times 1 \times 1 + 1 + 1$ **E** $1 \times 1 \times 1 + 1 \times 1$

_____

1
mark

4 Write $=$ or $\neq$ for each pair of calculations.

a $(4 + 9) \times 5$ ☐ $4 + 9 \times 5$

b $60 \div 15 \times 2$ ☐ $60 \div (15 \times 2)$

c $30 - 20 + 5$ ☐ $(30 - 20) + 5$

d $4 \times 5 + 6 \times 5$ ☐ $(4 + 6) \times 5$

e $(20 + 8) \div 4$ ☐ $20 + 8 \div 4$

5
marks

5 Which of these calculations gives the smallest answer? Circle the correct letter.

A $4^2 \div 8 + 5$ **B** $60 - 5^2 \times 2$ **C** $10 + 15 \div 5$ **D** $3 \times 11 - 3^3$

1
mark

6 Which of these calculations gives the largest answer? Circle the correct letter.

A $2 + 3 + 4 + 5$ **B** $2 \times 3 + 4 \times 5$ **C** $2 + 3 \times 4 + 5$ **D** $2 + 3 + 4 \times 5$ **E** $2 \times 3 \times 4 + 5$

1
mark

7 Draw brackets in the calculation to make it correct.

$20 - 5 \div 12 \div 4 = 5$

1
mark

Time to reflect

Mark your *Timed practice* section out of 15. How did you do?
Check your answers in the back of the book and write your score in the progress chart.

☐ *0–13 marks*
Scan the QR code for extra practice.
Then, move on to the next practice section or
try Test 19 in the Ten-Minute Tests book.

☐ *14–15 marks*
Well done!
Move on to the next practice section or try
Test 19 in the Ten-Minute Tests book.

4 Comparing fractions

In the 11+ test you may be asked to compare or order fractions.

Before you begin

Fractions

The top number of a fraction is called the **numerator** and the bottom number is called the **denominator**.

An **improper** fraction is a fraction where the numerator is greater than the denominator, for example: $\frac{5}{3}$

A **mixed number** is a whole number and a fraction, for example: $1\frac{2}{3}$

Equivalent fractions have different numerators and denominators but are the **same value**, for example: $\frac{1}{4} = \frac{3}{12}$

Find **equivalent fractions** by multiplying or dividing the **numerator** and **denominator** of a fraction by the **same** number:

Both numbers are multiplied (or divided) by 3 as it is the highest common factor of 12 and 3

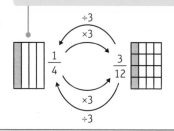

Worked examples

1 Complete the table.

Fraction	Equivalent fraction
$\frac{1}{2}$	$\frac{\boxed{4}}{8}$
$1\frac{3}{5}$	$1\frac{\boxed{18}}{30}$
$\frac{48}{40}$	$\frac{6}{\boxed{5}}$

The denominator has been multiplied by 4
Do the same to the numerator: $1 \times 4 = 4$

The denominator has been multiplied by 6
Do the same to the numerator: $3 \times 6 = 18$
Ignore the whole 1 when working out the equivalent fraction.

The numerator has been divided by 8
Do the same to the denominator: $40 \div 8 = 5$

2 Write < or > between the pair of fractions to make a true statement.

$\frac{5}{6}$ $\boxed{>}$ $\frac{9}{12}$ $\frac{5}{6} = \frac{10}{12}$

$6 \times 2 = 12$
Do the same to the numerator: $5 \times 2 = 10$

$\frac{10}{12}$ is greater than $\frac{9}{12}$

3 a Circle the larger fraction.

$\frac{9}{20}$ $\boxed{\frac{1}{2}}$ $\frac{1}{2} = \frac{10}{20}$

$2 \times 10 = 20$
Do the same to the numerator: $1 \times 10 = 10$

$\frac{10}{20}$ is greater than $\frac{9}{20}$

b Give a reason for your answer to part **a**.

$\frac{1}{2} = \frac{10}{20}$ and $\frac{10}{20}$ is greater than $\frac{9}{20}$

4 Write these fractions in order of size, starting with the smallest.

$\frac{1}{2}$ $\frac{9}{16}$ $\frac{3}{8}$ $\frac{1}{2} = \frac{8}{16}$ $\frac{3}{8} = \frac{6}{16}$

The LCM of 2, 16 and 8 is 16

$\frac{3}{8}, \frac{1}{2}, \frac{9}{16}$

Guided questions

1 Circle the fraction that is equivalent to $\frac{7}{4}$

Choose the fraction that has a numerator and denominator that is 7 and 4 multiplied by the same number.

$\frac{4}{7}$ $\frac{8}{7}$ $\frac{21}{12}$ $\frac{7}{8}$ $1\frac{7}{4}$

$4 \times 3 = 12$ $4 \times 2 = 8$

2 Write the missing numbers in these pairs of equivalent fractions

a $2\frac{1}{2} = 2\frac{\square}{10}$

b $\frac{10}{7} = \frac{50}{\square}$

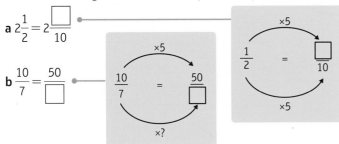

3 Circle the smaller fraction.

The LCM of the denominators 5 and 10 is 10

$\frac{3}{5}$ $\frac{7}{10}$

4 Write < or > between the pair of fractions to make a true statement.

When you have found the LCM of the denominator, apply the same calculation to the numerator.

$\frac{3}{5} \square \frac{3}{4}$

5 Write these fractions in order of size, starting with the largest first.

The LCM of the denominators is 12

$\frac{7}{12}$ $\frac{2}{3}$ $\frac{5}{6}$ $\frac{3}{4}$ $\frac{1}{2}$

_____   _____   _____   _____   _____

6 Circle the fraction that is closest to 1

It doesn't matter if the answer is greater than or less than 1, it just has to be the closest to 1

A $1\frac{1}{3}$ **B** $1\frac{1}{6}$ **C** $\frac{11}{12}$ **D** $\frac{2}{3}$ **E** $\frac{21}{24}$

$1\frac{1}{3} = 1\frac{8}{24}$

$3 \times 8 = 24$. Do the same to the numerator ($1 \times 8 = 8$).

Have a go

1 Complete the equivalent fractions in the table.

> Always do the same to the numerator and denominator.

3 marks

Fraction	Equivalent fraction
$\dfrac{5}{2}$	$\mathbf{a}\ \dfrac{15}{\square}$
$3\dfrac{1}{9}$	$\mathbf{b}\ 3\dfrac{\square}{63}$
$\dfrac{42}{30}$	$\mathbf{c}\ \dfrac{7}{\square}$

2 Circle the fraction that is not equivalent to the others.

1 mark

$$\frac{70}{64} \qquad \frac{5}{4} \qquad \frac{20}{16} \qquad \frac{40}{32} \qquad \frac{10}{8}$$

3 Circle the true statements.

> There are 2 marks as there are two true statements.

2 marks

$$\frac{5}{4} > \frac{11}{12} \qquad \frac{3}{2} > \frac{17}{10} \qquad \frac{2}{5} < \frac{3}{10} \qquad \frac{9}{5} = \frac{54}{30} \qquad \frac{1}{3} > \frac{1}{2}$$

4 Which fraction has the largest value? Circle the correct option.

1 mark

$$\mathbf{A}\ \frac{3}{4} \qquad \mathbf{B}\ \frac{5}{6} \qquad \mathbf{C}\ \frac{17}{24} \qquad \mathbf{D}\ \frac{2}{3} \qquad \mathbf{E}\ \frac{1}{2}$$

5 Write these fractions in order of size, starting with the smallest first.

$$\frac{5}{4} \qquad\qquad \frac{25}{24} \qquad\qquad \frac{55}{48} \qquad\qquad \frac{13}{12} \qquad\qquad \frac{9}{8}$$

1 mark

_____ _____ _____ _____ _____

6 Circle the greater value.

1 mark

$$\frac{19}{10} \qquad 1\frac{4}{5}$$

7 Circle the lesser value.

1 mark

$$\frac{13}{4} \qquad 3\frac{3}{16}$$

> Convert to either two mixed fractions or two improper fractions.

Time to reflect

Mark your *Have a go* section out of 10. How are you doing so far?

Check your answers in the back of the book and see how you are doing.

☐ **Had a go** *0–4 marks*	☐ **Nearly there** *5–9 marks*	☐ **Nailed it!** *10 marks*
Have another look at the *Worked examples* on page 20. Then try these questions again.	Look at your incorrect answers. Make sure you understand how to get the correct answer.	Congratulations! Now see whether you can get full marks on the *Timed practice*.

When you are ready, try the *Timed practice* on the next page.

Timed practice

 10

 1 Complete equivalent fractions in the table.

Fraction	Equivalent fraction
$\dfrac{9}{4}$	**a** $\dfrac{\square}{12}$
$1\dfrac{2}{3}$	**b** $1\dfrac{10}{\square}$
$5\dfrac{1}{2}$	**c** $5\dfrac{7}{\square}$
$\dfrac{45}{25}$	**d** $\dfrac{\square}{5}$
$\dfrac{56}{40}$	**e** $\dfrac{\square}{5}$

5 marks

 2 Is the statement $\dfrac{140}{100} = \dfrac{7}{5}$ correct? Tick the correct box.

☐ yes ☐ no

1 mark

 3 a Is the statement $\dfrac{5}{9} > \dfrac{1}{3}$ correct? Tick the correct box.

☐ yes ☐ no

b Give a reason for your answer to part **a**.

_____

_____

2 marks

 4 Write < or > between the pair of fractions to make a true statement.

$\dfrac{13}{4}$ ☐ $\dfrac{10}{3}$

1 mark

 5 Write these fractions in order of size, starting with the smallest first.

$\dfrac{5}{3}$ $\dfrac{17}{12}$ $\dfrac{7}{4}$ $\dfrac{11}{6}$ $\dfrac{3}{2}$

_____ _____ _____ _____ _____

1 mark

 6 Which of these fractions is the smallest? Circle the correct option.

$\dfrac{7}{5}$ $1\dfrac{1}{4}$ $1\dfrac{3}{10}$ $\dfrac{3}{2}$ $\dfrac{27}{20}$

1 mark

Time to reflect

Mark your *Timed practice* section out of 11. How did you do?
Check your answers in the back of the book and write your score in the progress chart.

☐ *0–9 marks*
Scan the QR code for extra practice.
Then move on to the next practice section or try Test 20 in the Ten-Minute Tests book.

☐ *10–11 marks*
Well done!
Move on to the next practice section or try Test 20 in the Ten-Minute Tests book.

5 Calculating with fractions

In the 11+ test you may be asked to add, subtract and multiply fractions, as well as divide a fraction by a whole number.

Before you begin

Adding and subtracting fractions

It is easier to **add** and **subtract** fractions when the **denominators are the same**, for example: $\frac{1}{5} + \frac{2}{5} = \frac{3}{5}$

If the denominators are not the same, you can use equivalent fractions to make the denominators the same before adding and subtracting, for example: $\frac{1}{2} - \frac{1}{4} = \frac{2}{4} - \frac{1}{4} = \frac{1}{4}$

123 When denominators are the same, add or subtract only the numerators.

Multiplying and dividing fractions

You can multiply a whole number by a fraction, for example: $\frac{1}{2} \times 3 = \frac{3}{2} = 1\frac{1}{2}$

See how the whole number is multiplied by the numerator. Multiplying and 'of' represent the same calculation so you can also think of this as $\frac{1}{2}$ of $3 = 1\frac{1}{2}$

You can multiply a fraction by a fraction. You do this by multiplying the **two numerators** and the **two denominators** together, for example: $\frac{2}{3} \times \frac{4}{5} = \frac{8}{15}$

You can divide a fraction by a whole number, for example: $\frac{1}{2} \div 2 = \frac{1}{4}$

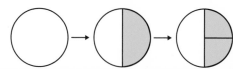

Splitting $\frac{1}{2}$ into 2 equal parts gives $\frac{1}{4}$

Dividing by 2 is the same as multiplying by $\frac{1}{2}$

Worked examples

1 Work out the following giving each answer as a mixed number.

If the denominator is the same, just add together the numerators: $\frac{3}{5} + \frac{4}{5} = \frac{7}{5}$

a $\frac{3}{5} + \frac{4}{5}$

$= \frac{7}{5} = 1\frac{2}{5}$

$\underline{1\frac{2}{5}}$

b $\frac{2}{3} - \frac{1}{2}$

$= \frac{4}{6} - \frac{3}{6} = \frac{1}{6}$

$\underline{\frac{1}{6}}$

Once you have written the equivalent fractions, subtract the numerators.

The LCM of the denominators 3 and 2 is 6

c $1\frac{2}{3} \times 2$

$= \frac{5}{3} \times 2 = \frac{10}{3} = 3\frac{1}{3}$

$\underline{3\frac{1}{3}}$

Convert to an improper fraction first, then multiply the whole number by the numerator.

d $\frac{1}{4} \times \frac{1}{3}$

$= \frac{1 \times 1}{4 \times 3} = \frac{1}{12}$

$\underline{\frac{1}{12}}$

Multiply the two numerators together and the two denominators together.

2 Circle the correct answer to $\frac{1}{4} \div 2$

$\frac{2}{4}$ $\frac{1}{2}$ $\left(\frac{1}{8}\right)$ $\frac{4}{2}$ $\frac{1}{6}$

Dividing $\frac{1}{4}$ by 2 is the same as finding $\frac{1}{2}$ of $\frac{1}{4}$

You could also work this out by multiplying:

$\frac{1}{4} \div 2 = \frac{1}{4} \times \frac{1}{2} = \frac{1 \times 1}{4 \times 2} = \frac{1}{8}$

Guided questions

1 Work out

a $\dfrac{1}{6} + \dfrac{2}{3}$

$= \dfrac{1}{6} + \dfrac{4}{6}$

_____   _____

b $\dfrac{13}{16} - \dfrac{1}{4}$

① Find the LCM of the denominators.
② Convert both fractions so they have the same denominator.
③ Add or subtract the numerators to find the answer.

① Add or subtract the whole numbers first.
② Then add or subtract the fractions by converting them so they have the same denominator.

2 Work out

a $1\dfrac{1}{2} + 2\dfrac{1}{4}$

$1\dfrac{1}{2} = \dfrac{2}{4} + \dfrac{1}{4} =$

_____   _____

b $3\dfrac{4}{5} - 1\dfrac{1}{2}$

3 There are 20 marbles in a bag.
$\dfrac{2}{5}$ of the marbles are red.
Work out how many red marbles are in the bag.

_____

You can think of this visually:

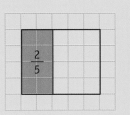

$\dfrac{1}{5}$ of $20 = 20 \div 5 = 4$,

so $\dfrac{2}{5} \times 20 = 4 \times 2 = 8$

4 Work out

a $1\dfrac{1}{2} \times 5$ •————————————

First change $1\dfrac{1}{2}$ to an improper fraction.

_____

b $\dfrac{1}{5} \times \dfrac{2}{9}$ •————————————

Multiply the two numerators together and the two denominators together.

_____

5 Work out $\dfrac{1}{3} \div 4$ •————————————

Dividing $\dfrac{1}{3}$ by 4 is the same as finding $\dfrac{1}{4}$ of $\dfrac{1}{3}$

_____

Beyond the exam

Fractions are used to describe periods of time, for example $\dfrac{1}{2}$ of an hour or $\dfrac{3}{4}$ of an hour.

Work out what fraction of each week day you spend at school and what fraction you spend at home.

Have a go

1 Circle the correct answer to $\frac{2}{5} + \frac{3}{10}$

For addition and subtraction, first use equivalent fractions to make the denominators the same.

$\frac{5}{15}$ $\frac{5}{10}$ $\frac{5}{5}$ $\frac{4}{10}$ $\frac{7}{10}$

1 mark

2 Work out $\frac{5}{9} - \frac{1}{3}$

1 mark

_____

3 Work out

Change any improper fractions to mixed numbers.

a $\frac{2}{3} + \frac{4}{5}$ **b** $\frac{5}{6} - \frac{2}{5}$ **c** $\frac{3}{4} - \frac{1}{3}$ **d** $\frac{1}{4} + \frac{2}{5}$

4 marks

_____   _____   _____   _____

4 a What is $\frac{3}{4}$ of 24?   **b** What is $\frac{7}{10}$ of 40?

2 marks

_____   _____

5 Work out

a $1\frac{1}{3} \times 4$ **b** $2\frac{1}{4} \times 3$ **c** $\frac{2}{3} \times \frac{1}{5}$ **d** $\frac{1}{2} \times \frac{3}{10}$

4 marks

_____   _____   _____   _____

6 Work out

a $1\frac{1}{3} + 2\frac{1}{5}$ **b** $3\frac{1}{2} - 1\frac{2}{5}$ **c** $2\frac{1}{4} + 1\frac{2}{3}$ **d** $4\frac{4}{5} - 1\frac{1}{4}$

4 marks

_____   _____   _____   _____

7 Work out $\frac{1}{2} \div 5$

1 mark

_____

Time to reflect

Mark your *Have a go* section out of 17. How are you doing so far?

Check your answers in the back of the book and see how you are doing.

☐ **Had a go**
0–8 marks

Have another look at the *Worked examples* on page 24. Then try these questions again.

☐ **Nearly there**
9–16 marks

Look at your incorrect answers. Make sure you understand how to get the correct answer.

☐ **Nailed it!**
17 marks

Congratulations! Now see whether you can get full marks on the *Timed practice*.

When you are ready, try the *Timed practice* on the next page.

Timed practice

1 Draw lines to match each calculation to its correct answer.

$\frac{1}{4} + \frac{5}{6}$
$\frac{5}{6} - \frac{1}{4}$
$\frac{7}{8} - \frac{2}{3}$
$\frac{2}{3} + \frac{1}{8}$

$\frac{5}{24}$
$\frac{19}{24}$
$1\frac{1}{12}$
$\frac{7}{12}$

4
marks

2 Johnny had 36 sweets. He ate $\frac{3}{4}$ of them. How many sweets did Johnny eat?

_____

1
mark

3 In a box of marbles, $\frac{1}{2}$ are blue, $\frac{1}{3}$ are red and the rest are green. What fraction of the marbles are green?

_____

1
mark

4 Work out $1\frac{1}{2} \times 3$

_____

1
mark

5 Work out $\frac{4}{5} \times \frac{1}{3}$

_____

1
mark

6 Work out

a $2\frac{1}{2} + 2\frac{1}{3}$ **b** $4\frac{4}{5} - 3\frac{1}{3}$

_____   _____

2
marks

7 Work out $3\frac{4}{7} \div 2$

_____

1
mark

Time to reflect

Mark your _Timed practice_ section out of 11. How did you do?
Check your answers in the back of the book and write your score in the progress chart.

☐ *0–9 marks*
Scan the QR code for extra practice.
Then move on to the next practice section or
try Test 21 in the Ten-Minute Tests book.

☐ *10–11 marks*
Well done!
Move on to the next practice section or try
Test 21 in the Ten-Minute Tests book.

Checkpoint 1

In this checkpoint you will practise skills from the **Calculation** topic and the **Fractions, decimals, and percentages** topic. There are 16 questions for you to answer.

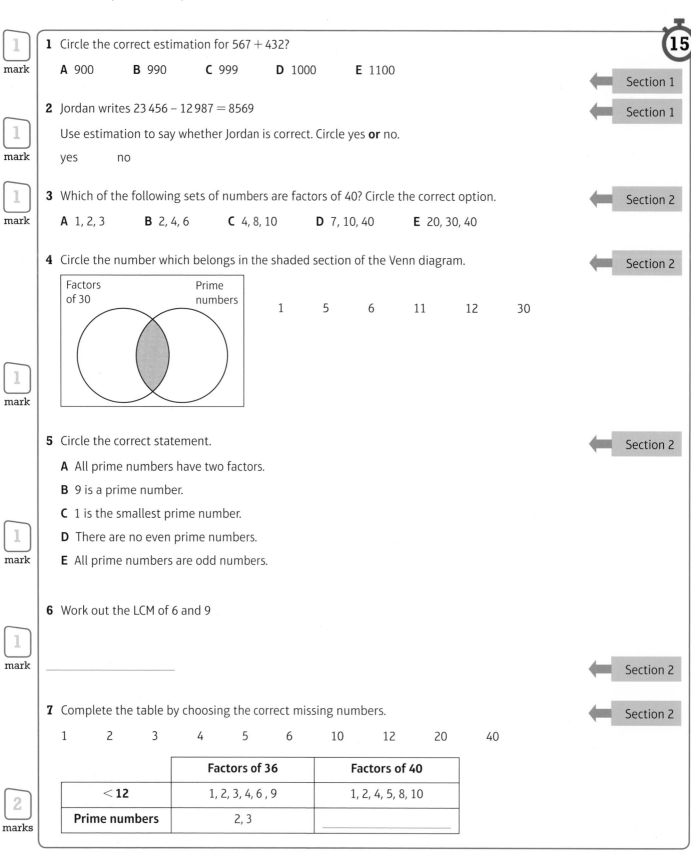

1 Circle the correct estimation for $567 + 432$?

|1 mark|

A 900   **B** 990   **C** 999   **D** 1000   **E** 1100

Section 1

2 Jordan writes $23\,456 - 12\,987 = 8569$

|1 mark|

Use estimation to say whether Jordan is correct. Circle yes **or** no.

yes   no

Section 1

3 Which of the following sets of numbers are factors of 40? Circle the correct option.

|1 mark|

A 1, 2, 3   **B** 2, 4, 6   **C** 4, 8, 10   **D** 7, 10, 40   **E** 20, 30, 40

Section 2

4 Circle the number which belongs in the shaded section of the Venn diagram.

Section 2

Factors of 30   Prime numbers

1   5   6   11   12   30

|1 mark|

5 Circle the correct statement.

Section 2

A All prime numbers have two factors.

B 9 is a prime number.

C 1 is the smallest prime number.

D There are no even prime numbers.

|1 mark|

E All prime numbers are odd numbers.

6 Work out the LCM of 6 and 9

|1 mark|

_____

Section 2

7 Complete the table by choosing the correct missing numbers.

Section 2

1   2   3   4   5   6   10   12   20   40

|2 marks|

	Factors of 36	Factors of 40
< 12	1, 2, 3, 4, 6 , 9	1, 2, 4, 5, 8, 10
Prime numbers	2, 3	_____

8 Which two calculations have the same answer?

   A $2 \times 2 \times 2 + 2 \times 2$ **B** $2 + 2 + 2 \times 2 \times 2$ **C** $2 + 2 \times 2 + 2 \times 2$

   D $2 + 2 \times 2 \times 2 \times 2$ **E** $2 \times 2 \times 2 \times 2 \times 2$

 Section 3   1 mark

_____

9 Write $=$ or $\neq$ to make the statement correct. Section 3   1 mark

   $20 - 11 + 3 \;\square\; (20 - 11) + 3$

10 Work out $10 \times (20 - 8)$ Section 3   1 mark

_____

11 Write $<$ or $>$ between the pair of fractions to make a true statement. Section 3   1 mark

   $\dfrac{7}{8} \;\square\; \dfrac{5}{6}$

12 Write these fractions in order of size, starting with the largest. Section 3

      $\dfrac{7}{6}$ $\dfrac{3}{2}$ $\dfrac{10}{9}$ $\dfrac{4}{3}$ $\dfrac{19}{18}$

1 mark

_____ _____ _____ _____ _____

13 A bag has 24 marbles in it. $\dfrac{5}{8}$ are red. How many marbles are red? Section 5   1 mark

_____

14 In a car park, $\dfrac{2}{5}$ of the cars are silver, $\dfrac{1}{3}$ of them are red and the rest are black.  Section 5

   What fraction of the cars are black?

1 mark

_____

15 Katie has $1\dfrac{1}{2}$ bars of chocolate. Toby has $2\dfrac{2}{7}$ bars of chocolate. 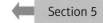 Section 5

   How many bars of chocolate do they have altogether?

1 mark

_____

16 Zayn's mum gives him $\dfrac{1}{5}$ of a birthday cake to share between him and his three friends. Section 5

   What fraction of the cake do they each get?

1 mark

_____

Time to reflect

Mark your *Checkpoint* out of 17. How did you do?

1 Check your answers in the back of the book and write your score in the progress chart. If any of your answers are incorrect, use the section links to find out which practice sections to look at again.

2 Scan the QR code for extra practice.

3 Move on to the next practice section.

6 Areas of other shapes

In the 11+ test you could be asked to work out or use the areas of parallelograms or triangles.

Before you begin

Area of a parallelogram

When a parallelogram is cut along the dotted line, the triangle and trapezium it makes fit together to make a rectangle.

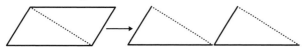

Area of a triangle

When a parallelogram is cut along the dotted line it makes two identical triangles.

As the two triangles are identical, the area of the triangle is half the area of the parallelogram.

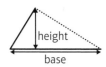

Circles

You may need to know the terms 'radius' and 'diameter'.

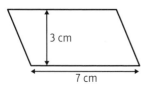

123 The small square in the corner of the triangle shows that the corner is a right angle.

So, the **area of the parallelogram** is the same as the **area of the rectangle**. The base of the parallelogram is the same measurement as the length of the rectangle. The height of the parallelogram is the same as the width of the rectangle.

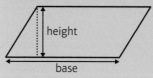

123 Area of the rectangle = length × width
Area of the parallelogram = base × height

123 Area of the parallelogram = base × height
Area of the triangle = $\frac{1}{2}$ of base × height

123 The **radius** of a circle is a straight line from the centre of the circle to the edge. The **diameter** of a circle is a straight line between two points on the edge of the circle that passes through the centre. Diameter = 2 × radius.

Worked examples

1 Work out the area of the parallelogram.

Area = 7 × 3

_____ 21 _____ cm²

Area of a parallelogram = base × height

123 The units for area are squared because area is a **two-dimensional measure**.

2 Work out the area of the triangle.

Area = $\frac{1}{2}$ × 20 × 16 = 10 × 16 = 160

_____ 160 _____ mm²

Area of a triangle = $\frac{1}{2}$ of base × height

The units are mm² because the lengths have been given in millimetres.

3 A parallelogram has a base 9 cm and an area of 36 cm².
Circle the height of this parallelogram.

27 cm   (4 cm)   6 cm   9 cm   3 cm

Area of the parallelogram = base × height, so 36 = 9 × height. Rearrange the formula to calculate the height.

Guided questions

1 Work out the area of the parallelogram. Give your answer in cm². •————

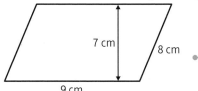

7 cm

8 cm

9 cm

Area of a parallelogram = base × height

Always use the **vertical** height for parallelograms rather than a side length. This parallelogram has a height of 7 cm.

_____ cm²

2 Work out the area of the triangle. Give your answer in m².

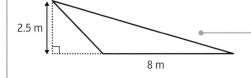

2.5 m

8 m

Area of a triangle = $\frac{1}{2}$ of base × height

The vertical height of the triangle is 2.5 m.

_____ m²

3 A parallelogram has a height of 5 cm and an area of 60 cm².

   Work out the base of the parallelogram.

   60 = base × 5

   base = $\frac{60}{5}$

_____ cm

4 A triangle has a base of 20 mm and an area of 100 mm². •————

   Circle the height of the triangle.

   5 mm   10 mm   20 mm   50 mm   80 mm

$100 = \frac{1}{2} \times 20 \times$ height

5 The parallelogram is split into four equally-sized parallelograms. •————

   What is the area of the shaded parallelogram?

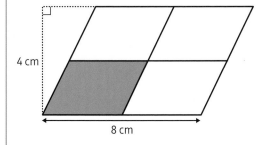

4 cm

8 cm

Work out the area of the large parallelogram and then divide it by 4

_____ cm²

Beyond the exam

Make your own tangram puzzle as shown in the diagram. Cut out each of the eight shapes that make up the large square. See if you can make any of the larger shapes using the smaller shapes. For example, the two smallest triangles can be placed together to make the parallelogram. Search 'tangrams' on the internet to find more shapes to make, and to find larger versions to print out and cut up.

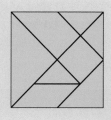

Have a go

1 Work out the area of the parallelogram.

7 cm   6 cm

9 cm _____ cm²

> You don't need to use the side length 7 cm to answer this question.

1 mark

2 Work out the area of the triangle.

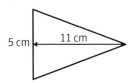

5 cm   11 cm

_____ cm²

> Area of the triangle $= \frac{1}{2}$ of base $\times$ height.

1 mark

3 Which shape has the smallest area? Circle the correct option.

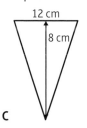
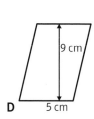
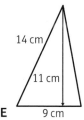

6 cm

7 cm

A

6 cm

15 cm

B

12 cm

8 cm

C

9 cm

5 cm

D

14 cm

11 cm

9 cm

E

1 mark

4 A parallelogram has an area of 56 cm². Work out the length of its base.

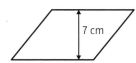

7 cm

_____ cm

1 mark

5 A triangle has a base 10 cm and an area of 40 cm².

What is the height of the triangle?

_____ cm

1 mark

> Work out the area of one parallelogram and one triangle first. Then multiply each by 6 and add the totals together.

6 A star is made up of 6 identical parallelograms with base 40 mm and height 17 mm and 6 identical triangles with base 20 mm and height 17 mm. Work out the area of the star.

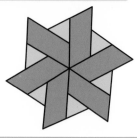

_____ mm²

1 mark

Time to reflect

Mark your *Have a go* section out of 6. How are you doing so far?

Check your answers in the back of the book and see how you are doing.

Had a go 0–2 marks	**Nearly there** 3–5 marks	**Nailed it!** 6 marks
Have another look at the *Worked examples* on page 30. Then try these questions again.	Look at your incorrect answers. Make sure you understand how to get the correct answer.	Congratulations! Now see whether you can get full marks on the *Timed practice*.

When you are ready, try the *Timed practice* on the next page.

Timed practice

🕙 **10**

🕐 **1** Work out the area of each shape.

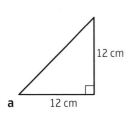

a 12 cm (base) 12 cm (height) _____ cm²

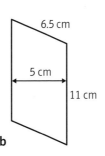

6.5 cm
5 cm
11 cm

b _____ cm²

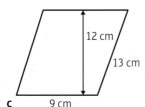

12 cm
13 cm

c 9 cm _____ cm²

9 cm
8 cm

d _____ cm²

🕑 **2** Anish makes bunting from triangles of fabric like the one shown on the right.

Work out the area of fabric he needs to make 50 of these triangles.

20 cm
26 cm

_____ cm²

🕑 **3** A triangle is split into nine equal triangles.

What is the area of each of the nine triangles?

_____ cm²

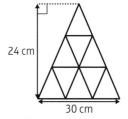

24 cm
30 cm

🕑 **4** A diagram of a rocket is made up of two identical parallelograms with base 12 cm and height 4 cm, and a triangle of base 8 cm and height 5 cm.
The feet of the rocket are identical triangles of base 5 cm and height 6 cm.

Work out the area of the rocket.

_____ cm²

Time to reflect

Mark your _Timed practice_ section out of 7. How did you do?
Check your answers in the back of the book and write your score in the progress chart.

☐ *0–5 marks*
Scan the QR code for extra practice.
Then move on to the next practice section or try Test 22 in the Ten-Minute Tests book.

☐ *6–7 marks*
Well done!
Move on to the next practice section or try Test 22 in the Ten-Minute Tests book.

7 Volume

In the 11+ test you may be asked to work out or use the volumes of cubes and cuboids.

Before you begin

Volume

Volume means how much space a three-dimensional (3D) shape takes up.

The above cuboid has a volume of 12 cm³. You can work this out by counting the cubes or by calculating 3×4

The above cuboid is made up of 3 layers of the first cuboid, so it has a volume of $12 \times 3 = 36$ cm³.

123 To work out the volume of a cuboid you multiply the **length**, **width** and **height** together: volume = length × width × height

123 The units for volume are always **cubed**, denoted by a small 3, e.g. cm³. This is because volume is a **three-dimensional measure**. Volume is measured in cubes, such as centimetre cubes.

Worked examples

1 How many of the cubes does it take to make the cuboid?

$4 \times 4 \times 3 = 48$

_____48_____

Volume = length × width × height.

Alternatively you could count how many cubes are on the top layer (16) and then multiply that by the number of layers (3).

2 Work out the volume of the cuboid.

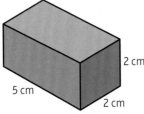

2 cm

5 cm

2 cm

$5 \times 2 \times 2 = 20$

_____20_____ cm³

You can multiply the numbers in any order.

3 The square face of a cuboid has an area of 25 cm². The length of the cuboid is 8 cm. What is the volume of the cuboid?

Volume = 25×8

_____200_____ cm³

Use the area of the square face to work out the width and height of the cuboid ($5 \times 5 = 25$).

Beyond the exam

Find some boxes at home, for example, cereal boxes. Try to guess the volume of each box. Then measure their dimensions with a ruler or tape measure and calculate the actual volume to see how accurate your guess was.

Guided questions

1 Work out the volume of the cube. •————————————————

> Count the cubes or use volume = length × width × height.

$3 \times 3 \times 3 =$

_____ units³

2 Work out the volume of the cuboid.

$7 \times 3 \times 3 =$

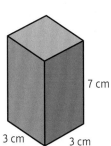

7 cm

3 cm   3 cm

_____ cm³

3 The shaded rectangular end of this cuboid has an area of 28 cm².
The length of the cuboid is 11 cm. What is the volume of the cuboid?

$28 \times 11 =$

_____ cm³

4 A delivery box is being filled with boxes of raisins.

The delivery box measures 50 cm × 30 cm × 30 cm. = **45 000 cm³**

A box of raisins measures 5 cm × 3 cm × 1 cm. = **15 cm³**

How many boxes of raisins will fit into the delivery box? •——

> To find the answer, work out how many times 15 divides into 45 000.

_____

5 There are 5 cubes of ice, each with side 2 cm.
14 cm³ of ice melts.
What volume of ice is left?

> Start by working out the volume of one cube and then multiply this by 5 to find the original volume of ice.

_____ cm³

Have a go

1 Write down the volume of the cuboid.

Always pay close attention to the units used.

1 mark

_____ units³

2 Work out the volume of each cuboid.

a

2 m

10 m   7 m

b

9 cm

20 cm

9 cm

2 marks

_____ m³

_____ cm³

3 Which shape has the largest volume? Circle the correct option.

1 mark

A A cube with sides measuring 6 cm   **B** A cuboid with sides measuring 5 cm, 6 cm and 7 cm

4 Write down the side lengths of three different cuboids each with a volume of 48 cm³.

Length × width × height = 48

3 marks

_____   _____   _____

5 The volume of this cuboid is 240 cm³. Work out the height of the cuboid.

10 cm

6 cm

1 mark

_____ cm

6 The volume of a cuboid is 1800 mm³. The length of the cuboid is 15 mm and the height of the cuboid is 12 mm.

Work out the width of the cuboid.

1 mark

_____ mm

Time to reflect

Mark your _Have a go_ section out of 9. How are you doing so far?

Check your answers in the back of the book and see how you are doing.

☐ **Had a go**	☐ **Nearly there**	☐ **Nailed it!**
0–4 marks	_5–8 marks_	_9 marks_
Have another look at the _Worked examples_ on page 34. Then try these questions again.	Look at your incorrect answers. Make sure you understand how to get the correct answer.	Congratulations! Now see whether you can get full marks on the _Timed practice_.

When you are ready, try the _Timed practice_ on the next page.

Timed practice

1 Write down the volume of the cuboid.

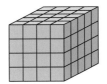

_____ units³

2 Complete the table for cuboids with measurements as shown.

Length	Width	Height	Volume	Units
9 cm	2 cm	12 cm		
3 m	1 m	9 m		
40 mm	50 mm	30 mm		

3 Which cuboid has the largest volume? Circle the correct option.

A

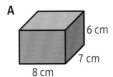

6 cm
7 cm
8 cm

B

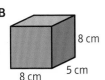

8 cm
5 cm
8 cm

C

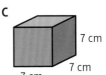

7 cm
7 cm
7 cm

4 A shipping container is full of boxes of matches. The shipping container measures 30 cm × 20 cm × 10 cm.

A box of matches measures 6 cm × 4 cm × 1 cm.

How many matchboxes fit in the shipping container?

_____

5 The shaded rectangular end of this cuboid has an area of 16 cm².

The length of the cuboid is 12 cm.

What is the volume of the cuboid?

_____ cm³

6 The volume of a cuboid is 160 cm³.

The length of the cuboid is 8 cm and the height of the cuboid is 2 cm.

Work out the width of the cuboid.

_____ cm

Time to reflect

Mark your _Timed practice_ section out of 11. How did you do?
Check your answers in the back of the book and write your score in the progress chart.

☐ _0–9 marks_
Scan the QR code for extra practice.
Then move on to the next practice section or
try Test 23 in the Ten-Minute Tests book.

☐ _10–11 marks_
Well done!
Move on to the next practice section or try
Test 23 in the Ten-Minute Tests book.

8 Square and cube numbers

In the 11+ test you could be asked to identify square and cube numbers. You may also need to use them in calculations.

Before you begin

Square numbers

Square numbers can be found by picturing a square. For example, to work out 3^2, think about a square with sides of length 3, and find its area.

123 A square number is a number multiplied by itself. For example $3^2 = 3 \times 3 = 9$ The small 2 after the number means 'squared'.

 The first square number is 1 (area $= 1 \times 1$, which can also be written as 1^2)

 The second square number is 4 (area $= 2 \times 2$ or 2^2)

 The third square number is 9 (area $= 3 \times 3$ or 3^2)

 The fourth square number is 16 (area $= 4 \times 4$ or 4^2)

Cube numbers

Cube numbers can be found by picturing a cube. For example, to work out 2^3, think about a cube with length, width and depth of 2

123 To cube a number, multiply it by itself twice. For example, $2^3 = 2 \times 2 \times 2 = 8$ The small 3 after the number means 'cubed'.

 The first cube number is 1 (volume $= 1 \times 1 \times 1$ or 1^3)

 The second cube number is 8 (volume $= 2 \times 2 \times 2$ or 2^3)

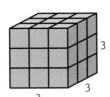 The third cube number is 27 (volume $= 3 \times 3 \times 3$ or 3^3)

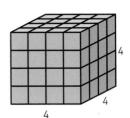 The fourth cube number is 64 (volume $= 4 \times 4 \times 4$ or 4^3)

Worked examples

1 Write down the ninth square number.
$9 \times 9 = 9^2 = 81$

Use the nine times table.

2 Work out 5^3
$5 \times 5 \times 5$
$= 25 \times 5$
$= 125$

Multiply two 5s together first and then multiply by 5 again.

3 Circle the square number.
30   32   (36)   39   40

$6 \times 6 = 36$

4 Work out 4×3^2
4×3^2
$= 4 \times 9$
$= 36$

Follow the correct order of operations: work out the indices before the multiplication.

1 Circle the value that is not a square number.

100   121   225   200   144

> $100 = 10 \times 10 = 10^2$ so 100 is a square number. $121 = 11 \times 11 = 11^2$ so 121 is a square number.

2 Circle the cube number.

3   6   9   18   27

> 1 is the first cube number (1^3) and 8 is the second cube number (2^3) so 3 and 6 cannot be cube numbers. Next work out the third cube number.

3 Write down the smallest square number.

_____

> To find the first square number work out 1^2

4 Circle the numbers which belong in the shaded section of the Venn diagram.

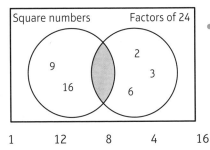

1   12   8   4   16

> A factor is a number that divides exactly into another number.

5 Work out 5×7^2

_____

> Follow the correct order of operations: work out the indices before the multiplication.

6 What is the product of the second square number and the second cube number?

_____

> **123** To find the product, multiply the two numbers together.

7 Matthew is thinking of a number and he squares it to get 225

What number is Matthew thinking of?

_____

> Find the number that you multiply by itself to get 225
> This operation is known as finding the **square root**.

Investigate some sums using only odd numbers. For example:

1

$1 + 3 =$

$1 + 3 + 5 =$

$1 + 3 + 5 + 7 =$

What do you notice?

Have a go

1 Circle the value that is not a square number.

121   144   169   178   196

> Use partitioning to help you multiply larger numbers.

1 mark

2 Work out

a 7^3 **b** 12^2 **c** 14^2 **d** 9^3

_____   _____   _____   _____

4 marks

3 Work out the total of 13^2 and 6^3

_____

1 mark

4 Tick the true statements.

☐ All square numbers are even numbers.

☐ The smallest square number is 1

☐ All square numbers have an odd number of factors.

☐ 100 is a cube number.

> There are 2 marks because there are two statements which are true.

> Numbers that aren't square have an even number of factors.

2 marks

5 Work out $3 + 2 \times 5^2$

_____

1 mark

6 Draw lines to match each calculation with its correct answer.

2^3	
8^3	
7^2	
13^2	

49	
169	
512	
8	

4 marks

7 Complete the table using numbers less than 100

	Square numbers	Cube numbers
< 20	1, 4, 9, 16	1, 8
Even numbers < 100	4, 16, 36, 64	_____

2 marks

Time to reflect

Mark your *Have a go* section out of 15. How are you doing so far?

Check your answers in the back of the book and see how you are doing.

☐ **Had a go**
0–7 marks
Have another look at the *Worked examples* on page 38. Then try these questions again.

☐ **Nearly there**
8–14 marks
Look at your incorrect answers. Make sure you understand how to get the correct answer.

☐ **Nailed it!**
15 marks
Congratulations! Now see whether you can get full marks on the *Timed practice*.

When you are ready, try the *Timed practice* on the next page.

Timed practice

10

1 Circle the value that is not a cube number.

27   64   1000   81   125

1 mark

2 Choose one number from the list to fit each description and write it on the answer line.

1   2   4   10   18   25   70

a An even square number. _____

b An odd cube number. _____

2 marks

3 Where does 100 belong in this table? Write a letter from the table.

	Square numbers	Cube numbers
Factors of 20	A	C
Multiples of 4	B	D

_____

1 mark

4 List all numbers that belong in the shaded section of the Venn diagram.

Cube numbers   Factors of 64

27   2

_____

3 marks

5 The three numbers 64, 121 and 196 are alike in some ways.

Circle the true statements.

A They are all multiples of 4   **B** They are all factors of 8

C They are all even numbers.   **D** They are all cube numbers.

E They are all square numbers.

1 mark

6 A square has an area of 144 cm². What is the length of the sides of the square?

_____ cm

1 mark

7 A cube has a volume of 1000 cm³. What is the length of the edges of the cube?

_____ cm

1 mark

Time to reflect

Mark your *Timed practice* section out of 10. How did you do?

Check your answers in the back of the book and write your score in the progress chart.

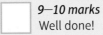 *0–8 marks*
Scan the QR code for extra practice.
Then move on to the next practice section or try Test 24 in the Ten-Minute Tests book.

9–10 marks
Well done!
Move on to the next practice section or try Test 24 in the Ten-Minute Tests book.

9 Triangles and quadrilaterals

In the 11+ test you may be asked to identify different triangles and quadrilaterals so you need to know their properties.

Before you begin

Triangles

A triangle has 3 straight sides. There are three different types of triangles. Each type has different properties.

Equilateral	Isosceles	Scalene
• 3 equal sides	• 2 equal sides	• No equal sides
• 3 equal angles	• 2 equal angles	• No equal angles

123   **Angles** in a shape that are marked with matching **arcs** are equal in size. **Dashes** on the sides of a shape mean that those **sides** are equal in length.

Quadrilaterals

A quadrilateral has 4 straight sides. There are different types of quadrilaterals, including **square**, **rectangle**, **parallelogram**, **rhombus**, **kite** and **trapezium**.

Name	Shape	Sides	Angles
Square		4 equal sides; 2 pairs of opposite sides are parallel	4 right angles
Rectangle		2 pairs of opposite sides are equal and parallel	4 right angles
Parallelogram		2 pairs of opposite sides are equal and parallel	2 pairs of opposite equal angles
Rhombus		4 equal sides; 2 pairs of opposite sides are parallel	2 pairs of opposite equal angles
Kite		2 pairs of adjacent sides are equal	1 pair of opposite equal angles
Trapezium		1 pair of opposite sides is parallel	Angles may all be different (but base angles are equal in regular trapeziums)

123   Single dashes and double dashes on a shape show pairs of lines that are the **same length**. For example, opposite sides in a parallelogram are the same length.

Worked examples

1 Which of these shapes is not a trapezium? Circle the correct letter. •—— A trapezium has one pair of parallel sides.

A   Ⓑ   C   D

2 A triangle has sides with lengths 5 cm, 5 cm and 7 cm. What type of triangle is it? •—— Two of the sides are equal and one is not.

Isosceles

Guided questions

1 For each triangle, write down if it is equilateral, isosceles or scalene.

> The angles in the triangles that have the same number of single or double arcs are equal.

a _____ b _____ c _____

2 Which of the shapes is **not** a quadrilateral? Circle the correct option.

> A quadrilateral has four straight sides.

A   **B**   **C**   **D**

3 Choose one shape from the list below that matches each description.

> A square, rectangle, parallelogram, rhombus and trapezium all have at least one pair of opposite parallel sides.

square   rectangle   parallelogram   rhombus   kite   trapezium

a A quadrilateral that has no parallel sides

_____

b A quadrilateral that has four right angles

> There are two quadrilaterals that have four right angles. Choose one.

_____

c A quadrilateral that has four sides that all measure 5 cm

> There are two quadrilaterals that have four equal sides. Choose one.

_____

d A quadrilateral that has only one pair of parallel sides

> The only quadrilaterals that do not have two pairs of parallel sides are a kite and a trapezium.

_____

4 List three properties of a rhombus.

> The three properties should relate to side length, parallel sides and angles.

_____

_____

_____

Have a go

1 Measure and label the side lengths of each triangle.
For each triangle, write down if it is equilateral, isosceles or scalene.

a

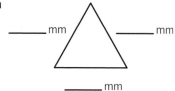

_____ mm   _____ mm

_____ mm

b

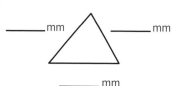

_____ mm   _____ mm

_____ mm

a = _____

b = _____

2 marks

2 Name each shape.

   ◇

A   **B**   **C**   **D**

4 marks

_____   _____   _____   _____

3 Name a quadrilateral that belongs in the shaded part of the Venn diagram.

> The shaded section should not include shapes with opposite parallel sides.

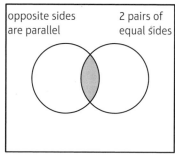

opposite sides are parallel   2 pairs of equal sides

_____

1 mark

4 Part of a parallelogram is drawn using the coordinates (1, 1), (5, 1) and (3, 5).
Write down the missing coordinate.

> You can sketch shapes or grids to helps you.

_____

1 mark

5 The radius of the circle is 4.5 cm.
What is the length of one side of the square?

> Look at practice section 6 for information about radius and diameter.

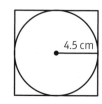

4.5 cm

_____

1 mark

Time to reflect

Mark your *Have a go* section out of 9. How are you doing so far?

Check your answers in the back of the book and see how you are doing.

☐ **Had a go**
0–3 marks
Have another look at the *Worked examples* on page 42. Then try these questions again.

☐ **Nearly there**
4–8 marks
Look at your incorrect answers. Make sure you understand how to get the correct answer.

☐ **Nailed it!**
9 marks
Congratulations! Now see whether you can get full marks on the *Timed practice*.

When you are ready, try the *Timed practice* on the next page.

Timed practice **10**

1 For each triangle, write down whether it is equilateral, isosceles or scalene.

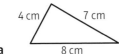

a _____

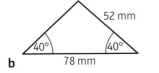

b _____

c A triangle with side lengths: 4.5 cm, 4.5 cm, 4.5 cm _____

d A triangle with side lengths: 53 mm, 32 mm, 53 mm _____

4 marks

2 This a picture of a tangram puzzle. Name the two quadrilaterals in the puzzle.

 _____

abc A tangram is a square that has been split up into seven pieces. The aim is to put the pieces back together in the correct way. Look at page 31 for more information about tangrams.

2 marks

3 Aisha draws a quadrilateral with sides 25 mm, 35 mm, 25 mm and 35 mm. Its opposite sides are parallel.

Name a quadrilateral that Aisha could have drawn.

_____

1 mark

4 List three properties of a parallelogram.

_____
_____
_____

3 marks

5 Two identical rectangles are drawn on a grid.

Write down the coordinates of *P*.

_____

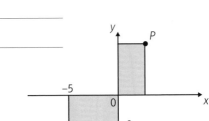

1 mark

Time to reflect

Mark your *Timed practice* section out of 11. How did you do?
Check your answers in the back of the book and write your score in the progress chart.

☐ *0–9 marks*
Scan the QR code for extra practice.
Then move on to the next practice section or try Test 25 in the Ten-Minute Tests book.

☐ *10–11 marks*
Well done!
Move on to the next practice section or try Test 25 in the Ten-Minute Tests book.

10 Polygons and 3D shapes

In the 11+ test you may be asked to identify regular and irregular polygons and 3D shapes and know some of their properties.

Before you begin

Polygons

A **polygon** is a shape with straight sides. The table shows the names of some polygons and how many sides they have.

Shape name	Number of sides
Triangle	3
Quadrilateral	4
Pentagon	5
Hexagon	6
Heptagon	7
Octagon	8

3D shapes

3D shapes are **three-dimensional** shapes. **Faces**, **edges** and **vertices** are parts of 3D shapes. A face, edge and vertex are each labelled on this diagram of a cuboid.

The 3D shapes you need to know are:

- Cube
- Cuboid
- Prisms
- Triangle-based pyramid
- Square-based pyramid

Prisms have the same shape if you cut them anywhere along their length parallel to its end faces. The shape of each end face is called the **cross-section**.

Here are three examples of prisms:

Cuboid   Triangular prism   Hexagonal prism

A **regular polygon** is a shape in which all the sides are equal and all the angles are equal.

An **irregular polygon** is a shape in which the sides and the angles are not all equal.

abc You need to know the correct terminology to talk about 3D shapes.

- Face: a flat surface on a 3D shape
- Edges: a line where two faces meet
- Vertex: a point where three or more edges meet
- Vertices: the plural of vertex

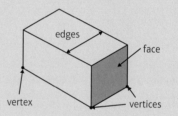

123 A **triangle-based pyramid** has a triangle at its base and then a triangle from each side of the base that meet at a vertex.

A **square-based pyramid** has a square at its base and then a triangle from each side of the base that meet at a vertex.

Worked example

1 Which of these shapes is a regular polygon? Circle the correct option.

A   B   C   (D)   E

Shape **D** has equal sides and equal angles so is 'regular'.

Guided questions

1 Circle the hexagons. ———————————————————— Hexagons have 6 sides.

  A   B   C   D   E

2 Circle the prisms. ———— Prisms have the same shape throughout the solid, known as the cross-section.

  A   B   C   D   E

3 This is a square-based pyramid.

Write down its number of:

Remember to include the base when you are counting the number of faces.

a faces   _____

b edges   _____   Edges are where two faces meet.

c vertices _____   Vertices are corners where 3 or more edges meet.

4 Which of these shapes has 6 faces, 12 edges and 8 vertices?

  A   B   C   D

_____

Beyond the exam

Go on a shape hunt around your home. Look for as many different polygons and 3D shapes as you can and try to name them.

Have a go

1 How many sides does an octagon have?

1 mark

_____

2 A pentagon has five equal sides of 4 cm each and five equal angles of 108° each. Is it a regular or irregular pentagon?

1 mark

_____

3 Choose the correct word that matches each definition.

> 'Vertices' is the plural of vertex.

face   edge   vertex   vertices

a _____ : a point where edges meet.

3 marks

b _____ : a 2D surface on a 3D shape.

> A pyramid has a triangle from each side of the base that meet at a vertex. Prisms have the same shape throughout the solid, known as the cross-section.

c _____ : where two faces meet.

4 Use these shape names to label each diagram.

Cuboid   Triangle-based pyramid   Square-based pyramid

3 marks

a _____   **b** _____   **c** _____

5 Complete the table.

Shape	Number of faces	Number of edges	Number of vertices
Triangle-based pyramid			
Triangular prism			
Pentagonal prism			

9 marks

Time to reflect

Mark your *Have a go* section out of 17. How are you doing so far?

Check your answers in the back of the book and see how you are doing.

	Had a go		Nearly there		Nailed it!
☐	0–8 marks	☐	9–16 marks	☐	17 marks

Had a go
0–8 marks

Have another look at the *Worked examples* on page 46. Then try these questions again.

Nearly there
9–16 marks

Look at your incorrect answers. Make sure you understand how to get the correct answer.

Nailed it!
17 marks

Congratulations! Now see whether you can get full marks on the *Timed practice*.

When you are ready, try the *Timed practice* on the next page.

Timed practice

⏱ **10**

⊘ **1** Name each of these polygons.

a

b

c

d

[4 marks]

⊘ **2** A shape has 5 sides. What is the name of the shape?

[1 mark]

⊘ **3** State whether each shape is a regular or an irregular polygon.

a

b

c
110°
75°   75°
140°   140°

[3 marks]

⊘ **4** This solid has been made by sticking two 3D shapes together. Name the two shapes that were used.

1.5 m
1.5 m

[2 marks]

⊘ **5** This is a hexagonal prism. Write down the number of:

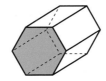

a faces _____

b edges _____

c vertices _____

[3 marks]

Time to reflect

Mark your _Timed practice_ section out of 13. How did you do?
Check your answers in the back of the book and write your score in the progress chart.

☐ _0–11 marks_
Scan the QR code for extra practice.
Then move on to the next practice section or
try Test 26 in the Ten-Minute Tests book.

☐ _12–13 marks_
Well done!
Move on to the next practice section or try
Test 26 in the Ten-Minute Tests book.

11 Angles

In the 11+ test you may be asked to name, estimate and compare angles.

Before you begin

Types of angles

There are three types of angles:

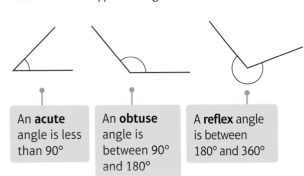

An **acute** angle is less than 90°

An **obtuse** angle is between 90° and 180°

A **reflex** angle is between 180° and 360°

There are some special angles that you need to be able to recognise:

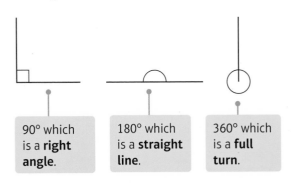

90° which is a **right angle**.

180° which is a **straight line**.

360° which is a **full turn**.

123 **Angles** are measured in **degrees** and the degree symbol is °

Estimating angles

When estimating an angle:

1 First decide which type of angle it is. This will help you to make an estimation within the correct range. For example, if you identify the angle as acute, you know your estimate should be less than 90°

2 Then decide how close the angle is to the lowest or highest possible value. For example, in the case of an acute angle, think about whether it is closer to 0° or 90°. Use this to narrow down your estimate.

Measuring angles

To measure an angle use a protractor. Place your protractor over the angle, like in the image below, and read off the measurement. Remember to start at 0. It's unlikely that you will have to use a protractor to measure angles in the 11+ test, but this practice will improve your ability to estimate the size of angles.

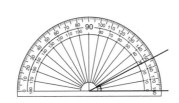

To measure a reflex angle you can measure the other side of the angle and then subtract this from 360°

Worked examples

1 Name each angle as acute, obtuse or reflex.

a

b

c

Obtuse

Reflex

Acute

a The angle is between 90° and 180°

b The angle is between 180° and 360°

c The angle is less than 90°

2 **a** Estimate the size of the angle shown.

____30____ °

The angle is acute so it must be less than 90°. It looks to be about one third of a right angle so the estimate is 30°

b Measure the angle shown to check your answer.

____27____ °

Use a protractor.

Guided questions

1 Identify each angle as acute, obtuse or reflex.

a ⎯ The angle is less than 90°

b

_____ _____

c The angle is between 180° and 360°

d

_____ _____

e The angle is between 90° and 180°

f

_____ _____

2 a Estimate the size of the angle. ⎯ The angle is acute so is less than 90°
It is closer to 0° than 90°

_____ °

b Measure the angle to check your answer. ⎯ Use a protractor: remember to start measuring from 0

_____ °

3 a Estimate the size of the angle. ⎯ The angle is obtuse so is between 90° and 180°
It is about half way between 90° and 180°

_____ °

b Measure the angle to check your answer.

_____ °

Beyond the exam

Play an angle guessing game with a friend. Draw an angle using a ruler and pencil and both guess the angle in secret. The player with the closest guess wins.

Have a go

1 Circle the obtuse angles.

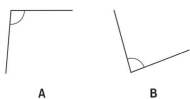   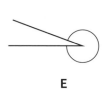

A   B   C   D   E

2 marks

2 Estimate the size of each angle.

a    b   c   d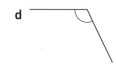

_____ °   _____ °   _____ °   _____ °

4 marks

3 Measure each of the angles in question 2 to check your estimates.

a _____ °

b _____ °

c _____ °

d _____ °

4 marks

4 a Estimate size of the obtuse angle in the triangle.

_____ °

b Measure the obtuse angle to check your estimate.

_____ °

2 marks

Time to reflect

Mark your *Have a go* section out of 12. How are you doing so far?

Check your answers in the back of the book and see how you are doing.

	Had a go 0–5 marks		**Nearly there** 6–11 marks		**Nailed it!** 12 marks

Had a go
0–5 marks
Have another look at the *Worked examples* on page 50. Then try these questions again.

Nearly there
6–11 marks
Look at your incorrect answers. Make sure you understand how to get the correct answer.

Nailed it!
12 marks
Congratulations! Now see whether you can get full marks on the *Timed practice*.

When you are ready, try the *Timed practice* on the next page.

Timed practice

⏱ **10**

🕐 **1** Circle the angle that is not a reflex angle.

A   B   C   D

🕐 **2** Circle the correct measurement for the angle.

55°   125°

🕐 **3 a** Estimate the size of the angle.

_____ °

b Measure the angle to check your estimate.

_____ °

🕐 **4 a** Name the type of angle labelled *a* in the triangle.

_____

b Estimate the size of angle *a*.

_____ °

a

c Measure angle *a* to check your estimate.

_____ °

Time to reflect

Mark your *Timed practice* section out of 7. How did you do?
Check your answers in the back of the book and write your score in the progress chart.

☐ *0–5 marks*
    Scan the QR code for extra practice.
Then move on to the next practice section or
try Test 27 in the Ten-Minute Tests book.

☐ *6–7 marks*
    Well done!
Move on to the next practice section or try
Test 27 in the Ten-Minute Tests book.

12 Angle properties

In the 11+ test you may be asked to work out missing angles using knowledge of right angles, angles on a straight line, angles in a full turn, and the angle properties of triangles and quadrilaterals.

Before you begin

Angles

There are **90°** in a **right angle**.

$a = 50°$ because $90 - 40 = 50$

There are **180°** on a **straight line**.

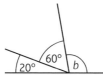

$b = 100°$ because
$180 - 20 - 60 = 100$

When two lines cross to form **vertically opposite angles**, the angles are equal.

$d = 60°$ because the angles 60° and d are vertically opposite each other.

There are **360°** in a **full turn**.

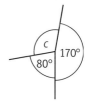

$c = 110°$ because
$360 - 80 - 170 = 110$

Triangles and quadrilaterals

The internal angles in a **triangle** total **180°**

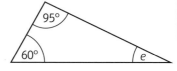

$e = 25°$ because
$95° + 60° + 25° = 180°$

The internal angles in a **quadrilateral** total **360°**

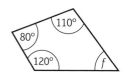

$f = 50°$ because
$120° + 80° + 110° + 50° = 360°$

Worked example

1 Work out the angles marked with a letter in each diagram.

a

$90 - 65 = 25$
$a = \underline{\qquad 25 \qquad}°$

A right angle is 90°

b

$90 + 142 + 67 = 299$
$360 - 299 = 61$
$b = \underline{\qquad 61 \qquad}°$

A full turn is 360°

Remember that the little square means that angle is a right angle.

c

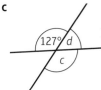

$c = \underline{\qquad 127 \qquad}$

Vertically opposite angles are equal.

$180 - 127 = 53$
$d = \underline{\qquad 53 \qquad}°$

The angles 127° and d make a straight line which totals 180°

Beyond the exam

Use a ruler and pencil to draw a large triangle, mark the angles on it and cut it out. Tear off each of the angles. Place them together side by side. What do you notice? Does this work for any triangle? Do the same for a quadrilateral.

Guided questions

1 Work out each angle labelled with a letter.

$a =$ _____ °

● A right angle is 90°

$b =$ _____ °

● There are 180° on a straight line.

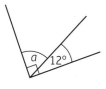

$c =$ _____ °

● There are 360° in a full turn.

2 Work out the missing angle.

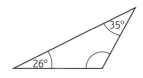

_____ °

● The angles in a triangle total 180°

3 Work out the angles marked with a letter.

a

b

c

$x =$ _____ °

$y =$ _____ °

$z =$ _____ °

The angles in a triangle total 180°
Use the fact that this is an equilateral triangle to help you.

This is a right-angled triangle.

The angles in a quadrilateral total 360°

4 Work out the size of angle P.

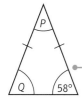

The angles in a triangle total 180°
This is an isosceles triangle, so angle Q is also 58°

$P =$ _____ °

5 Work out the size of angle q.

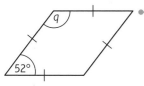

This shape is a rhombus so opposite angles are equal and adjacent angles total 180°

123 **Adjacent** means 'next to'.

$q =$ _____ °

Have a go

1 a Work out the size of angle *x*.

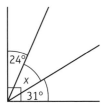

x = _____ °

b Work out the size of angles *x* and *y*.

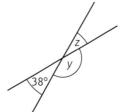

y = _____ °

x = _____ °

3 marks

2 Work out the size of angle *a*.

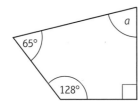

a = _____ °

1 mark

3 Work out the value of *x*.

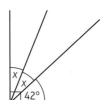

x = _____ °

The angles labelled *x* are equal.

1 mark

4 A regular hexagon is made of 6 equilateral triangles. What is the size of the shaded angle shown?

_____ °

1 mark

5 The diagram shows a parallelogram. What is the size of angle *w*?

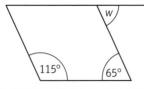

w = _____ °

1 mark

Time to reflect

Mark your *Have a go* section out of 7. How are you doing so far?

Check your answers in the back of the book and see how you are doing.

☐ **Had a go**
0–2 marks
Have another look at the *Worked examples* on page 54. Then try these questions again.

☐ **Nearly there**
3–6 marks
Look at your incorrect answers. Make sure you understand how to get the correct answer.

☐ **Nailed it!**
7 marks
Congratulations! Now see whether you can get full marks on the *Timed practice*.

When you are ready, try the *Timed practice* on the next page.

Timed practice ⏱ ⑩

🕐 **1** Work out the size of each angle labelled with a letter.

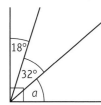

18°
32°
a

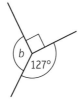

b
127°

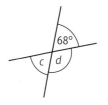

68°
c d

a = _____ °   b = _____ °   c = _____ °

d = _____ °

🕐 **2** Work out the size of angles w and x.

w

33°   w = _____ °

x
45°   x = _____ °

🕐 **3** What is the total of angles w, x, y and z? Circle the correct answer.

90°   180°   270°   300°   360°

w
x
z   y

🕐 **4** Work out the value of y.

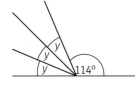

y
y
y   114°   y = _____ °

🕐 **5** Angle a is 52° and angle b is 76°

   a What is the size of angle c? _____ °

   b What is the size of angle d? _____ °

b
c d
a

🕐 **6** The diagram shows a kite. Work out the size of angle k.

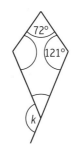

72°
121°

k

k = _____ °

Time to reflect

Mark your *Timed practice* section out of 11. How did you do?
Check your answers in the back of the book and write your score in the progress chart.

☐ *0–9 marks*
Scan the QR code for extra practice.
Then move on to the next practice section or
try Test 28 in the Ten-Minute Tests book.

☐ *10–11 marks*
Well done!
Move on to the next practice section or try
Test 28 in the Ten-Minute Tests book.

Checkpoint 2

In this checkpoint you will practise skills from the **Shapes and their properties** topic. There are 12 questions for you to answer.

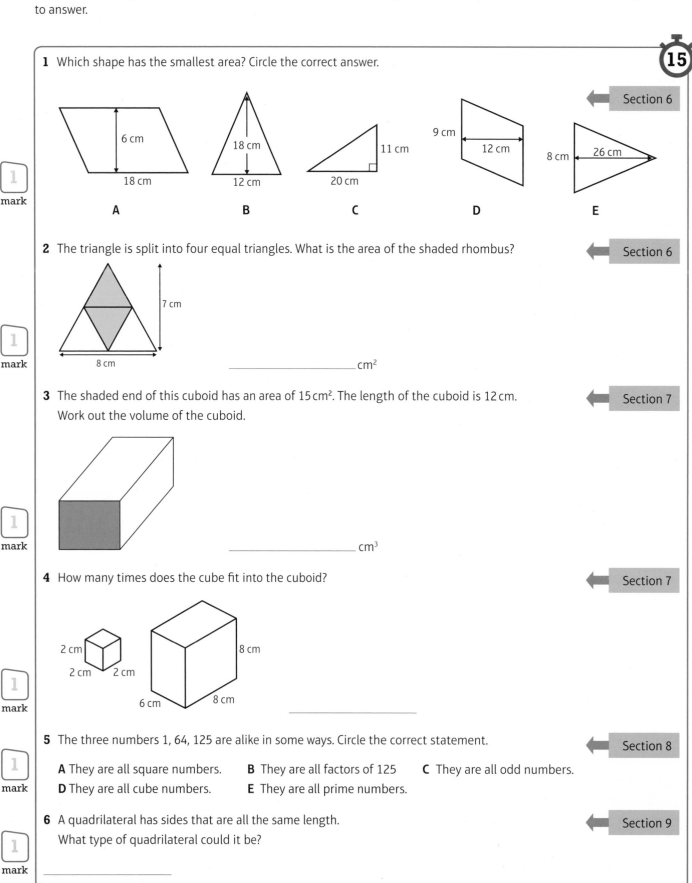

1 Which shape has the smallest area? Circle the correct answer.

15

← Section 6

6 cm
18 cm

A

18 cm
12 cm

B

11 cm
20 cm

C

9 cm
12 cm

D

8 cm
26 cm

E

1 mark

2 The triangle is split into four equal triangles. What is the area of the shaded rhombus?

← Section 6

7 cm
8 cm

_____ cm²

1 mark

3 The shaded end of this cuboid has an area of 15 cm². The length of the cuboid is 12 cm. Work out the volume of the cuboid.

← Section 7

_____ cm³

1 mark

4 How many times does the cube fit into the cuboid?

← Section 7

2 cm
2 cm   2 cm

8 cm
6 cm   8 cm

_____

1 mark

5 The three numbers 1, 64, 125 are alike in some ways. Circle the correct statement.

← Section 8

A They are all square numbers.   **B** They are all factors of 125   **C** They are all odd numbers.
D They are all cube numbers.   **E** They are all prime numbers.

1 mark

6 A quadrilateral has sides that are all the same length.
What type of quadrilateral could it be?

← Section 9

_____

1 mark

7 Which of these shapes are **not** parallelograms? Circle the **two** correct options.

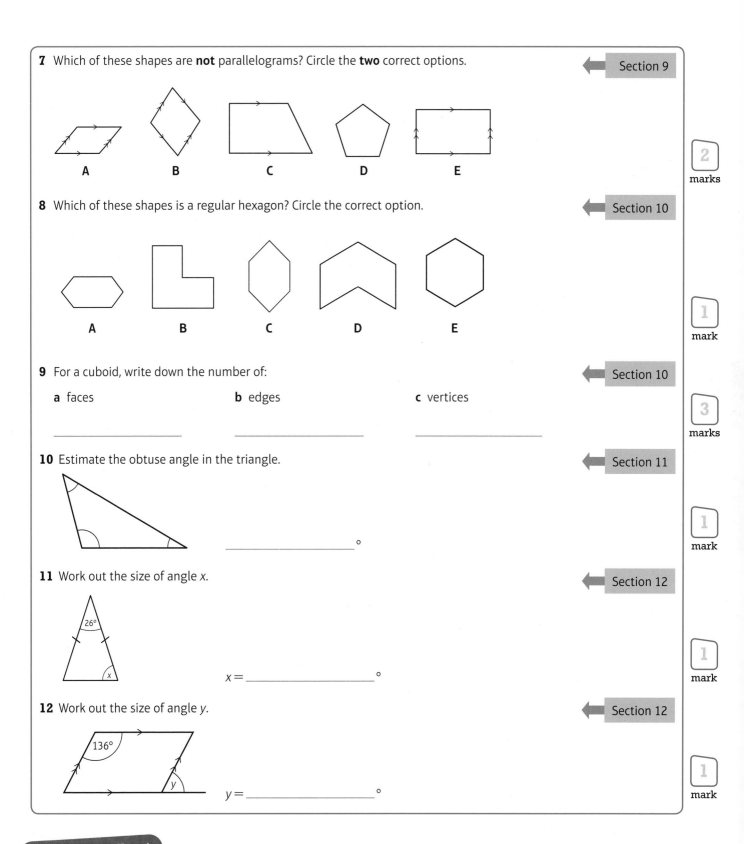

A   B   C   D   E

Section 9

2 marks

8 Which of these shapes is a regular hexagon? Circle the correct option.

A   B   C   D   E

Section 10

1 mark

9 For a cuboid, write down the number of:

a faces   b edges   c vertices

_____   _____   _____

Section 10

3 marks

10 Estimate the obtuse angle in the triangle.

_____ °

Section 11

1 mark

11 Work out the size of angle x.

26°

x

x = _____ °

Section 12

1 mark

12 Work out the size of angle y.

136°

y

y = _____ °

Section 12

1 mark

13 Equations and formulae

In the 11+ test you may be asked to write expressions, use formulae to work out values and solve problems using equations.

Before you begin

Writing expressions

You can write an **expression** by using letters as replacements for numbers. For example, a letter like x can be used to represent a number. So, 5 more than x can be written as $x + 5$

Solving equations

Solving an **equation** means working out the value of the unknown number which is represented by a letter. You can use **bar models** to help you visualise equations. For example, to solve $a + 9 = 15$:

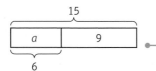

The whole bar represents 15. Part of the bar is a and the other part is 9. To work out the value of a you need to subtract 9 from 15. So, $a = 6$

Using formulae

A **formula** is a rule for working out different values using words or letters. You can use **formulae** (the plural of 'formula') to work out an unknown value when you are given the other values.

9 cm

Here you are given one value: the length of one side = 9 cm. If you wanted to work out the perimeter you could use the formula $P = 4L$ (where P means perimeter and L means length).

This is because the shape is a square so you know that there are four sides with equal lengths.

Once you have a formula, substitute in the numbers you know.

So $P = 4 \times 9 = 36$. Therefore, the perimeter of the square is 36 cm.

Worked examples

1 Ewan is c years old. His brother Zach is 3 years older than him. How old is Zach? Give your answer in terms of c.

$c + 3$

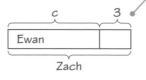

You could draw a bar model to help you picture the information given in the question. 'In terms of c' means that your answer needs to involve the letter c.

2 Solve $x - 7 = 14$ by working out the value of x.

$x = 21$

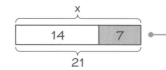

The whole bar represents x; part of the bar is 14 and the other part is 7
To work out the value of x, add 14 and 7

3 A phone company uses the formula $B = 1000 + 10m + 5t$ to work out a monthly bill.

B = bill (in pence)

m = the number of minutes used

t = the number of text messages sent

Work out the monthly bill for 124 minutes and 47 text messages. Give your answer in pounds.

$B = 1000 + (10 \times 124) + (5 \times 47)$

$= 1000 + 1240 + 235$

$= 2475$

£ ___24.75___

The question asks for the answer in pounds so divide by 100 to convert your answer at the end.

Guided questions

1 Ava has *s* amount of sweets. She eats 4 of them. How many sweets does
she have left? Give your answer in terms of *s*.

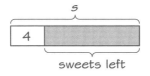

Use the bar model to help you.

_____

2 Solve $2x + 5 = 21$

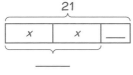

Complete the bar model to help you.
As there are two *x*'s in the equation,
there are two *x*'s on the bar model.

_____

3 Using the formula $2a + 3b = 22$, work out the value of *a* when $b = 4$

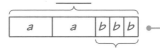

Complete the bar model to help you.

_____

4 The formula for the area of a parallelogram is $A = b \times h$,
where *b* is the base and *h* is the height of the parallelogram.
If $A = 20$ cm² and $b = 4$ cm, what is the value of *h*.

Make sure you know the formula
for the area of a parallelogram from
memory – it might not be provided
in the exam.

$h =$ _____ cm

5 Ryan thinks of a number. He doubles it and then adds 15
The answer is 41. What is Ryan's number?

Put the information in a bar model
to help you.

_____

As the cost of the banana is in pence,
convert £10 to pence.

6 A banana costs *x* pence. James buys 8 bananas.

How much change will he get from £10? Write your answer as an expression in terms of *x*.

£ _____

Have a go

1 Jenny is y years old. Her sister is 6 years younger. Circle the expression for her sister's age.

$y - 6$ $6y$ $y + 6$ $6 - y$ $y \div 6$

> 1 mark

2 Solve $19 - a = 12$

$a = $ _____

> 1 mark

3 $2a + b = 17$

Write a possible whole number value for a and for b.

$a = $ _____

$b = $ _____

> What number can you double and then by adding another number make 17?

> 2 marks

4 There are x people on a bus.

8 people get off at the first stop and y people get off at the second stop.

Write an expression for the number of people on the bus after two stops.

_____

> 1 mark

5 Solve $3x - 8 = 28$

$x = $ _____

> 1 mark

6 $3a + 2b = 13$

List the possible whole number combinations of a and b that satisfy the equation.

_____

> There are 2 marks because there are two different combinations of a and b that work in the equation.

> 2 marks

7 A regular hexagon has sides each with a length of x cm.
Write an expression for the perimeter of the hexagon.

_____

> A regular hexagon has 6 equal sides and its perimeter is the total of its 6 sides.

> 1 mark

8 Finn will be n years old in three years' time. How old was Finn 7 years ago? Give your answer in terms of n.

_____

> 1 mark

Time to reflect

Mark your *Have a go* section out of 10. How are you doing so far?

Check your answers in the back of the book and see how you are doing.

☐ **Had a go**	☐ **Nearly there**	☐ **Nailed it!**
0–4 marks	*5–9 marks*	*10 marks*
Have another look at the *Worked examples* on page 60. Then try these questions again.	Look at your incorrect answers. Make sure you understand how to get the correct answer.	Congratulations! Now see whether you can get full marks on the *Timed practice*.

When you are ready, try the *Timed practice* on the next page.

Timed practice

1 A number is t less than 25. Write an expression for the number in terms of t.

_____

1 mark

2 Solve $x + 45 = 63$

$x =$ _____

1 mark

3 $P = 5x - 2y$

Work out the value of P when $x = 7$ and $y = 4$

$P =$ _____

1 mark

4 $5x - 3y = 28$

Write a possible whole number value for x and a whole number value for y.

$x =$ _____ $y =$ _____

1 mark

5 Using the formula $a + 2b = 15$, work out the value of a when $b = 4$

$a =$ _____

1 mark

6 A regular octagon has sides of length L cm. Write a formula for the perimeter, P, of the octagon.

_____

1 mark

7 Anita thinks of a number. She subtracts 7 and then doubles the result. Her answer was 50. What was Anita's original number?

_____

1 mark

8 An angle of $a°$ is forms part of a straight line. Write an expression, in terms of a, for the remaining angle on the straight line.

_____

1 mark

9 A swimming pool is 50 metres long, and half as wide. The volume of the pool is 3750 m^3.

Find the depth of the pool.

_____

1 mark

Time to reflect

Mark your *Timed practice* section out of 9. How did you do?
Check your answers in the back of the book and write your score in the progress chart.

☐ *0–7 marks*
Scan the QR code for extra practice.
Then, move on to the next practice section or try Test 29 in the Ten-Minute Tests book.

☐ *8–9 marks*
Well done!
Move on to the next practice section or try Test 29 in the Ten-Minute Tests book.

14 Linear sequences

In the 11+ test you may be asked to work out the rule for a sequence or write missing numbers in a sequence. You may also be asked to identify or use the *n*th term of a sequence.

Before you begin

Linear sequences

A **linear sequence** is a sequence that is ascends (goes up) or descends (goes down) by the same amount with each jump. For example, the sequence '3, 8, 13, 18, 23…' is ascending by 5 with each jump.

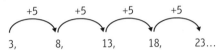

+5   +5   +5   +5

3,   8,   13,   18,   23…

To write down a missing term in a sequence, you need to know what the rule is. The rule of the sequence '3, 8, 13, 18, 23…' is 'add 5' so to find the next term in the sequence, work out $23 + 5$. The next term is 28

nth term

The rule for a sequence can be given using an expression that includes an **nth term.** The *n*th term corresponds to the position of the number in the sequence. For example, if you are looking for the third number in the sequence, *n* becomes 3. If the *n*th term of a sequence is given by the expression $7n + 3$, the sequence is as follows: 10, 17, 24, 31, 38… The workings for each term up to the 5th term are shown here in a table.

Position	Value of *n*	Calculation	Term
1st	1	$7 \times 1 + 3 = 10$	10
2nd	2	$7 \times 2 + 3 = 17$	17
3rd	3	$7 \times 3 + 3 = 24$	24
4th	4	$7 \times 4 + 3 = 31$	31
5th	5	$7 \times 5 + 3 = 38$	38

By using the *n*th term you can jump ahead to a specific number in the sequence, without having to work out all the other numbers before it in the sequence. For example, to work out the 10th term of this sequence:

Position	Value of *n*	Calculation	Term
10th	10	$7 \times 10 + 3 = 73$	73

Worked examples

1 What is the next number in this sequence? •————

2,   5,   8,   11   …

+3   +3   +3   +3

_____ 14 _____

> The rule for this ascending sequence is 'add 3'

> Draw arrows for the jumps to help you to see the pattern in the sequence.

2 Work out the 20th term in the sequence with *n*th term $3n - 5$ •————

$3 \times 20 - 5 = 60 - 5 = 55$

_____ 55 _____

> Substitute $n = 20$ into the expression $3n - 5$

Beyond the exam

Work out: $1 \times 1, 11 \times 11, 111 \times 111, 1111 \times 1111$

Can you predict what will be next in the pattern? When will the pattern stop? Can you explain why?

Guided questions

1 Work out the rule for this sequence.

7,   13,   19,   25   31   …

+   +   +   +   +

> Work out what you add to 7 to make 13 and then what you add to 13 to make 19, and so on.

_____

2 What is the next number in this sequence?

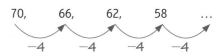

70,   66,   62,   58   …

−4   −4   −4   −4

_____

3 Write down the first five terms of the sequence with nth term $8n - 5$

Position	Value of n	Calculation	Term
1st	1	$8 \times 1 - 5 = 3$	3
2nd	2	$8 \times 2 - 5 = \ldots$	_____
3rd	3	_____	_____
4th	_____	_____	_____
5th	_____	_____	_____

4 Circle the linear sequence.

> A linear sequence ascends or descends by the same amount with each jump.

2, 4, 8, 16, 32…   1, 1, 2, 3, 5…   3, −3, 3, −3, 3…

3, 7, 12, 18, 25…   50, 44, 38, 32, 26…

5 Circle the correct expression for the nth term of the sequence 5, 9, 13, 17, 21…

> Substitute in the different values for n (1, 2, 3…) into each expression to see whether they give the numbers in the sequence.

$5n$ $5n + 9$ $4n + 1$ $4n + 5$ $4n + 9$

$n = 1$: $5n = 5$

$n = 2$: $5n = 10$ so the nth term is not $5n$

6 Is 36 in the sequence with nth term $3n$?

Give a reason for your answer.

> Work out whether n is a whole number when $36 = 3n$.

Have a go

1 Write down the next two terms in the sequence.

2, 13, 24, 35, 46…

> Draw arrows and write down the jump between each term to help you.

_____

2 Write the first five terms of a sequence that has a first term of 90 and a rule of 'subtract 7'.

_____

3 Write down the missing terms in each sequence.

> These sequences ascend or descend by the same amount with each jump.

a 4, 8, _____, 16, 20, _____, 28

b 60, 51, _____, _____, 24, 15

c _____, _____, 57, 63, 69, 75

4 Is 60 part of the sequence 7, 13, 19, 25…?

Give a reason for your answer.

_____

_____

5 Write down the first five terms of the sequence with *n*th term 6*n* + 5

_____

6 Write down the 15th term of the sequence with *n*th term 3*n* + 4

_____

7 Which is the correct expression for the *n*th term of the sequence 1, 3, 5, 7, 9…? Circle the correct answer.

A *n*   **B** *n* + 3   **C** 2*n*   **D** 2*n* + 1   **E** 2*n* − 1

1 mark

1 mark

3 marks

2 marks

1 mark

1 mark

1 mark

Time to reflect

Mark your *Have a go* section out of 10. How are you doing so far?

Check your answers in the back of the book and see how you are doing.

☐ **Had a go**
0—4 marks

Have another look at the *Worked examples* on page 64. Then try these questions again.

☐ **Nearly there**
5—9 marks

Look at your incorrect answers. Make sure you understand how to get the correct answer.

☐ **Nailed it!**
10 marks

Congratulations! Now see whether you can get full marks on the *Timed practice*.

When you are ready, try the *Timed practice* on the next page.

Timed practice

10

1 Write down the next term in the sequence.

24, 31, 38, 45, 52…

_____

1 mark

2 Write the first five terms of a sequence that has a first term of 5 and a rule of 'add 12'.

_____

1 mark

3 Write down the missing terms in each sequence.

a 9, 18, _____, 36, 45, _____

b 51, 48, _____, _____, 39, 36

c _____, _____, 51, 64, 77, 90

3 marks

4 Write down the first five terms of the sequence with nth term $3n - 2$

_____

1 mark

5 a Circle the number from the list that is in the sequence 2, 8, 14, 20, 26…

33   45   55   67   74

b Give a reason for your answer.

_____

2 marks

6 Write down the 25th term of the sequence with nth term $5n - 3$

_____

1 mark

7 Is 45 in the sequence with nth term $2n - 1$?

Give a reason for your answer.

_____

1 mark

Time to reflect

Mark your *Timed practice* section out of 10. How did you do?
Check your answers in the back of the book and write your score in the progress chart.

☐ *0–8 marks*
Scan the QR code for extra practice.
Then, move on to the next practice section or
try Test 30 in the Ten-Minute Tests book.

☐ *9–10 marks*
Well done!
Move on to the next practice section or try
Test 30 in the Ten-Minute Tests book.

15 Tables, charts and graphs

In the 11+ test you may be asked to interpret information in tables and timetables. You could also be asked questions about the data given in bar charts, line graphs and pie charts.

Before you begin

Tables

- A **frequency table** shows how many of each value there are in a data set.
- A **timetable** shows a time schedule. For example, a bus timetable shows the times that buses leave each stop.

Charts and graphs

- A **bar chart** displays data with bars of equal width.
- A **pie chart** displays data in a circle. The circle is divided into slices, called sectors.
- A **line graph** displays values in a data set over time. For example, the changes in temperature during a day.

123 Timetables usually use **24 hour time** which starts at 00.00 (midnight) and goes up to 23.59 (11.59pm). At midnight the time resets to 00.00 again.

Worked examples

1 A class of children was asked about their favourite subjects. The bar chart shows the results. What percentage of the children chose maths?

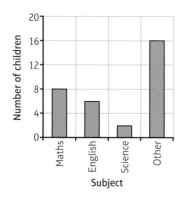

_____25_____ %

1 Work out the total number of children in the class by reading the height of each bar and adding the values: $8 + 6 + 2 + 16 = 32$

2 Look at how many children chose maths: 8

3 Work out the percentage: $\left(\dfrac{8}{32}\right) \times 100 = 25$

You could simplify this fraction to $\dfrac{1}{4}$

2 30 children choose their favourite colour from the options red, orange or blue. The pie chart shows the results.

a What fraction of the children chose blue? Circle the correct fraction.

$\dfrac{1}{8}$ $\dfrac{1}{6}$ $\dfrac{1}{3}$ $\dfrac{1}{2}$ $\dfrac{1}{5}$

Calculate 60° as a fraction of 360°.

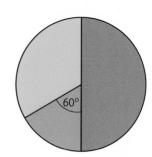

b How many children chose yellow?

$\dfrac{1}{3}$ of $30 = 30 \div 3$

_____10_____

Add the two other angles together and take them away from 360°: $360 - (60 + 180) = 120$

As a fraction of the whole pie chart this can be written as $\dfrac{120}{360}$ which simplifies to $\dfrac{1}{3}$. The pie chart represents 30 children, so for the colour yellow, work out $\dfrac{1}{3}$ of 30

Beyond the exam

Tables, charts and graphs are often used to display data. Try to find any tables, bar charts, line graphs and pie charts in a newspaper or on a website and explain the information being displayed.

Guided questions

1 Here is part of a bus timetable.

Buxton	07.45	09.06	10.53
Bakewell	08.15	09.33	11.19
Darley Dale	08.25	09.42	11.28
Matlock	08.35	09.51	11.37

a A bus leaves Bakewell at 09.33

How long does it take to get to Darley Dale?

_____

b Jamie regularly catches the bus from Buxton to Matlock. •——
Out of the three buses, how long does the shortest bus ride take?

_____

> The 07.45 bus takes from 07.45 to 08.35
> To make this calculation easier, this can be broken down into 07.45 to 08.00 which is 15 minutes, and 08.00 to 08.35 which is 35 minutes. $15 + 35 = 50$ minutes.

2 Some children were asked what their favourite animal is. Complete the table of results.

Animal	**Number of children**
Dog	_____
Cat	_____
Rabbit	_____
Guinea pig	_____
Other	6

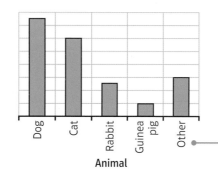

> The table shows that 6 children chose 'Other'. Use this to label the vertical axis on the bar chart to help you complete the table.

3 The pie chart shows how 228 children travel to school.

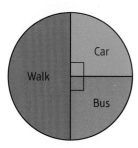

a What percentage of the children walk to school?

_____ %

b How many children travel to school by bus?

_____

> The pie chart shown that half of the children walk to school. Write $\frac{1}{2}$ as a percentage.

> First, work out the angle of the sector for bus, then write this as a fraction of the whole pie chart. Now multiply 228 by this fraction.

Have a go

1 The line graph shows the temperature in a town during a day.

a What time of day was the warmest?

_____

b What time of day was it after the temperature had increased the most?

The temperature increased the most at the steepest part of the graph.

_____

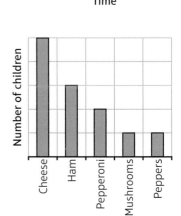

2 marks

2 48 children were asked to name their favourite pizza topping. The bar chart shows the results.

a Work out the number of children who chose cheese.

_____

b Which pizza topping was chosen by 8 children?

There is no scale on the y-axis but you can use the information that there were 48 children asked altogether to work out the answers.

_____

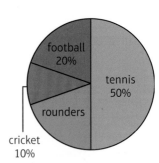

2 marks

3 240 people are asked to choose their favourite sport.

The pie chart shows the results.

a What percentage of people chose rounders?

_____ %

b How many people chose rounders?

Use your answer from part **a**.

_____

2 marks

Time to reflect

Mark your _Have a go_ section out of 6. How are you doing so far?

Check your answers in the back of the book and see how you are doing.

☐ **Had a go**
 0—2 marks

Have another look at the _Worked examples_ on page 68. Then try these questions again.

☐ **Nearly there**
 3—5 marks

Look at your incorrect answers. Make sure you understand how to get the correct answer.

☐ **Nailed it!**
 6 marks

Congratulations! Now see whether you can get full marks on the _Timed practice_.

When you are ready, try the _Timed practice_ on the next page.

Timed practice

 1 Here is part of a train timetable.

London Euston	07.20	07.35	08.00	08.20	08.40
Milton Keynes	07.50	08.06	-	08.50	-
Stoke-on-Trent	08.48	-	09.25	09.48	-
Stockport	09.17	09.37	09.55	10.17	10.37
Manchester	09.25	09.45	10.04	10.28	10.46

a A train leaves Milton Keynes at 08.06

How long does it take to get to Manchester? Give your answer in hours and minutes.

_____

b Sophie lives in London. She wants to arrive at Stockport before 09.45

What times could she catch the train from London Euston?

_____

2
marks

 2 The bar chart shows the different types of items Ayesha recycled during a week.

a Which type of item did Ayesha recycle the most?

_____

b Ayesha recycled 50 items in total.
Work out how many tin items she recycled.

_____

c What percentage of the recycled items were card?

_____ %

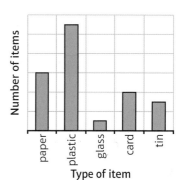

3
marks

 3 168 people are asked to choose their favourite type of book.
The pie chart shows the results.

Work out how many people chose science fiction.

_____

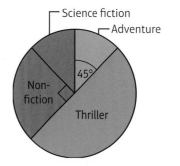

1
mark

Time to reflect

Mark your _Timed practice_ section out of 6. How did you do?

Check your answers in the back of the book and write your score in the progress chart.

☐ _0–4 marks_
Scan the QR code for extra practice.
Then move on to the next practice section or try Test 31 in the Ten-Minute Tests book.

☐ _5–6 marks_
Well done!
Move on to the next practice section or try Test 31 in the Ten-Minute Tests book.

16 Mean average

In the 11+ test you may be asked to work out the mean of a data set or use the mean to work out a missing number in a data set.

Before you begin

Mean

An **average** is a typical value that is used to represent a data set. There are different types of average, one of which is called the **mean**. To work out the mean, find the total of the numbers in the data set and then divide the total by how many numbers there are in the set. For example, to work out the mean of the numbers on the cards:

 4   7   9   9   11

1 First work out the total: $4 + 7 + 9 + 9 + 11 = 40$
2 Then divide by 5 because there are five cards: $40 \div 5 = 8$

So the mean of 4, 7, 9, 9 and 11 is 8
The formula for calculating the mean of a data set is:
Mean = total of the values ÷ number of values

Worked example

1 The table shows the highest temperature in London each day for a week in March.

Day of the week	Temperature in °C
Monday	7
Tuesday	6
Wednesday	9
Thursday	5
Friday	11
Saturday	8
Sunday	10

Work out the mean of these temperatures.

$7 + 6 + 9 + 5 + 11 + 8 + 10 = 56$ ● — First work out the total of the temperatures.

$56 \div 7 = 8$ ● — Then divide your total by 7 because there are 7 temperatures.

_____8_____ °C

2 Here are the number of points scored by a team in five rugby matches: ● — Mean score = total ÷ 5 = 34

13, 41, 23, x and 47

The mean score is 34

Work out the score x.

You can rearrange the formula for calculating the mean to give 'Total = Mean × number of values'. Put the values you know into this equation to calculate the total.

Total = $34 \times 5 = 170$ ●

$13 + 41 + 23 + x + 47 = 170$ ● — Use the total of the five scores (170) to work out score x.

$124 + x = 170$

$x =$ _____46_____

Guided questions

1 Work out the mean of 13, 19, 16, 14 and 13 •————— First work out the total and then divide by 5 as there are 5 numbers.

_____

2 The table shows the heights of some school children.

Work out the mean height.

First work out the total of the heights and then divide by the number of children.

Name	Height in cm
Sameer	133
Elliot	141
Ben	135
Bartosz	144
Ava	138
Emma	131

_____ cm

3 Here are five number cards: •—————

| 21 | 14 | 17 | 13 | |

One card is face down.

The mean of the five numbers is 16

Work out the number on the card that is face down.

Mean = total ÷ number of cards, therefore $16 = total ÷ 5$
Use this to work out the total before you work out the number on the card that is face down. Let the missing number equal x and form an equation.

_____

4 Grace has a times tables test every week. •—————

The average score for her first three tests is 12

After the fourth test her average score is 14

How much did she score in the fourth test?

$12 \times 3 = 36$

$14 \times 4 = 56$

First work out the total for the first three test scores by multiplying the number of tests by the mean. Then work out the total for the four test scores in the same way, and find the difference between the totals to work out the fourth test score.

_____

5 The mean of four numbers in a data set is 13 •—————

The number 18 is added to the data set.

Work out the mean of the five numbers.

First work out the total for the first four numbers, then work out the total for the five numbers and divide it by 5 to find the new mean.

_____

Beyond the exam

Work out the mean average for data from your everyday life. For example:

- What is the mean age of the people living in your home?
- What is the mean number of pets per person between you and your friends?
- What is the mean length of songs on your favourite album?

Have a go

1 Work out the mean of 47, 37, 43, 46, 41 and 44

1 mark

_____

2 The table shows the temperature at midnight in a town for a week in January.

Work out the mean of these temperatures.

> You can use number lines to help you with negative temperatures.

Day of the week	Temperature in °C
Monday	0
Tuesday	−2
Wednesday	1
Thursday	0
Friday	3
Saturday	5
Sunday	7

1 mark

_____ °C

3 Circle the true statement.

A The mean is the middle number.

B The mean is the difference between the largest and smallest number.

C The mean is the most common number.

D The mean is always one of the numbers in the data set.

E Mean = total of the values ÷ number of values

1 mark

4 Josh writes down the number of cars that pass his house every hour for 4 hours. He then calculates the mean number of cars. The number of cars counted in the fourth hour has been crossed out.

16,   7,   2,   ~~5~~

Mean = 12

Work out the missing number of cars.

1 mark

_____

5 Ryan buys a 12-pack of crisps for £3 and a 6-pack of crisps for £2.40

What is the average cost per packet of all the packets of crisps he buys?

> You need to know the total cost and the total number of bags of crisps.

1 mark

_____ p

Time to reflect

Mark your *Have a go* section out of 5. How are you doing so far?

Check your answers in the back of the book and see how you are doing.

☐ **Had a go**
0–2 marks

Have another look at the *Worked examples* on page 72. Then try these questions again.

☐ **Nearly there**
3–4 marks

Look at your incorrect answers. Make sure you understand how to get the correct answer.

☐ **Nailed it!**
5 marks

Congratulations! Now see whether you can get full marks on the *Timed practice*.

When you are ready, try the *Timed practice* on the next page.

Timed practice

1 Harry took part in a project to cycle instead of using his car for 4 weeks. The table shows the distance he cycled each week.

Week	1	2	3	4
Distance in kilometers	53	58	65	72

Work out the mean distance Harry cycled each week.

_____ km

2 The table shows the lowest recorded temperature each month in a city during the first half of a year.

Month	Jan	Feb	Mar	Apr	May	Jun
Temperature in °C	−11	−5	2	4	11	17

Work out the mean temperature.

_____ °C

3 Shey works out that the mean number of aces a tennis player scored in three matches is 14. During the next match the tennis player scored 18 aces. Work out the mean number of aces the player has scored after the fourth match.

_____

4 Alfie recorded the amount of rainfall during a week at school.

Day	Monday	Tuesday	Wednesday	Thursday	Friday
Rainfall in millimeters	24	0	12	5	

He worked out that the mean rainfall each day for the week is 18 mm.

Complete the table.

5 Amelia buys a 6-pack of water for £3.40 and a 4-pack of water for £2.60

What is the average cost of a bottle of water across both packs?

_____ p

Time to reflect

Mark your _Timed practice_ section out of 5. How did you do?
Check your answers in the back of the book and write your score in the progress chart.

☐ _0–3 marks_
Scan the QR code for extra practice.
Then move on to _Checkpoint 3_ or try Test 32
in the Ten-Minute Tests book.

☐ _4–5 marks_
Well done!
Move on to _Checkpoint 3_ and the _Progress test_,
or try Test 32 in the Ten-Minute Tests book.

Checkpoint 3

In this checkpoint you will practise skills from the **Algebra** topic and the **Statistics** topic. There are 15 questions for you to answer.

(15)

1 Use the formula $P = 5x + y$ to list the possible whole number combinations of x and y that satisfy the formula when $P = 16$

1 mark

Section 13

2 Using the formula $3a - 2b = 25$, work out the value of a when $b = 7$

1 mark

Section 13

$a = $ _____

3 A regular pentagon has a length L cm. Write an expression for the perimeter, P, of the pentagon.

1 mark

Section 13

4 Maisie thinks of a number. She multiplies it by 4 and then subtracts 5. Her answer is 31

What is Maisie's number?

1 mark

Section 13

5 An angle of $x°$ is part of a right angle. Write an expression, in terms of x, for the remaining angle.

1 mark

Section 13

6 Hannah is a years old and Abdul is b years old.
3 times Hannah's age plus double Abdul's age is 35

How old could Hannah and Abdul be?

1 mark

Section 13

7 Write down the next two terms in the sequence.

61, 57, 53, 49, 45…

1 mark

Section 14

8 State whether 75 is in the sequence 6, 14, 22, 30, 38…

Give a reason for your answer.

1 mark

Section 14

9 Write down the first five terms of the sequence with nth term $2n + 7$

1 mark

Section 14

10 Write down the 20th term of the sequence with nth term $5n - 2$

1 mark

Section 14

11 Circle the correct expression for the *n*th term of the sequence 7, 12, 17, 22, 27…

$7n$ $7n + 12$ $5n$ $5n + 7$ $5n + 2$

Section 14

1 mark

12 Some children were asked for their fastest swimming stroke. The partially completed table and bar chart show the results. Complete the table.

Section 15

Stroke	Number of children
Front crawl	12
Backstroke	_____
Breast stroke	_____
Butterfly	_____

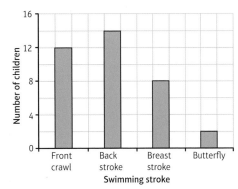

3 marks

13 The pie chart shows the number of medals a team won in a competition.

The team won a total of 48 medals.

Work out how many gold medals the team won.

Section 15

_____

1 mark

14 The table shows the number of cars entering a car park during a week in May.

Section 16

Day	Monday	Tuesday	Wednesday	Thursday	Friday	Saturday	Sunday
Number of cars	124	105	98	112	108	134	54

Work out the mean number of cars in the car park per day.

_____

1 mark

15 Josh works out that the mean amount of rainfall over 4 days is 32 mm per day. The following day, there is 67 mm of rain. Work out the new mean rainfall.

Section 16

_____ mm

1 mark

Time to reflect

Mark your *Checkpoint* out of 17. How did you do?

1 Check your answers in the back of the book and write your score in the progress chart. If any of your answers are incorrect, use the page links to find out which practice sections to look at again.

2 Scan the QR code for extra practice.

Progress test

Complete this test once you have worked through all the practice sections in this book. It covers all the topics in this book and is as hard as a real 11+ test.

(45)

1 Brody has written $4000 + 600 = 4600$ as an estimate for $4500 + 555$

Which number has Brody rounded incorrectly, 4500 or 555?

Section 1

1 mark

_____

2 Circle the number that is not a prime number.

2   3   7   13   19   25   31

Section 2

1 mark

3 The three numbers 8, 64 and 1000 are alike in some ways. Circle the correct statement.

A They are all prime numbers.   **B** They are all multiples of 9

C They are all odd numbers.   **D** They are all square numbers.

E They are all cube numbers.

Section 2 and 8

1 mark

4 Circle the set of numbers that are all multiples of 9

3, 6, 9   3, 9, 18   6, 18, 24   27, 54, 81   36, 45, 55

Section 2

1 mark

5 Circle the correct statement.

A Square numbers can be odd or even numbers.

B Multiples are numbers that divide exactly into another number.

C Prime numbers have only 1 factor.

D 100 is a cube number.

E 3 is a factor of 100

Section 2 and 8

1 mark

6 Circle the sum of the factors of 20

A 20   **B** 21   **C** 22   **D** 41   **E** 42

Section 2

1 mark

7 Work out the highest common factor of 48 and 60

Section 2

1 mark

_____

8 Work out $70 - (3 + 9) \div 4$

Section 3

1 mark

_____

9 Add one set of brackets to make the calculation correct.

$10 - 6 - 4 = 8$

Section 3

1 mark

10 Work out $5 + 7^2$

Section 3 and 8

1 mark

_____

11 Write < or > between the pair of fractions to make the statement correct.

$\frac{7}{20}$ ☐ $\frac{2}{5}$

Section 4

1 mark

12 Circle the value that is the odd one out.

$\frac{6}{4}$ $\frac{12}{8}$ $1\frac{1}{2}$ $\frac{50}{40}$ $1\frac{10}{20}$

Section 4

1 mark

13 Work out

a $\frac{4}{9} + \frac{1}{3}$ **b** $4\frac{5}{6} - 1\frac{3}{4}$

Section 5

2 marks

14 Harriet has 60 counters. $\frac{7}{12}$ of the counters are red. Work out how many red counters Harriet has.

Section 5

1 mark

15 Work out

a $2\frac{1}{3} \times 7$ **b** $\frac{6}{7} \times \frac{3}{5}$

Section 5

2 marks

16 Work out $\frac{5}{6} \div 2$

Section 5

1 mark

17 Work out the area of the triangle.

8 cm

11 cm   _____ cm²

Section 6

1 mark

18 A parallelogram has an area of 112 cm² and its height is 8 cm.
What is the length of the base of the parallelogram?

Section 6

1 mark

_____ cm

19 The parallelogram is made up of four identical triangles. The base of the parallelogram is 9 cm and the height is 8 cm.

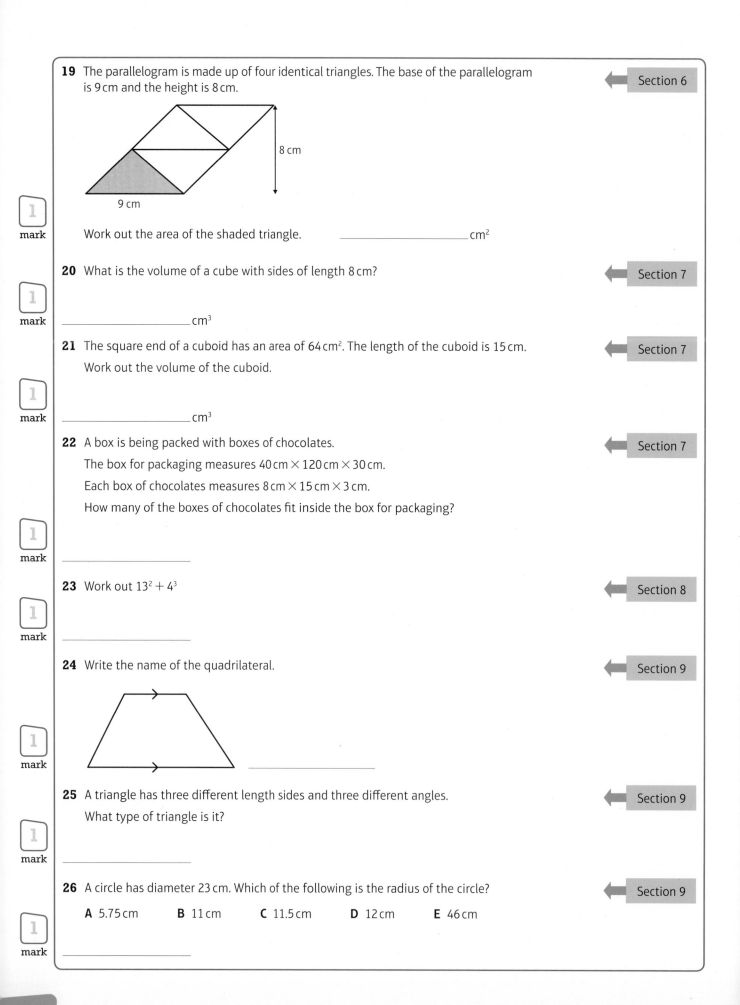

8 cm

9 cm

`1` mark

Work out the area of the shaded triangle. _____ cm²

Section 6

20 What is the volume of a cube with sides of length 8 cm?

`1` mark

_____ cm³

Section 7

21 The square end of a cuboid has an area of 64 cm². The length of the cuboid is 15 cm.
Work out the volume of the cuboid.

`1` mark

_____ cm³

Section 7

22 A box is being packed with boxes of chocolates.
The box for packaging measures 40 cm × 120 cm × 30 cm.
Each box of chocolates measures 8 cm × 15 cm × 3 cm.
How many of the boxes of chocolates fit inside the box for packaging?

`1` mark

_____

Section 7

23 Work out $13^2 + 4^3$

`1` mark

_____

Section 8

24 Write the name of the quadrilateral.

`1` mark

_____

Section 9

25 A triangle has three different length sides and three different angles.
What type of triangle is it?

`1` mark

_____

Section 9

26 A circle has diameter 23 cm. Which of the following is the radius of the circle?

    A 5.75 cm   **B** 11 cm   **C** 11.5 cm   **D** 12 cm   **E** 46 cm

`1` mark

_____

Section 9

27 How many sides does a hexagon have?

Section 10

1 mark

_____

28

Section 10

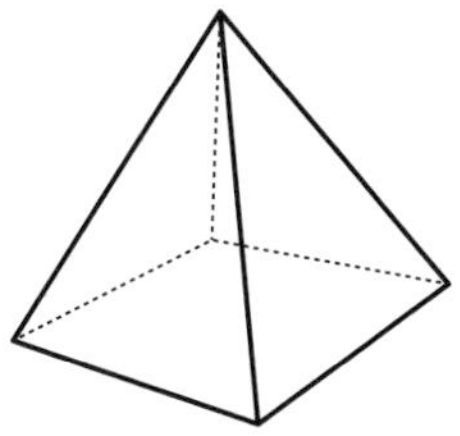

a Write the name of this shape.

_____

b How many faces does the shape have?

_____

c How many edges does the shape have?

_____

d How many vertices does the shape have?

_____

4 marks

29 Here is an irregular octagon.

Section 11

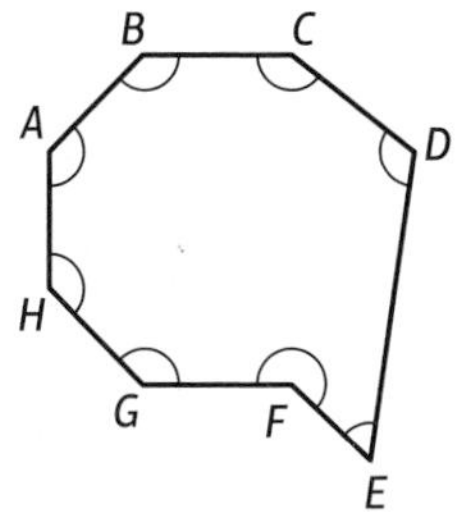

a Circle the letter showing the acute angle in the irregular octagon.

A   B   C   D   E   F   G   H

b Estimate size of the angle at **B** in the irregular octagon.

_____ °

2 marks

30 Work out the size of angles _a_ and _b_.

Section 12

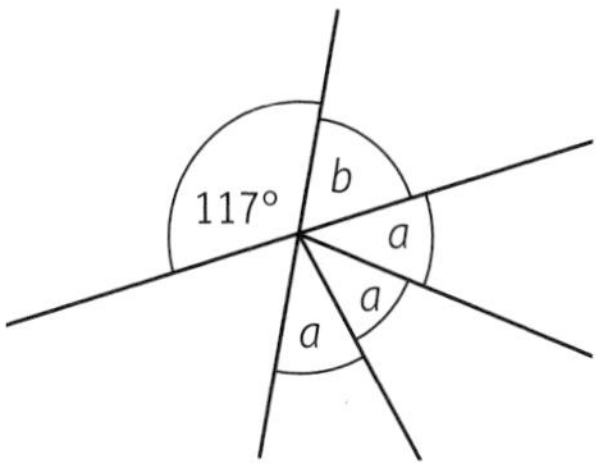

$a =$ _____ °

$b =$ _____ °

2 marks

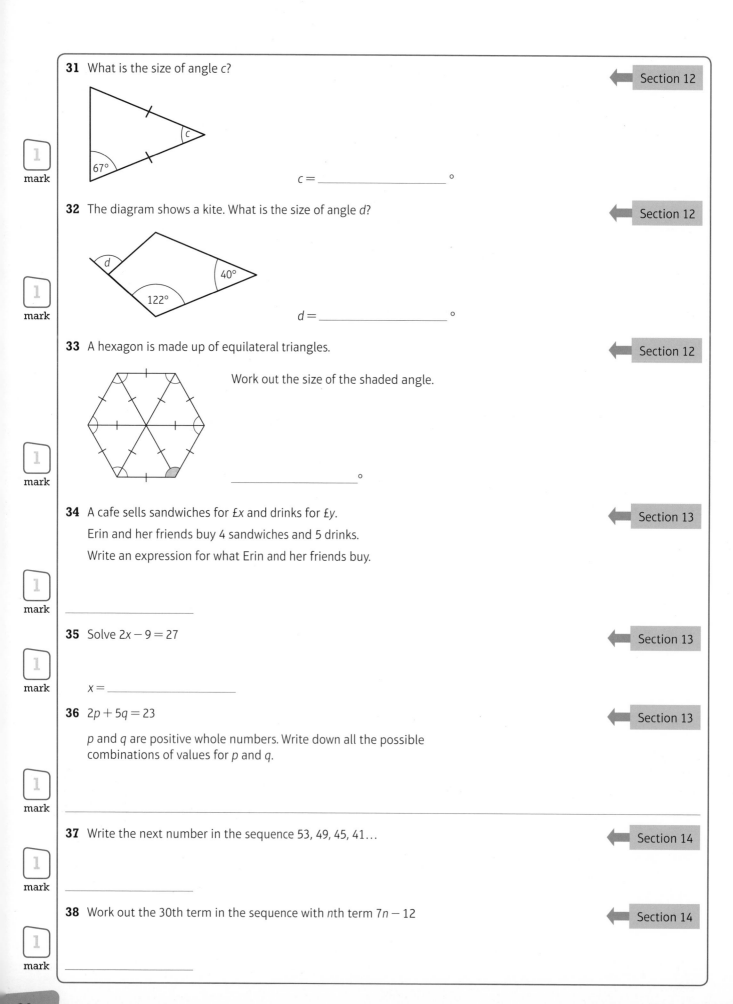

31 What is the size of angle *c*?

Section 12

67°

c = _____ °

1 mark

32 The diagram shows a kite. What is the size of angle *d*?

Section 12

d

40°

122°

d = _____ °

1 mark

33 A hexagon is made up of equilateral triangles.

Section 12

Work out the size of the shaded angle.

_____ °

1 mark

34 A cafe sells sandwiches for £*x* and drinks for £*y*.

Erin and her friends buy 4 sandwiches and 5 drinks.

Write an expression for what Erin and her friends buy.

Section 13

_____

1 mark

35 Solve $2x - 9 = 27$

Section 13

x = _____

1 mark

36 $2p + 5q = 23$

p and *q* are positive whole numbers. Write down all the possible combinations of values for *p* and *q*.

Section 13

_____

1 mark

37 Write the next number in the sequence 53, 49, 45, 41…

Section 14

_____

1 mark

38 Work out the 30th term in the sequence with *n*th term $7n - 12$

Section 14

_____

1 mark

39 Some children were asked what their favourite school trip was from the last four years.
Complete the table of results.

Section 15

Trip	Number of children
Museum	_____
Zoo	_____
Science park	_____
Castle	6

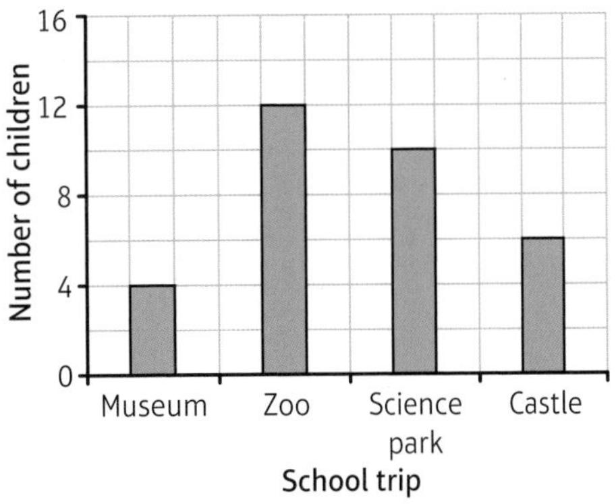

3 marks

40 252 children were asked what their favourite flavour of crisps is. The pie chart shows the results.
How many children chose cheese and onion?

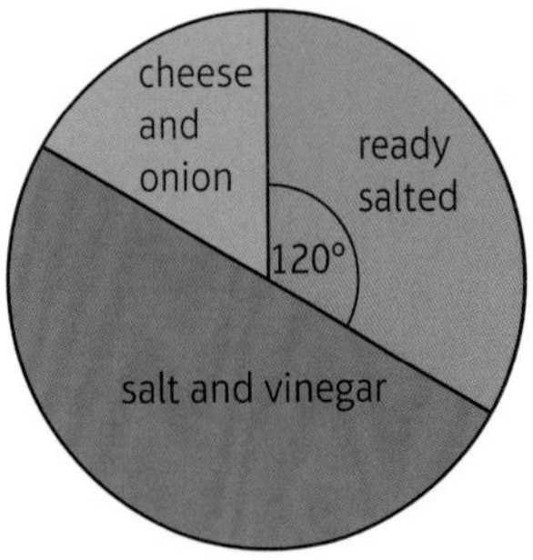

Section 15

_____

1 mark

41 Isabel has four coins. The mean value of the coins is 70p.

Isabel is given a £1 coin.

Work out the new mean for Isabel's coins.

Section 16

_____p

1 mark

42 Sandeep buys a pack of 3 apples for £1.08 and a pack of 6 apples for £1.80
What is the average cost per apple of all the apples Sandeep buys?

Section 16

_____p

1 mark

Time to reflect

Mark your *Progress test* out of 51. How did you do?

☐ *0–41 marks*
Use the page links to identify your strengths and weaknesses. Revisit the practice sections you scored the lowest in and then scan the QR code to try more mixed questions.

☐ *42–51 marks*
Use the page links to identify your strengths and weaknesses. You might want to revisit the practice sections you scored the lowest in.

Answers

Diagnostic test

Pages 2–7

1 $800 \times 80 = 64\,000$ so no, Tia is incorrect as $64\,000$ is much larger than 6568

2 **C** 2 is the only even prime number.

> 2 is an even number as it is divisible by 2. The factors of 2 are 1 so it is a prime number as it has two factors.

3 **D** 1, 4, 16

4 12

5 11

> Work out $2 + 6$ in the brackets first then divide 32 by your answer. Lastly, add the 7

6 $82 - 12 \times 5 = 82 - (12 \times 5)$

7 $9 \times (5 - 3) = 18$

> To make 18 using the 9, you can either add 9 or multiply by 2 Using the 5 and 3 in the brackets, you cannot make 9 but you can make 2 using subtraction.

8 $5^2 = 25$ and $2 \times 25 = 50$, so the correct answer is 50

> Zahra has worked out $2 \times 5 = 10$ and has then squared 10 to give 100, which is not the correct order of operations.

9 **B** $\dfrac{29}{30}$

10 $1\dfrac{13}{32}, \dfrac{23}{16}, \dfrac{3}{2}, 1\dfrac{5}{8}, \dfrac{7}{4}$

> Use equivalent fractions to change the fractions so that they all have the same denominator $3\dfrac{1}{2} = 3\dfrac{15}{30}, \dfrac{31}{10} = 3\dfrac{3}{30},$ $\dfrac{7}{3} = \dfrac{70}{30} = 2\dfrac{10}{30}, \dfrac{17}{6} = \dfrac{85}{30} = 2\dfrac{25}{30}$

11 **a** $\dfrac{5}{8}$ **b** $5\dfrac{13}{20}$

12 18

> Work out $\dfrac{3}{8}$ of 48 by working out $\dfrac{1}{8}$ first and then multiplying by 3

13 **a** $\dfrac{4}{21}$ **b** $8\dfrac{1}{3}$

14 $\dfrac{1}{5}$

> Area of a parallelogram = base × vertical height = $9\,\text{cm} \times 5\,\text{cm} = 45\,\text{cm}^2$. The side length of 6 cm is not used.

15 $45\,\text{cm}^2$

> Area = $14\,\text{cm} \times \text{height} = 84\,\text{cm}^2$
> Height = $84\,\text{cm}^2 \div 14\,\text{cm} = 6\,\text{cm}$

16 6 cm

17 $240\,\text{mm}^2$

> The area of one parallelogram = $5\,\text{mm} \times 6\,\text{mm} = 30\,\text{mm}^2$, and the area of one triangle = $\dfrac{1}{2}$ of $10\,\text{mm} \times 6\,\text{mm} = 30\,\text{mm}^2$.

18 **A**

19 4500

> Work out the volume of each shape and then see how many times the volume of the cuboid divides into the volume of the cube.

20 6 cm

21 4

> V = $8\,\text{cm} \times 7\,\text{cm} \times \text{height} = 336\,\text{cm}^3$
> $56\,\text{cm}^2 \times \text{height} = 336\,\text{cm}^3$
> height = $336\,\text{cm}^3 \div 56\,\text{cm}^2 = 6\,\text{cm}$

22 **a** equilateral **b** scalene **c** isosceles

23 rhombus

> The only quadrilaterals with four equal sides are a square and a rhombus. A square has four right angles but a rhombus has opposite equal angles.

24 **C** 13 cm

25 hexagonal prism

> The diameter is double the radius.

26 **a** 6 **b** 12 **c** 8

27 **B**

> **b** The edges are where two faces meet.
> **c** The vertices are where three or more edges meet.

28 a The closer your angle is to 124° the more accurate you are.

b It is an isosceles triangle so the two acute angles are the same.

29 a $x = 27°$ **b** $x = 61°, y = 58°$ **c** $z = 72°$

d 120° — The angles in a triangle total 180° and the angles in the equilateral triangle are equal.

e 125° — Adjacent angles in a parallelogram total 180°

30 225°

31 $2R + T$

32 $b = 9$ — Substitute $a = 4$ into the formula and then solve the equation to work out b.

33 11 — Form an equation and solve it.

34 45 — The sequence decreases by 6 each time, so work out $51 - 6$

35 $11n - 8$

36 1424 — $100\% - 50\% - 20\% - 20\% = 10\%$.

37 26

38 7 hours — Total for four days $= 8 \times 4 = 32$
Total for five days $= 32 + 3 = 35$
Mean $= 35 \div 5 = 7$ hours

39 $x = 27$

1 Estimating

Page 9
Guided questions

1 40, 600, 80, 12 000, 50 000

2 a 500 **b** 5000 **c** 5500 — $500 + 5000 = 5500$

3 50 — Round 93 and 36 to the nearest 10 to give 90 and 40

4 3000 — Round 4682 and 2279 to the nearest 1000 to give 5000 and 2000

5 a 259 **b** 475 — 475 needs to be rounded to the nearest 100, not the nearest 10

6 140 — Round 23 to the nearest 10 to give 20

Page 10
Have a go

1 600

2 7000

3 a 700 **b** 400 **c** 300 — **c** $700 - 400 = 300$

4 a 800 **b** 400 **c** no — **c** $800 + 400 = 1200$ and 1200 is nearly 200 more than 1026, so 1026 is too low.

5 920 — Round 953 to the nearest 100 to give 1000
Round 77 to the nearest 10 to give 80

6

$154 + 683$	$500 + 400$
$145 + 638$	$100 + 600$
$451 + 386$	$400 + 400$
$415 + 368$	$200 + 700$

Round each number to the nearest 100

7 4000 — 6438 and 1725 rounded to the nearest 1000 are 6000 and 2000

8 $50 \times 4 = 200$ — 53 rounded to the nearest 10 is 50

Timed practice

1 800, 70, 9000, 8300, 70 000

2 a 80   **b** 500   **c** 580

30 000 − 10 000 = 20 000 which is too high compared to 15 678, so the answer is no.

3 no

4000 + 2000 = 6000

4 6000

800 − 100 = 700

5 700

6 C 4500 + 3825 → 4000 + 4000 = 8000

4500 rounds to 5000, not 4000 so **C** is incorrect.

7 An estimate of 479 × 62 is 500 × 60 = 30 000 which is not close to Emily's answer so she must be incorrect.

479 rounded to the nearest 100 is 500 and 62 rounded to the nearest 10 is 60

2 Multiples and factors

Page 13

Guided questions

1 63, 70, 80

28 = 4 × 7 and 28 = 2 × 14 so 4, 7 and 14 are all factors of 28

2 4, 7, 14

3 2

1 only has one factor so it is not a prime number. The factors of 2 are 1 and 2, so 2 is a prime number.

4 a 15   **b** 16

5 10

a 15 is a common multiple of 3 and 5
b 16 is a multiple of 1, 2, 4, 8 and 16 but not 3 or 5

6 24

The factors of 30 are 1, 2, 3, 5, 6, 10, 15 and 30
The factors of 50 are 1, 2, 5, 10, 25 and 50
10 is the highest number that is a factor of both 30 and 50

Page 14

Have a go

1 9, 18, 27, 36, 45

The multiples of 6 are 6, 12, 18, 24, 30, 36…
The multiples of 8 are 8, 16, 24, 32, 40, 48…
24 is the lowest number that is a multiple of both 6 and 8

2 B Prime numbers all have two factors.
   E 23 is a prime number.

3 E 24

4 a 1, 2, 3, 4, 6, 8, 12, 24
   b 1, 2, 4, 5, 8, 10, 20, 40

8 is the highest number that is a factor of both 24 and 40

   c 8

The multiples of 4 are 4, 8, 12, 16, 20, 24, 28…
The multiples of 7 are 7, 14, 21, 28, 35…
28 is the lowest number that is a multiple of both 4 and 7

5 28

6 27 = multiple of 9 (3 × 9 = 27)
    8 = factor of 40 (40 = 8 × 5)
    15 = factor of 30 (30 = 15 × 2)
    19 = prime number (19 has two factors which are 1 and 19)

7 2 and 5

From the list 1, 2, 5, 10, 25 and 50 are all factors of 50 but of these, only 2 and 5 are prime numbers.

Page 15

Timed practice

1 1, 2, 5, 10

1 × 10 = 10 and 2 × 5 = 10

2 a 18   **b** 70   **c** 15 and 1   **d** 2

3 E None of these

56 is a multiple of 1, 2, 4, 7, 8, 19, 28 and 56 but not 6 or 9

4 3

3 is a factor of both 9 and 12 because 3 × 3 = 9 and 4 × 3 = 12

5 A They are prime numbers.

$3 = 1 \times 3, 5 = 1 \times 5$ and $11 = 1 \times 11$ so 3, 5 and 11 all have two factors each.

6 12

3 Order of operations

Page 17

Guided questions

1 26

$12 + 2 \times 7 = 2 + 14 = 26$

2 6

$20 - (12 + 4 + 11) = 20 - (3 + 11) = 20 - 14 = 6$

3 $20 - 4 \times 5$, $20 - 5 \times 4$ and $20 \div 4 - 5$

4 12

After the brackets there is only multiplication and division left, so work from left to right: $3 \times 8 \div 2 = 24 \div 2 = 12$

5 a $\neq$ **b** $\neq$ **c** $=$ **d** $=$ **e** $\neq$

6 13

$20 - 12 + 5 = 8 + 5 = 13$

7 12

Square the result of 6 − 4, don't square the 6 and the 4 separately. $(6 - 4)^2 \times 3 = 2^2 \times 3 = 4 \times 3 = 12$

8 $\times$ and $+$

$1 \times (2 + 3) - 4 = 1 \times 5 - 4 = 5 - 4 = 1$

Page 18

Have a go

a Once you've worked out the multiplication, work from left to right. Work out the addition and then subtract the answer to 2×4

1 a 12 **b** 42

b $6 \times (12 - 5) = 6 \times 7 = 42$

2 1

$48 \div (3 + 9) - 3 = 48 \div 12 - 3 = 4 - 3 = 1$

3 a No

b Toby has worked out $20 - 6 = 14$, then divided by 2 to give 7 and then added on 5 to give 12. He should have worked out $6 \div 2$ first to give $20 - 3 + 5 = 17 + 5 = 22$

4 $10 \times 9 + 8 \times 7$ and $8 \times 7 + 9 \times 10$ are equal

5 27

$(9 - 3 \times 2)^3 = (9 - 6)^3 = 3^3 = 27$

6

$1 + 3 \times 8 \div 4 = 7$

$(1 + 3) \times 8 \div 4 = 8$

$1 \times 3 \times 8 \div 4 = 6$

$1 + 3 \times 8 - 4 = 21$

$1 + 3 \times (8 - 4) = 13$

7 D E B A C

Page 19

Timed practice

1 19, 28, 35, 19, 26

2 18

$6 + 12 = 18$

3 C $1 + 1 \times 1 + 1 \times 1$

D $1 \times 1 \times 1 + 1 + 1$

A $= 5$, **B** $= 4$, **C** $= 3$, **D** $= 3$, **E** $= 2$

4 a $\neq$ **b** $\neq$ **c** $=$ **d** $=$ **e** $\neq$

5 D $3 \times 11 - 3^3$

A $= 7$, **B** $= 10$, **C** $= 13$, **D** $= 6$

6 E $2 \times 3 \times 4 + 5$

A $= 14$, **B** $= 26$, **C** $= 19$, **D** $= 25$, **E** $= 29$

7 $(20 - 5) \div (12 \div 4) = 5$

Think about which two numbers you can use in a division or a subtraction to make 5, and see if you can make any of them from parts of the calculation.

4 Comparing fractions

Guided questions

1 $\dfrac{21}{12}$ ———————————— Multiply the numerator and denominator of $\dfrac{7}{4}$ by 3, because 3 is the LCM of 4 and 12

2 **a** 5   **b** 35

3 $\dfrac{3}{5}$ ———————————— $\dfrac{3}{5} = \dfrac{6}{10}$

4 < ———————————— $\dfrac{3}{5} = \dfrac{12}{20}$ and $\dfrac{3}{4} = \dfrac{15}{20}$

5 $\dfrac{5}{6}, \dfrac{3}{4}, \dfrac{2}{3}, \dfrac{7}{12}, \dfrac{1}{2}$

6 C $\dfrac{11}{12}$ ———————————— $1\dfrac{1}{3} = 1\dfrac{8}{24}, 1\dfrac{1}{6} = 1\dfrac{4}{24}, \dfrac{11}{12} = \dfrac{22}{24}, \dfrac{2}{3} = \dfrac{16}{24}$

Page 22

Guided questions

1 **a** 6   **b** 7   **c** 5

2 $\dfrac{70}{64}$ ———————————— $\dfrac{5}{4} = \dfrac{80}{64}, \dfrac{20}{16} = \dfrac{80}{64}, \dfrac{40}{32} = \dfrac{80}{64}, \dfrac{10}{8} = \dfrac{80}{64}$

3 $\dfrac{5}{4} > \dfrac{11}{12}, \dfrac{9}{5} = \dfrac{54}{30}$

4 B $\dfrac{5}{6}$ ———————————— $\dfrac{3}{4} = \dfrac{18}{24}, \dfrac{5}{6} = \dfrac{20}{24}, \dfrac{2}{3} = \dfrac{16}{24}, \dfrac{1}{2} = \dfrac{12}{24}$

5 $\dfrac{25}{24}, \dfrac{13}{12}, \dfrac{9}{8}, \dfrac{55}{48}, \dfrac{5}{4}$

6 $\dfrac{19}{10}$ ———————————— $1\dfrac{4}{5} = \dfrac{9}{5} = \dfrac{18}{10}$ so $\dfrac{19}{10}$ is the largest.

7 $3\dfrac{3}{16}$ ———————————— $\dfrac{13}{4} = 3\dfrac{1}{4} = 3\dfrac{4}{16}$ so $3\dfrac{3}{16}$ is the smallest.

Page 23

Timed practice

1 **a** 27   **b** 15   **c** 14   **d** 9   **e** 7

2 yes ———————————— $140 \div 20 = 7$ and $100 \div 20 = 5$

3 **a** yes   **b** As $\dfrac{1}{3} = \dfrac{3}{9}$ and $\dfrac{5}{9} > \dfrac{3}{9}, \dfrac{5}{9} > \dfrac{1}{3}$

4 < ———————————— $\dfrac{13}{4} = \dfrac{39}{12}$ and $\dfrac{10}{3} = \dfrac{40}{12}$, so $\dfrac{13}{4} < \dfrac{10}{3}$

5 $\dfrac{17}{12}, \dfrac{3}{2}, \dfrac{5}{3}, \dfrac{7}{4}, \dfrac{11}{6}$ ———————————— $\dfrac{5}{3} = \dfrac{20}{12}, \dfrac{7}{4} = \dfrac{21}{12}, \dfrac{11}{6} = \dfrac{22}{12}, \dfrac{3}{2} = \dfrac{18}{12}$

6 $1\dfrac{1}{4}$ ———————————— $\dfrac{7}{5} = \dfrac{28}{20}, 1\dfrac{1}{4} = \dfrac{5}{4} = \dfrac{25}{20}, 1\dfrac{3}{10} = \dfrac{13}{10} = \dfrac{26}{20}, \dfrac{3}{2} = \dfrac{30}{20}$

5 Calculating with fractions

Page 25

Guided questions

a Convert both fractions so they have the same denominator. The LCM of the denominators 6 and 3 is 6

b The LCM of the denominators 16 and 4 is 16
$\dfrac{13}{16} - \dfrac{1}{4} = \dfrac{13}{16} - \dfrac{4}{16} = \dfrac{9}{16}$

1 **a** $\dfrac{5}{6}$ **b** $\dfrac{9}{16}$ ————————————

2 **a** $3\dfrac{3}{4}$ **b** $2\dfrac{3}{10}$ ————————————

a First add the whole numbers, $1 + 2$. Then add the fractions by converting both fractions so they have the same denominator.

3 8

b $3\dfrac{4}{5} - 1\dfrac{1}{2} = 2\dfrac{8}{10} - \dfrac{5}{10} = 2\dfrac{3}{10}$

4 a $7\frac{1}{2}$ **b** $\frac{2}{45}$ •————————— **a** $1\frac{1}{2} \times 5 = \frac{3}{2} \times 5 = \frac{15}{2} = 7\frac{1}{2}$ **b** $\frac{1}{5} \times \frac{2}{9} = \frac{1 \times 2}{5 \times 9} = \frac{2}{45}$

5 $\frac{1}{12}$ •————————— $\frac{1}{3} \div 4 = \frac{1}{3} \times \frac{1}{4} = \frac{1 \times 1}{3 \times 4} = \frac{1}{12}$

Page 26

Have a go

1 $\frac{7}{10}$ •————————— $\frac{2}{5} + \frac{3}{10} = \frac{4}{10} + \frac{3}{10} = \frac{7}{10}$

2 $\frac{2}{9}$ •————————— $\frac{5}{9} - \frac{1}{3} = \frac{5}{9} - \frac{3}{9} = \frac{2}{9}$

3 a $1\frac{7}{15}$

b $\frac{13}{20}$ $\frac{2}{3} + \frac{4}{5} = \frac{10}{15} + \frac{12}{15} = \frac{22}{15} = 1\frac{7}{15}$

c $\frac{5}{12}$ $\frac{5}{6} - \frac{2}{5} = \frac{25}{30} - \frac{12}{30} = \frac{13}{30}$

d $\frac{13}{20}$

4 a 18   **b** 28 •————————— $\frac{1}{4}$ of $24 = 24 \div 4 = 6$, $\frac{3}{4}$ of $24 = 6 \times 3 = 18$

5 a $5\frac{1}{3}$ **b** $6\frac{3}{4}$ **c** $\frac{2}{15}$ **d** $\frac{3}{20}$

6 a $3\frac{8}{15}$ **b** $2\frac{1}{10}$ **c** $3\frac{11}{12}$ **d** $3\frac{11}{20}$ •— First add or subtract the whole numbers. Then add or subtract the fractions by converting them using equivalent fractions so they have the same denominator.

7 $\frac{1}{10}$ •————————— $\frac{1}{2} \div 5 = \frac{1}{2} \times \frac{1}{5} = \frac{1 \times 1}{2 \times 5} = \frac{1}{10}$

Page 27

Timed practice

1 $\frac{1}{4} + \frac{5}{6} = 1\frac{1}{12}$ •— First use equivalent fractions to make the denominators the same. For the answers, change any improper fractions to mixed numbers.

$\frac{5}{6} - \frac{1}{4} = \frac{7}{12}$

$\frac{7}{8} - \frac{2}{3} = \frac{5}{24}$

$\frac{2}{3} + \frac{1}{8} = \frac{19}{24}$

2 27 •————————— $\frac{1}{4}$ of $36 = 36$, $4 = 9$, $\frac{3}{4}$ of $36 = 9 \times 3 = 27$

3 $\frac{1}{6}$ •————————— $\frac{1}{2} + \frac{1}{3} = \frac{3}{6} + \frac{2}{6} = \frac{5}{6}$

$1 - \frac{5}{6} = \frac{1}{6}$

4 $4\frac{1}{2}$

5 $\frac{4}{15}$ First add or subtract the whole numbers. Then add or subtract the fractions by converting them using equivalent fractions so they have the same denominator.

6 a $4\frac{5}{6}$ •

b $1\frac{7}{15}$ Firstly convert the mixed number to an improper fraction by splitting it up: $3\frac{4}{7} = \frac{21}{7} + \frac{4}{7} = \frac{25}{7}$

Then multiply by $\frac{1}{2}$, as that is the same as dividing by 2:

7 $1\frac{11}{14}$ •————————— $\frac{25}{7} \times \frac{1}{2} = \frac{25}{14} = 1\frac{11}{14}$

Checkpoint 1

Pages 28–29

1 **D** 1000

2 no ●————————————————— $20\,000 - 10\,000 = 10\,000$

3 **C** 4, 8, 10

4 5 ●————————————————— 1, 5, 6 and 30 are all factors of 30, but 5 is the only factor that is a prime number.

5 **A** All prime numbers have two factors. ●—— 9 has three factors (1, 3, 9) so is not a prime number. 1 has only one factor so is not a prime number. 2 has two factors so is an even prime number.

6 18

7 2, 5

8 **A** $2 \times 2 \times 2 + 2 \times 2$ ●————— **A** $2 \times 2 \times 2 + 2 \times 2 = 8 + 4 = 12$
   B $2 + 2 + 2 \times 2 \times 2$ **B** $2 + 2 + 2 \times 2 \times 2 = 2 + 2 + 8 = 12$

9 $20 - 11 + 3 = (20 - 11) + 3$ ●—— $20 - 11 + 3 = 9 + 3 = 12$ and $(20 - 11) + 3 = 9 + 3 = 12$

10 120

11 > ●————————————————— Use equivalent fractions to make the denominators the same before comparing the fractions.

12 $\dfrac{3}{2}, \dfrac{4}{3}, \dfrac{7}{6}, \dfrac{10}{9}, \dfrac{19}{18}$ ●——

$\dfrac{3}{2} = \dfrac{27}{18}, \dfrac{4}{3} = \dfrac{24}{18}, \dfrac{7}{6} = \dfrac{21}{18}, \dfrac{10}{9} = \dfrac{20}{18}$

13 15

14 $\dfrac{4}{15}$

15 $3\dfrac{11}{14}$

16 $\dfrac{1}{20}$ ●————————————————— $\dfrac{1}{5} \div 4 = \dfrac{1}{5} \times \dfrac{1}{4} = \dfrac{1 \times 1}{5 \times 4} = \dfrac{1}{20}$

6 Areas of other shapes

Page 31

Guided questions

1 63 cm² ●————————————————— Area of the parallelogram = base × height. Always use the vertical height.

2 10 m² ●————————————————— Area of a triangle = $\dfrac{1}{2}$ of base × height.

3 12 cm

4 10 mm ●————————————————— Height = 100 mm² ÷ 10 mm = 10 mm

5 8 cm² ●————————————————— The area of the small parallelogram is $\dfrac{1}{4}$ of 32 cm²

Page 32

Have a go

1 54 cm²
2 27.5 cm²
3 **A** ●—————

A $7 \times 6 = 42$ **D** $5 \times 9 = 45$
B $\dfrac{1}{2}$ of $15 \times 6 = \dfrac{1}{2}$ of $90 = 45$ **E** $\dfrac{1}{2}$ of $9 \times 11 = \dfrac{1}{2}$ of $99 = 49.5$
C $\dfrac{1}{2}$ of $12 \times 8 = \dfrac{1}{2}$ of $96 = 48$

4 8 cm
5 8 cm ●—————

Area of parallelogram = 40 mm × 17 mm = 680 mm²
Area of triangle = $\dfrac{1}{2}$ of 20 mm × 17 mm = 170 mm²

6 5100 mm² ●————————————————— Total area = 6 × 680 mm² + 6 × 170 mm² = 4080 mm²
                                   + 1020 mm² = 5100 mm²

90

Timed practice

1 a 72 cm²

  b 55 cm²

  c 108 cm²

  d 36 cm²

2 13 000 cm² —————————————— Work out the area of one triangle first, then multiply it by 50

3 40 cm² —————————————— The small triangle has an area $\frac{1}{9}$ that of the large triangle.

4 146 cm² —————————————

7 Volume

Page 35

Guided questions

Area of parallelogram $= 12 \times 4 = 48$
Area of blue triangle $= \frac{1}{2}$ of $8 \times 5 = \frac{1}{2}$ of $40 = 20$
Area of red triangle $= \frac{1}{2}$ of $5 \times 6 = \frac{1}{2}$ of $30 = 15$
Total area $= (2 \times 48) + 20 + (2 \times 15) = 96 + 20 + 30 = 146$

1 27 units³

2 63 cm³ —————————————— Volume = length × width × height.

3 308 cm³

4 3000

5 26 cm³ ——————————————

$V = 2\,cm \times 2\,cm \times 2\,cm = 8\,cm^3$
Total volume $= 5 \times 8\,cm^3 = 40\,cm^3$
Volume left $= 40\,cm^3 - 14\,cm^3 = 26\,cm^3$

Page 36

Have a go

1 90 units³ —————————————— $V = 6 \times 5 \times 3 = 90$ units³

2 a 140 m³   **b** 1620 cm³

3 A ——————————————

A $V = 6\,cm \times 6\,cm \times 6\,cm = 216\,cm^3$
B $V = 5\,cm \times 6\,cm \times 7\,cm = 210\,cm^3$

4 1 cm × 1 cm × 48 cm, 1 cm × 2 cm × 24 cm, 1 cm × 3 cm × 16 cm,
1 cm × 4 cm × 12 cm, 1 cm × 6 cm × 8 cm, 2 cm × 2 cm × 12 cm,
2 cm × 3 cm × 8 cm, 2 cm × 4 cm × 6 cm, 3 cm × 4 cm × 4 cm

Any 3 different cuboids with these dimensions.

5 4 cm —————————————— $V = 10\,cm \times 6\,cm \times height = 240\,cm^3$

6 10 mm ——————————————

$15\,mm \times 12\,mm = 180\,mm^2$
$1800\,mm^3 = 180\,mm^2 \times width$
$width = 1800\,mm^3 \div 180\,mm^2 = 10\,mm$

Page 37

Timed practice

1 80 units³ —————————————— As there are no units, units³ are used.

2 216 cm³, 27 m³, 60 000 mm³

3 C

4 250 ——————————————

Volume of display box $= 30\,cm \times 20\,cm \times 10\,cm = 6000\,cm^3$
Volume of box of matches $= 6\,cm \times 4\,cm \times 1\,cm = 24\,cm^3$
Number of boxes of matches $= 6000 \div 24 = 250$

5 192 cm³

6 10 cm

8 Square and cube numbers

Page 39
Guided questions

1 200 isn't a square number.

2 E 27 ────────────── $3 \times 3 \times 3 = 27$, so 27 is a cube number.

3 1 ────────────── $1^2 = 1 \times 1 = 1$ so 1 is the smallest square number.

4 1 and 4

5 245 ────────────── Work out the indices before multiplication.

6 32 ────────────── $2^2 \times 2^3 = 4 \times 8 = 32$

7 15 ────────────── $225 = 15 \times 15$

Page 40
Have a go

1 178 ────────────── $11^2 = 121, 12^2 = 144, 13^2 = 169$ and $14^2 = 196$

2 a 343   **b** 144   **c** 196   **d** 729

3 385 ────────────── $13^2 + 6^3 = 169 + 216 = 385$

4 C The smallest square number is 1
   D all square numbers have an odd number of factors

5 53 ────────────── $3 + 2 \times 25 = 3 + 50 = 53$

6 $2^3 = 8, 8^3 = 512, 7^2 = 49, 13^2 = 169$ ────── $2^3 = 2 \times 2 \times 2 = 8, 8^3 = 8 \times 8 \times 8 = 512, 7^2 = 7 \times 7 = 49,$
                                              $13^2 = 13 \times 13 = 169$
7 8, 64

Page 41
Timed practice

1 81 ────────────── $81 = 9 \times 9$, and therefore is a square number but not a cube number.

2 a 4   **b** 1 ────────────── The only cube number in the list is 1, which is an odd number.

3 B

                                              The cube numbers are 1, 8, 27, 64, 125… and of these 1, 8 and 64
4 1, 8, 64 ────────────── are factors of 64

5 E ────────────── $64 = 8^2, 121 = 11^2$ and $196 = 14^2$

6 12 cm

7 10 cm

9 Triangles and quadrilaterals

Page 43
Guided questions

                                              A 3 angles are equal.
1 A equilateral   **B** isosceles   **C** scalene ───── **B** 2 angles are equal.
                                              C No angles are equal.
2 C

3 a kite

   b square or rectangle ────────────── A square and a rhombus have 4 equal sides.

   c square or rhombus

   d trapezium ────────────── A kite does not have any parallel sides.

4 4 equal sides, opposite sides are parallel, opposite angles are equal

Page 44
Have a go

1 **a** Equilateral triangle with side lengths of 1.9 cm.
   b Scalene triangle with side lengths 1.7 cm, 1.5 cm and 1.9 cm.

2 **A** trapezium   **B** kite

   C rhombus   **D** rectangle

A 1 pair of parallel sides.
B 2 pairs of adjacent sides and 1 pair of opposite angles are equal.
C 4 equal sides, opposite sides are parallel and opposite angles are equal.
D Opposite sides are equal and parallel, 4 right angles.

3 kite

In a kite, adjacent sides are equal.

4 (7, 5)

5 9 cm

$4.5 \times 2 = 9$ cm

Page 45
Timed practice

1 **A** scalene   **B** isosceles

   C equilateral   **D** isosceles

A All 3 sides are different.
B 2 angles are equal.
C 3 equal sides.
D 2 equal sides.

2 square and parallelogram

You needed to spot the shapes with four sides.

3 rectangle or parallelogram

4 Opposite sides are parallel, opposite sides are equal, opposite angles are equal

Opposite sides are parallel and equal.

5 (3, 5)

10 Polygons and 3D shapes

Page 47
Guided questions

1 **B**, **C** and **E**

2 **B**, **C** and **E**

There is the square base and 4 triangular faces.

3 **a** 5
   b 8

There are 4 edges on the base and 4 edges connecting the 4 triangular faces.

   c 5

There are 4 vertices on the base and 1 vertex where the triangular faces meet at the top.

4 **D**

A cuboid has 6 faces, 12 edges and 8 vertices.

Page 48
Have a go

1 8

2 regular

The sides and angles are all the same length.

3 **a** vertex   **b** face   **c** edge

4 a square-based pyramid

> A square-based pyramid has 5 vertices.

   b triangle-based pyramid

> A triangle-based pyramid has 4 triangular faces.

   c cuboid

5 Triangle-based pyramid: 4, 6, 4
   Triangular prism: 5, 9, 6
   Pentagonal prism: 7, 15, 10

Page 49

Timed practice

1 a hexagon **b** octagon **c** pentagon **d** quadrilateral

2 pentagon

3 a regular **b** regular **c** irregular

4 cuboid and square-based pyramid

> Make a sketch of each shape separately to help you.

5 a 8   **b** 18   **c** 12

11 Angles

Page 51

Guided questions

1 a acute   **b** obtuse   **c** reflex

   d acute   **e** obtuse   **f** reflex

2 a The closer your answer is to 12°,
    the more accurate your estimate is.

   b 12°

> Any answer in the range of 10° to 14° is acceptable.

3 a The closer your answer is to 133°,
    the more accurate your estimate is.

   b 133°

> Any answer in the range of 131° to 135° is acceptable.

Page 52

Have a go

1 A and D

2 a 17°   **b** 172°   **c** 66°   **d** 116°

> The closer your answer is, the more accurate your estimate is.

3 a 17°   **b** 172°   **c** 66°   **d** 116°

4 a The closer your answer is to 112°, the more accurate your estimate is.

   b 112°

Page 53

Timed practice

1 C

2 125°

3 a The closer your answer is to 55°, the more accurate your estimate is.

   b 55°

4 a acute

   b The closer your answer is to 36°, the more accurate your estimate is.

   c 36°

12 Angle properties

Page 55

Guided questions

1 $a = 78°$ $b = 132°$ $c = 208°$

> a $90 - 12 = 78$ b $180 - 48 = 132$
> c $125 + 27 = 152, 360 - 152 = 208$

2 $x = 119°$

> $26 + 35 = 61, 180 - 61 = 119$

3 a $x = 60°$ b $y = 48°$ c $z = 113°$

4 $P = 64°$

> $58 + 58 = 116, 180 - 116 = 64$

5 $q = 128°$

> $180 - 52 = 128$

Page 56

Have a go

1 a $x = 35°$ b $x = 38°; y = 142°$

> a Vertically opposite angles are equal.
> b $180 - 38 = 142, y = 142°$

2 $a = 77°$

> $65 + 128 + 90 = 283, 360 - 283 = 77$

3 $x = 24°$

4 $300°$

5 $w = 65°$

> In a parallelogram vertically opposite angles are equal so the angle on the straight line with w is 115°.

Page 57

Timed practice

1 $a = 40°$ $b = 143°$ $c = 68°; d = 134°$

> a $18 + 32 = 50, 90 - 50 = 40$
> b $90 + 127 = 217, 360 - 217 = 143$

2 $w = 57°$ $x = 135°$

> w $33 + 90 = 123, 180 - 123 = 57, w = 57°$
> x $90 + 90 + 45 = 225, 360 - 225 = 135, x = 135°$

3 $360°$

> The angles in a quadrilateral total 360°

4 $y = 22°$

5 a $c = 52°$
   b $d = 308°$

> $360 - 52 = 308$

6 $k = 134°$

> $72 + 121 + 121 = 314, 360 - 314 = 46, 180 - 46 = 134$

Checkpoint 2

Pages 58–59

1 E

2 $14\,cm^2$

3 $180\,cm^3$

4 48

> Work out the volumes of both shapes and then divide the volume of the cuboid by the volume of the cube.

5 D

6 square or rhombus

7 C and D

> Shapes **A**, **B** and **E** all have two pairs of opposite parallel and equal sides, shape **C** only has one pair of parallel sides and shape **D** has no parallel sides.

8 E

9 a 6   b 12   c 8

10 Any angle within 20° of 105°

> The obtuse angle is the largest angle in the triangle. It is more than 90° but less than 180°. It is closer to 90° than it is to 180°

11 $x = 77°$ •⎯⎯⎯⎯⎯⎯⎯⎯⎯⎯⎯⎯⎯⎯⎯ $180 - 26 = 154, 154 \div 2 = 77$

12 $y = 44°$ •⎯⎯⎯⎯⎯ Opposite angles in a parallelogram are equal so the angle next to y on the straight line is also 136°. The angles on a straight line total 180°

13 Equations and formulae

Page 61

Guided questions

1 $s - 4$ •⎯⎯⎯⎯⎯⎯⎯⎯⎯⎯⎯⎯⎯ Ava now has 4 fewer sweets than the number she started with.

2 $2x = 16$
   $x = 8$

3 $a = 5$ •⎯⎯⎯⎯⎯⎯⎯⎯⎯⎯⎯⎯⎯ $2a + 12 = 22, 2a = 10$

4 $h = 5\,cm$ •⎯⎯⎯⎯⎯⎯⎯⎯⎯ $20 = 4 \times h; h = 20 \div 4$

5 $x = 13$ •⎯⎯⎯⎯⎯⎯⎯⎯⎯⎯
$2x + 15 = 41$
6 $1000 - 8x$ $2x = 26$

Page 62

Have a go

1 $y - 6$ •⎯⎯⎯⎯⎯ $6y$ would be 6 times older, $y + 6$ would be 6 years older than Jenny, $6 - y$ would be 6 years younger than Jenny and $y \div 6$ would be one sixth of Jenny's age.

2 $a = 7$

3 Possible answers include:
   $a = 1$ and $b = 15$, $a = 2$ and $b = 13$,
   $a = 3$ and $b = 11$, $a = 4$ and $b = 9$,
   $a = 5$ and $b = 7$, $a = 6$ and $b = 5$,
   $a = 7$ and $b = 3$ or $a = 8$ and $b = 1$

4 $x - 8 - y$ •⎯⎯⎯⎯ There are x people to start with and then as people get off the bus, keep subtracting from this amount.

5 $x = 12$

6 $a = 1$ and $b = 5$, $a = 3$ and $b = 2$

7 $6x$

8 $n - 10$ •⎯⎯⎯⎯⎯⎯⎯⎯⎯ $n - 3 - 7 = n - 10$

Page 63

Timed practice

1 $25 - t$
                      $18 + 45 = 63$
2 $x = 18$ •⎯⎯⎯⎯⎯⎯⎯⎯⎯

3 27 •⎯⎯⎯⎯⎯⎯ Substitute the values $x = 7$ and $y = 4$ into the formula $P = 5x - 2y$
                  $P = 5 \times 7 - 2 \times 4 = 35 - 8 = 27$

4 Possible answers include:
   $x = 8$ and $y = 4$, $x = 14$ and $y = 14$, $x = 20$
   and $y = 24$

5 $a = 7$ •⎯⎯⎯⎯ Substitute $b = 4$ into the formula $a + 2b = 15$ and then solve it:
                $a + 2 \times 4 = 15, a + 8 = 15$

6 $P = 8L$

7 32 •⎯⎯⎯⎯⎯⎯⎯⎯ $(n - 7) \times 2 = 50$
                  $n - 7 = 25$

8 $180 - a$

                  Volume = length $\times$ width $\times$ depth
9 $3\,m$ •⎯⎯⎯⎯⎯⎯ $3750 = 50 \times 25 \times$ depth
                  depth $= 3750 \div 1250$

14 Linear sequences

Page 65

Guided questions

1 Add 6

2 54 •————————————— $58 - 4 = 54$

3

Position	Value of n	Calculation	Term
1st	1	$8 \times 1 - 5 = 3$	3
2nd	2	$8 \times 2 - 5 = 11$	11
3rd	3	$8 \times 3 - 5 = 19$	19
4th	4	$8 \times 4 - 5 = 27$	27
5th	5	$8 \times 5 - 5 = 35$	35

4 50, 44, 38, 32, 26... •————

5 $4n + 1$

This sequence decreases by the same amount each time and so it is linear.

6 Yes, $3n = 36$
$n = 12$ so 36 is the 12th term.

Page 66

Have a go

The sequence increases by jumps of 11 each time.

1 57 and 68 •————

2 90, 83, 76, 69, 62 •————

90, $90 - 7 = 83$, $83 - 7 = 76$, $76 - 7 = 69$, $69 - 7 = 62$

3 **a** 12 and 24   **b** 42 and 33   **c** 45 and 51 •————

a The rule is 'add 4'   **b** The rule is 'subtract 9'   **c** The rule is 'add 6'

4 No, 60 is an even number but all of the
numbers in the sequence are odd numbers.

Alternately, you could find the nth term of the sequence:
$6n + 1 = 60$
$6n = 59$
59 is not divisible by 6, therefore 60 is not a term in the sequence.

5 11, 17, 23, 29, 35 •————

6 49

7 **E** $2n - 1$

$6 \times 1 + 5 = 11$, $6 \times 2 + 5 = 17$, $6 \times 3 + 5 = 23$, $6 \times 4 + 5 = 29$,
$6 \times 5 + 5 = 35$

Page 67

Timed practice

1 59

2 5, 17, 29, 41, 53 •————

5, $5 + 12 = 17$, $17 + 12 = 29$, $29 + 12 = 41$, $41 + 12 = 53$

3 **a** 27 and 54 •————

The rule is 'add 9'. $18 + 9 = 27$ and $45 + 9 = 54$

  b 45 and 42 •————

The rule is 'subtract 3'. $48 - 3 = 45$ and $45 - 3 = 42$

  c 25 and 38 •————

4 1, 4, 7, 10, 13 •————

Work backwards by subtracting 13 to find the second term and then the first term: $51 - 13 = 38$ and $38 - 13 = 25$

5 **a** 74

  b The numbers in the sequence are all
even numbers and 74 is the only
number in the list that is even.

$3 \times 1 - 2 = 1$, $3 \times 2 - 2 = 4$, $3 \times 3 - 2 = 7$, $3 \times 4 - 2 = 10$,
$3 \times 5 - 2 = 13$

6 122

7 Yes

$2n - 1 = 45$

$2n = 46$

$n = 23$

So 45 is the 23rd number in the sequence $2n - 1$

Form an equation and solve it. If you get a whole number answer then 45 is in the sequence.

15 Tables, charts and graphs

Guided questions

1 a 9 minutes   **b** 44 minutes

2 15, 12, 5, 2

> 6 children chose 'Other', which is 3 blocks high on the bar chart, so 1 block = 6 ÷ 3 = 2 children. Use this to label the y axis scale on the bar chart. Start at zero and go up in 2s.

3 a 50%

  b 57 children

> The angle for bus = 90°, so the fraction for bus = $\frac{90}{360} = \frac{1}{4}$
> There are 228 children so work out $\frac{1}{4}$ of 228

Page 70

Have a go

1 a 3.00pm   **b** 12.00pm

2 a 20   **b** pepperoni

> The temperature increased to the most between 9.00 am and 12.00 pm as this is the steepest part of the graph.

3 a 100% − 50% − 20% − 10% = 20%

  b 48 people

> 10% of 240 = 240 ÷ 10 = 24
> 20% = 10% × 2, so 20% of 240 = 24 × 2 = 48

Page 71

Timed practice

1 a 1 hour and 39 minutes   **b** 07.20 or 07.35

> The 07.20 train arrives in Stockport at 09.17, the 07.35 train arrives at 09.37, but the 08.00 train arrives at 09.55 which is too late. The 07.20 and 07.35 trains are the only two options.

2 a plastic   **b** 6   **c** 16%

3 21 people

> The angle for science fiction = 45°, so the fraction for
> science fiction = $\frac{45}{360} = \frac{1}{8}$
> There are 168 children so work out $\frac{1}{8}$ of 168

16 Mean average

Page 73

Guided questions

1 15

2 137 cm

3 15

> Total of the five cards = 16 × 5 = 80
> The four remaining cards total 21 + 14 + 17 + 13 = 65
> So the card face down = 80 − 65 = 15

4 20

5 14

> First work out the total for the first four numbers: 13 × 4 = 52
> Then work out the total for the five numbers: 52 + 18 = 70
> Finally divide it by 5 to find the new mean.

Page 74

Have a go

1 43

2 2 °C

3 E Mean = total of the values ÷ number of values

> Total of all 4 hours = 12 × 4 = 48.
> Total of first 3 hours = 16 + 7 + 2 = 25
> The difference: 48 − 25 = 23

4 23

5 30p

> Mean = total cost ÷ number of bags of crisps.

Page 75

Timed practice

1 62 km

2 3 °C

3 15

4 49

First work out the total for the first three matches: $14 \times 3 = 42$
Then work out the total for the four matches: $42 + 18 = 60$
Finally divide it by 4 to find the new mean.

5 60p

Checkpoint 3

Pages 76–77

1 $x = 1$ and $y = 11$, $x = 2$ and $y = 6$
or $x = 3$ and $y = 1$

2 $a = 13$

3 $P = 5L$

A pentagon has 5 sides so the perimeter of the pentagon is 5 times the length, L.

4 9

$4n - 5 = 31$, $4n = 36$, $n = 36 \div 4 = 9$

5 $90 - x$

6 Any answer pair from:
H:1 and A:16,
H:3 and A:13,
H:5 and A:10,
H:7 and A:7,
H:9 and A:4,
H:11 and A:1

7 41 and 37

The sequence is decreasing by 4 each time so $45 - 4 = 41$ and $41 - 4 = 37$

8 No, because 75 is an odd number but all of the numbers in the sequence are even numbers.

9 9, 11, 13, 15, 17

10 98

11 **E** $5n + 2$

$7n$ gives the sequence 7, 14, 21, 28, 35…
$7n + 12$ gives the sequence 19, 26, 33, 40, 47…
$5n$ gives the sequence 5, 10, 15, 20, 25…
$5n + 7$ gives the sequence 12, 17, 22, 27, 32…

12 14, 8, 2

12 children chose front crawl which is 3 blocks high on the bar chart, so 1 block $= 12 \div 3 = 4$ children. Use this to label the y axis scale on the bar chart, start at zero and go up in 4s.

13 16

14 105 cars

15 39 mm

The angle for gold $= 360° - (180° + 60°) = 120°$,

so the fraction for gold $= \dfrac{120}{360} = \dfrac{1}{3}$

There are 48 medals so work out $\dfrac{1}{3}$ of 48.

Progress test

Pages 78–83

1 4500

2 25

Prime numbers have exactly 2 factors. For example, the factors of 2 are 1 so 2 is prime as it has 2 factors.

3 **E** They are all cube numbers

$2^3 = 8$, $4^3 = 64$ and $10^3 = 1000$

4 27, 54, 81

5 **A** Square numbers can be odd or even numbers

The factors of 20 are 1, 2, 4, 5, 10 and 20

6 **E** 42

7 12

The factors of 48 are 1, 2, 3, 4, 6, 8, 12, 16, 24, 48. The factors of 60 are, 1, 2, 3, 4, 5, 6, 10, 12, 15, 20, 30, 60. The highest factor in both lists is 12

8 67

Work out the calculation in the brackets first then divide by 4, then subtract your answer from 70

9 $10 - (6 - 4) = 8$

Work out the indices first, $7^2 = 49$, and then add this to 5

10 54

11 $<$

Use equivalent fractions to make the denominators the same:
$$\frac{2}{5} = \frac{8}{20}$$

12 $\frac{50}{40}$

Simplify the fractions so they all have the same denominator:
$$\frac{6}{4} = \frac{3}{2}, \frac{12}{8} = \frac{3}{2}, 1\frac{1}{2} = \frac{3}{2}, \frac{50}{40} = \frac{5}{4}, 1\frac{10}{20} = \frac{30}{20} = \frac{3}{2}$$

13 **a** $\frac{7}{9}$ **b** $3\frac{1}{12}$

14 35

15 **a** $16\frac{1}{3}$

Change the mixed number to an improper fraction, multiply the numerator by 7 and then change your answer back to a mixed number.

b $\frac{18}{35}$

Multiply the numerators together and the denominators together.

16 $\frac{5}{12}$

17 44 cm^2

$A = \text{base} \times 8 \text{ cm} = 112 \text{ cm}^2$
$\text{Base} = 112 \text{ cm}^2 \div 8 \text{ cm} = 14 \text{ cm}$

18 14 cm

19 18 cm^2

Work out the area of the parallelogram and then divide by 4 to work out the area of the triangle.

20 512 cm^3

21 960 cm^3

$V = \text{area} \times \text{length} = 64 \text{ cm}^2 \times 15 \text{ cm} = 960 \text{ cm}^3$

22 400

$13^2 = 169$
$4^3 = 64$
$169 + 64 = 233$

23 233

24 trapezium

A trapezium has one pair of parallel lines.

25 scalene

26 **C** 11.5 cm

27 6

28 **a** square-based pyramid **b** 5 faces **c** 8 edges **d** 5 vertices

29 **a** E

An acute angle is less than 90°

b The closer your angle is to 148° the more accurate you are.

30 $a = 39°$ $b = 63°$

The angles on a straight line total 180° and vertically opposite angles are equal. $a = 117 \div 3 = 39$, $b = 180 - 117 = 63$

31 46°

32 104°

There is one pair of opposite equal angles in a kite and the angles total 360°: $360 - 122 - 122 - 40 = 76$
The angles on a straight line total 180°, so $d = 180 - 76 = 104$

33 120°

34 $4x + 5y$

35 $x = 18$

36 $p = 9$ and $q = 1$, $p = 4$ and $q = 3$

Try different values for p and q to see which values work for the equation.
q cannot be an even number or else p won't be a whole number.

37 37

38 198 •————————— Substitute $n = 30$ into the nth term $7n - 12$
$7 \times 30 - 12 = 198$

39 4, 12, 10 •
6 children chose the castle which is 1.5 blocks on the bar chart. $6 \div 1.5 = 4$, so each block on the bar chart represents 4 children. Label the y axis on the bar chart starting at zero and go up in 4's.

40 42 children

41 76p •—————————
Total for four coins $= 70p \times 4 = 280p$
Total for five coins $= 280p + £1 = 380p$
Mean $= 380p \div 5 = 76p$

42 32p •

Average $= 288 \div 9 = 32p$

Published by Pearson Education Limited, 80 Strand, London, WC2R 0RL.

www.pearsonschools.co.uk

Text © Pearson Education Limited 2018
Edited, typeset and produced by Elektra Media Ltd
Original illustrations © Pearson Education Limited
Illustrated by Elektra Media Ltd
Cover design by Lukas Bischoff

The right of Diane Oliver to be identified as author of this work has been asserted by her in accordance with the Copyright, Designs and Patents Act 1988.

First published 2018

21 20 19 18
10 9 8 7 6 5 4 3 2 1

British Library Cataloguing in Publication Data

A catalogue record for this book is available from the British Library

ISBN: 978 1 292 24651 2

Printed in Slovakia by Neografia

Acknowledgements

We would like to thank Nik Prowse and Amanda Booth for their invaluable help in the development and trialling of this publication.

Note from the publisher

Pearson has robust editorial processes, including answer and fact checks, to ensure the accuracy of the content in this publication, and every effort is made to ensure this publication is free of errors. We are, however, only human, and occasionally errors do occur. Pearson is not liable for any misunderstandings that arise as a result of errors in this publication, but it is our priority to ensure that the content is accurate. If you spot an error, please do contact us at resourcescorrections@pearson.com so we can make sure it is corrected.

Progress chart

Use this chart to keep track of your 11+ journey. Fill in your marks as you complete each *Timed practice* section and check off any extra practice you do.

	Timed practice	Digital questions	Ten-minute test
Diagnostic test	☐ / 51		
1 Estimating	☐ / 14	☑	☑
2 Multiples and factors	☐ / 9	☑	☑
3 Order of operations	☐ / 15	☑	☑
4 Comparing fractions	☐ / 11	☑	☑
5 Calculating with fractions	☐ / 11	☑	☑
Checkpoint 1	☐ / 17	☑	
6 Areas of other shapes	☐ / 7	☑	☑
7 Volume	☐ / 11	☑	☑
8 Square and cube numbers	☐ / 10	☑	☑
9 Triangles and quadrilaterals	☐ / 11	☑	☑
10 Polygons and 3D shapes	☐ / 13	☑	☑
11 Angles	☐ / 7	☑	☑
12 Angle properties	☐ / 11	☑	☑
Checkpoint 2	☐ / 15	☑	
13 Equations and formulae	☐ / 9	☑	☑
14 Linear sequences	☐ / 10	☑	☑
15 Tables, charts and graphs	☐ / 6	☑	☑
16 Mean average	☐ / 5	☑	☑
Checkpoint 3	☐ / 17	☑	
Progress test	☐ / 51	☑	